Every Pilgrim's Guide to the Journeys of the Apostles

Greece, Turkey, Cyprus,
Italy, Lebanon, Malta,
Syria and the Holy Land

MICHAEL COUNSELL

author of *Every Pilgrim's Guide to Oberammergau*

CANTERBURY
PRESS
N o r w i c h

Text, maps and colour photography © Michael Counsell 2002

Scripture quotations from the New Revised Standard Version of the
Bible © 1989 by the Division of Christian Education of the National
Council of Churches of Christ in the USA, are used by permission.
All rights reserved.

First published in 2002 by The Canterbury Press Norwich
(a publishing imprint of Hymns Ancient and Modern Limited,
a registered charity)
St Mary's Works, St Mary's Plain,
Norwich, Norfolk, NR3 3BH

Michael Counsell has asserted his right under the Copyright, Design
and Patents Act, 1988, to be identified as the Author of this Work

British Library Cataloguing in Publication Data

A catalogue record for this book is available from the British Library

ISBN 1-85311-444-8

Typeset by Regent Typesetting, London
and printed by Nørhaven A/S, Viborg, Denmark

Contents

Contents

Preface

Many pilgrims have found that a visit to the Holy Land made them feel closer to Jesus, and to see the places he knew helped them to understand his teaching better. Jesus lived, taught and thought within the culture of a first-century Jew, which was basically that of the Old Testament, but with much influence from the Greek-speaking culture of the Mediterranean Roman empire. He appointed apostles, however, to take his message beyond the area in which he worked during his lifetime. There are many apostles mentioned in the New Testament; the word means 'people who were sent out', or as we would put it, 'missionaries'. This book concentrates on the travels of St Peter, St Paul, and St John the author of 'The Revelation to John', also called 'The Apocalypse', with a short note on 'The Twelve who were also called apostles' (Mark 3:14; Luke 6:13).

Why are those first apostles so important? It is because they, and especially Paul, pioneered the task of carrying the message of Jesus out of its original Jewish context and translating it into the terms which would carry meaning to people across the world from many different backgrounds. If they had not done this, Christianity could have vanished, together with many other obscure Jewish sects, after the destruction of Jerusalem in AD 70.

Paul was brought up as a strict Jew, yet not in the Jewish homeland, but as a Roman citizen in a Greek-speaking city. When his call came, he travelled over most of the Roman empire to carry the message of Jesus. I believe that these journeys were part of a systematic strategy to convert the whole world as it was then known, to faith in Jesus. What a vision!

This book will concentrate on places mentioned in 'The Acts of the Apostles' (and 'The Revelation to John') which can be visited by a modern pilgrim. Many pilgrims are finding that a visit today to the places where Paul, and the other apostles, received their vision and began to work out what it meant, helps us to understand their teachings and share their inspiration. An enjoyable holiday in Greece or Turkey; Malta, Cyprus or Italy; Lebanon or Syria, is turned into a voyage of discovery when it is combined with an exploration of the journeys and the teachings of the apostles. Jesus said that if his disciples kept silent even the stones would cry out in praise of God (Luke 19:40); the experience of pilgrims to biblical places is that by their silent witness to the biblical narrative the archaeological remains do just that. The most important monuments at each site are highlighted in bold type so that modern visitors can identify quickly what they are looking at and its significance. Even to remain at home and read about the places the apostles visited can bring their writings vividly alive in a totally new way. It is to help all such pilgrims and armchair travellers that this book is written. I sincerely hope that none of my readers will follow my interpretation of Paul, Peter or John at all points, but that in working out their reasons for disagreeing with me they will learn to reassess the apostles, who were among the greatest creative geniuses in the history of human thought.

Anyone who wishes to be reassured about security before visiting these countries could seek the F.C.O. website http://www.fco.gov.uk or contact the nearest branch of the tourist information offices listed on pages 5 and 6.

I have visited all the places mentioned in this book except Albania, Alexandria, Lebanon, Syria and Tarragona. I should like to acknowledge the assistance of the Cyprus Tourist Organisation; Mgr John Azzopardi of the Mdina Cathedral Museum, Malta; George Filotheou of the Cyprus Museum, Nicosia; the Rev. Jonathan Boardman and the Anglican Centre in Rome; the British Institute of Archaeology at Ankara; the British School at Athens; the Rev. Dr Donald D. Binder of Southern Methodist University, Dallas, Texas; Askar Suleyman of Sahin Tours, Antakya, and his father Husein Suleyman; Hüssamettin Altunay of Seleukos Tourism, Antakya; Cengiz Topal of Karaman Museum; and to thank Brian Broughton of Nicosia, Cyprus, for the drawings.

Michael Counsell
2001

Practical Details for Travelling to Greece and Crete, Turkey, Cyprus, Israel, Italy, Lebanon, Malta and Syria

GENERAL INFORMATION

Travellers from the USA

Travellers from the USA can obtain a booklet *Your Trip Abroad* from The Superintendent of Documents, P.O. Box 371954, Pittsburgh PA 15250-7954, Telephone 202 512 1800, for about $1.25, which gives information of visa requirements, customs regulations, medical care, etc. in various countries.

On the Internet

A list of national travel offices, full though incomplete, is at http://www.towd.com. Travel information by country is listed at http://www. wtg-online.com and http://www. travel-library.com. Details of all British Representatives abroad and travel advice can be found at http://www.fco.gov.uk and http://www.lonelyplanet. com has a section called subWWWay which links you to travel resources elsewhere on the web.

GREECE AND CRETE

Nationals of the USA, Canada, Australia, or New Zealand with a valid passport, and the countries of the European Union with a passport or identity card, are allowed to stay for up to three months without a visa in Greece. Hotels do not have the right to detain your passport, but carrying a photocopy is advisable. Entry is refused to any whose passports show that they have visited Turkish-occupied North Cyprus, so visitors to that territory should have their visas stamped on a separate piece of paper. Drivers need an International Driving Permit or an EU driving licence (photocard), and a 'green card' (international third party insurance) is recommended. Warning triangles and seat belts are compulsory. Camping and caravanning are forbidden outside official sites. If you are taking medication you will need to produce a doctor's certificate to import the drugs into Greece. Smuggling of drugs and the export of antiquities, including even the smallest item from an archaeological site, are punished severely.

TURKEY

Turkey is a secular society, so visitors should not wear clerical dress, a prominent cross or other symbols identifying their religion. Nationals of Australia, Belgium, Canada, Denmark, Finland, France, Germany, Greece, Holland, Iceland, Japan, New Zealand, Norway, Sweden and Switzerland need no visas to enter Turkey. Nationals of Austria, Ireland, Israel, Italy, Portugal, Spain, the UK and the USA may buy a visa at the airport; an English ten pound note or US$45 in cash will be needed by UK and USA nationals respectively.

Drivers should carry with them their national car registration documents and drivers' licences at all times, and display oval nationality plates on the vehicle. A green card valid for the whole country ('Asian Turkey' as well as 'European Turkey') or a Turkish insurance policy, purchasable near the border, is obligatory. Accidental damage to vehicles imported into Turkey must be reported to the police and the local customs office.

When travelling by sea from Greece to Turkey always submit your passport to the ferry company the previous day. Smuggling of drugs and the export of antiquities, including even the smallest item from an archaeological site, are punished severely.

Visitors to Turkey will be encouraged to visit a carpet factory. There is no need to buy a carpet, though you will get a good bargain if you do, and they will even ship it home for you on payment of a deposit. But the making of a carpet is a fascinating process to watch, and a very ancient tradition using natural dyes and meticulous hand labour. Every pattern has a meaning, and comes from a particular area. Carpet-making is also an important part of Turkey's economy, and of the tourist industry. If you are lucky you may also see outside the factory a tent woven from goats' hair just like those from which St Paul used to make his living.

CYPRUS

A passport or EU photo-identity card is essential; keep it with you at all times. Nationals of EU countries, the USA, Australia, Canada, New Zealand and Singapore may enter both the Republic of Cyprus and Northern Cyprus without a visa for up to three months; for South Africans it is 30 days. EU citizens need only a domestic driving licence to drive in Cyprus; for others an International Driving Permit is advisable. If bringing your own vehicle, the registration document and a 'green card' to prove insurance cover (validated to include Cyprus) are necessary; however the customs procedures in Lemesos port are somewhat tedious. Vehicles drive on the left all over Cyprus.

The Turkish Republic of Northern Cyprus occupies about 35% of the island, with Turkish as the official language, but is recognized only by Turkey. Access is available by air and ferry from Turkey. It is impossible to travel between Turkey and Greece or Israel via Cyprus, however. The Republic of Cyprus occupies the south of the island; Greek is spoken there, sometimes with a dialect which differs from the Greek used on the mainland.

There are air and ferry connections from many places to the Republic of Cyprus (see below under Getting to Cyprus). Try to get immigration to stamp a separate paper, not your passport when you enter North Cyprus. You can enter the north from the south on a day trip, when Turkish Cypriot officials will issue a cost-free day pass. But you cannot enter the south from the north unless you came from the south in the first place; if you try you will be arrested, returned to the north and probably never be allowed into the south again. All postal addresses in the north must be followed by 'Mersin 10, Turkey', not by 'North Cyprus'.

ISRAEL

At the time this book was finalized there were not many pilgrims visiting Israel because of the Intifada. Guidance is given, however, for the situation as it was before, in the hope that peace will return. Visitors need a passport which is valid for at least six months after the date of return. Visas are not required except for those with passports from parts of Africa and Central America; India; Singapore, and some former Soviet republics. Avoid any stamp in the passport which would show you have visited Israel and might prevent subsequent visits to an Arab country. For your protection, luggage examination and questioning of passengers is usually a lengthy business when entering Israel by land or air; allow plenty of time for check-in, and do not include anything in your luggage that you have not packed yourself.

The National Parks green card gives free admission to many archaeological sites, and can be obtained from The National Parks Authority, 4 Rav Alluf M. Makleff Street, P.O. Box 7028, Hakirya, 61070 Tel Aviv, Tel. (03) 6952281, fax (03) 6967643, or the ticket office at most sites. Drivers in Israel need their domestic driving licence. Ferries run between Haifa in Israel and Piraeus in Greece via Limassol in Cyprus, and sometimes Crete and Rhodes; for details visit **www. greekislands.gr/greece.htm,**

www.Ferries.gr/Poseidon, or **www.viamare.com/salamis /salpre.htm**

ITALY

EU citizens need only a passport or national identity card to enter Italy and can remain there indefinitely; citizens of the USA, Canada, Australia and many other countries need only have their passports stamped on entry if they are coming for a purpose other than tourism, or intending to stay more than three months. There are limits on the amount of tobacco and alcohol that can be imported. Drivers should have a national driving licence (photocard) from an EU country or an international driving licence if they live outside the EU, and insurance cover; a 'green card', though not compulsory is useful evidence of this. Red triangles must be used in event of a breakdown; dipped headlights in poor visibility; priority is to the right at crossroads; on the spot fines can be given for crossing a solid white line. Tolls are levied on most autostrada.

LEBANON

Lebanon is now open to tourists after the end of the civil war, and attractions for visitors are being restored. All nationalities need a visa (which will take up two pages in the passport); visas can be obtained at Beirut airport for most nationalities, and at the border if entering from Syria, but they are cheaper obtained from the Lebanese Embassy or consulate in your home country; two passport photos, a fee, and a letter from your employer to show that you are returning to your job are usually needed. Passports must not contain any stamp which shows that you have ever entered or left Israel, and you must not give a 'yes' answer to questions as to whether you have ever or ever intend to visit Israel or 'Occupied Palestine'. Keep your passport with you at all times. Drivers need an International Driving Permit, and if bringing your own car a carnet. The cash charges levied on vehicles entering Lebanon make it uneconomical to bring in your own vehicle for a short visit.

MALTA

No visas are needed for a stay of up to three months in Malta. There are restrictions on the amount of Maltese currency that can be carried when entering or leaving the republic. Drivers taking vehicles in on a ferry need the vehicle's registration document, a 'green card' and a domestic driving licence; in Malta you drive on the left. Seat belts are compulsory; it is illegal to drive with any alcohol in the blood; if involved in an accident, do not move your vehicle until the police arrive.

SYRIA

All foreigners entering Syria need a visa; they must be obtained from the Syrian Embassy in your home country before setting out, as they cannot be obtained at the border or the airport. Visas obtained at the Syrian Embassies at Ankara or İstanbul can be expensive depending on your nationality, and you will need to take with your application two passport photos and a letter of recommendation from the Embassy there of your home country, which can also be expensive. Passports must not contain any stamp which shows that you have ever entered or left Israel, and you must not give a 'yes' answer to questions as to whether you have ever or ever intend to visit Israel or 'Occupied Palestine'. Visas must be used within three months of issue (six months for multiple entry visas) and are valid for fifteen days in Syria after which they must be renewed. Carry the yellow or white entry card, and your passport, at all times. Owners bringing vehicles into Syria must take out a Third Party Insurance; a Carnet de Passage and an International Driving Licence are required. Tax can be levied on video cameras, computers, etc. brought into the country. There is no Internet access in Syria.

NATIONAL TOURIST OFFICES

See the telephone directory of your capital city for local tourist offices, or consult the Internet sites below. Most towns have a **Tourist Information centre** indicated with the international 'i' symbol.

Greece and Crete

http://www.gnto.gr
EOT (Ellenikos Organismos Tourismou), Amerikis 2, Athens 10564, Greece. Tel. +30 1-327 1300 / 2, email info@gnto.gr
Dodecanese islands:
http://www.ando.gr/eot/
Hellenic Tourism Organization, Directorate for the Dodecanese Islands, Makariou and Papagou corner, 85100 Rhodos, Greece. Tel. +30 241 23255 or 21921 or 27466, Fax. +30 241 26955, email eot-rodos@otenet.gr
Greek ferry information:
http://www.ferries.gr
http://www. agapitos-ferries.gr
http://www.anak.gr
http://www.minoan.gr
http://www.strintzis.gr
http://www.superfast.com
http://www.ventouris.gr

Turkey

Karakoy Liman, İstanbul, Turkey. Tel. +90 (91) 1 49 57 76

Cyprus

http://www.cyprustourism. org
Cyprus Tourism Organization, P.O. Box 24535, CY 1390 Lefkosia (Nicosia), Cyprus.

Tel. +357 (2) 337715, Fax. +357 (2) 331644/331698, email cytour@cto.org.cy http://www.windowoncyprus.com, http://www.cosmosnet.net/azias/cyprus/c-main.html, and http://www.welcometocyprus.com also give travel information.

Turkish Republic of North Cyprus

http://www.cypnet.com/cyradise/cyradise.html North Cyprus Tourist Office, Bedrettin Demirel Caddesi, Lefkosa (North Nicosia), Mersin 10, Turkey. Tel. +90 392 228 1057, Fax. +90 392 228 5625

Israel

http://www.infotour.co.il Israel Government Tourist Office, POB 97911, Jerusalem, Israel. Tel. +97 (02) 280382 Christian Information Centre, P.O. Box 14308, by the Jaffa Gate, Jerusalem, Israel. Tel. +97 (02) 627 2692, Fax. +97 (02) 628 6417

Italy

http://www.enit.it/Eng Ente nazionale italiano per il turismo, via Marghera no. 2, 00185 Roma, Italy. Tel. +39 6 49711, Fax. +39 6 44 63379

Lebanon

http://www.lebanon-tourism.gov.lb http://www.lebanon-directory.com http://www.embofleb.org/waiver.htm

email mot@lebanon-tourism.gov.lb P.O. Box 11-5344, 550 rue Banque du Liban, Hamra, Beirut, Lebanon. Tel. +961 (01) 343073, Fax. +961 (01) 340945

Malta

http://www.visitmalta.com Malta Tourism Authority, 280 Republic Street, Valletta, CMR 02, Malta. Tel. +356 22 4444 / 4445 / 5048 / 5049, Fax. +356 22 0401, email info@visitmalta.com See also http://www.searchmalta.com.

Syria

http://www.syriatourism.org Ministry of Tourism, Abu firas al Hamandi Street, 3050 Damascus, Syria Arab Republic. Tel. +963 (11) 223 7490 or 224 2852, Fax. +963 (11) 224 2636, email mintourism@syriatel.net

NOTES FOR TRAVELLERS

Climate

In most countries referred to in this book the winters are wet but mild, the summers very hot and dry, and the spring and autumn the best times for touring. Bring warm clothes in winter, light clothes at other times, with cotton being preferable to man-made fabrics, but warm sweaters for the evenings, waterproofs, stout shoes for walking and light shoes for evenings, swimming gear, insect repellents and sun creams.

Distances

are in kilometres (km); approximately 8 kilometres = 5 miles; 1 mile = 1.6 kilometres; 1 kilometre = 0.62 miles; 100 kilometres = 62.14 miles

Dress codes

Modest dress is required when visiting churches and mosques; women should ensure that their shoulders and upper arms are covered, at least by a shawl, and men or women in shorts will not be admitted. When visiting Muslim countries, women should not wear tight or revealing clothing: loose cotton trousers or a long skirt, with a baggy long-sleeved top, are always acceptable and not too hot to wear.

Driving

is on the right except in North Cyprus, the Republic of Cyprus and Malta. In all other countries give way to traffic approaching from the right, unless the main road is indicated by a yellow diamond sign. The following regulations apply in nearly all countries: seat belts must be worn, carry a warning triangle, a first aid kit, a fire extinguisher and a set of spare bulbs, and a 'green card' or equivalent for insurance; motor cyclists must wear helmets; do not carry petrol (gasoline) cans; use dipped headlights in tunnels and conditions of poor visibility; do not cross a solid white line; and report all accidents to the police and complete a European Accident Statement which you should obtain from your insurance company in advance of setting off on your trip. International road signs are used in all countries, but they are not the same as those used in the USA and Canada.

Electrical equipment

Current is 220 volts AC 50 Hz; in Malta and both parts of Cyprus the British-style plugs with three flat pins are used; elsewhere plug sockets are of the European two-pronged design, so a travel adaptor may be necessary. Airlines require electrical equipment to be carried in hand luggage. A pocket torch can be helpful in some places. (See below for Radio Reception.)

Emergency services

Police: Cyprus Republic 199; Greece 100, or 109 in Athens suburbs; Israel 100; Italy 113 (Carabinieri 112); Lebanon 01112; North Cyprus 155; Malta 191; Syria 112 (traffic police 115); Turkey 155 (Traffic Police 154, Jandarma 156)

Fire Brigade: Cyprus Republic 119; Greece 199; Israel 102; Italy 115; Lebanon 01175; Malta 199; North Cyprus 199; Syria 113

Ambulance: Cyprus Republic 119; Israel 911; Italy 118;

Speed limits, in kilometres (and miles) per hour and other motoring information

Country	In towns	Open roads	Motorways	Blood alcohol	Motor assistance
Cyprus (N)	50 (31)	100 (62)	–	–	None
Cyprus (S)	50 (31)	80 (50)	100 (62)	.009mg/100 ml	313 233
Greece	50 (31)	90 (55)	120 (75)	0.05%	104
Italy	50 (31) Major roads: 100 (62)	90 (55) Motorways 110 (67) if under 1100cc.	130 (80)	0.08%	116
Malta	40 (25)	65 (40)	–	None permitted	241665
Syria	60 (37) Major roads: 110 (69)	70 (44)	–	–	–
Turkey	50 (31)	90 (55)	130 (80) max. 40 (25) minimum	–	212–282 8140

Lebanon 372 803/4; Malta 196; Syria 110; in less urgent situations call the local ambulance service, using the local telephone number from the telephone directory.

Medical Emergencies: in Greece call the tourist police 171; or in Athens the ambulance on 166; in North Cyprus 112.

Hospitals are indicated by a road sign with an 'H' on it.

Finance

Banking hours

Cyprus: Monday to Friday 08.30–12.30, plus 15.15–16.45 on Monday

Greece: Monday to Thursday 08.00–14.00, Friday 08.00–13.00

Israel: Sunday, Tuesday, Thursday: 08.30–12.30, 16.00–18.00; Monday and Wednesday 08.30–12.30; Friday and eve of Jewish Holy Days 08.30–12.00

Italy: Monday to Friday 08.30–13.30, 15.00–16.00

Lebanon: Monday to Friday 08.30–12.30 and 08.30–12.00 on Saturday

Malta: Monday to Friday 08.30–12.30; Saturday 08.30–11.30 (12.00 from 1 October to 14 June)

Syria: 08.00–14.00 daily, closed on Fridays

Turkey: Monday to Friday 08.30–12.00 and 13.30–17.00

Turkish North Cyprus: Monday to Friday 08.00–12.00 and 14.00–17.00 in winter; 08.00–13.30 and 14.30–17.00 in summer

Local currency is in Turkish lira; Cyprus pounds in the south and Turkish lira in the north; Israeli shekels; Lebanese lira; Maltese liri; and Syrian pounds.

In January 2002 Euro banknotes and coins were introduced in Austria, Belgium, Finland, France, Germany, Greece, Ireland, Italy, Luxembourg, Netherlands, Portugal and Spain; for further information see www.europa.eu.int and www.ecb.int

It is advisable to carry passports and all money and credit cards in a money belt and beware of pickpockets and handbag thieves. Eurocheques can be cashed on presentation of a Eurocard in Greece, Turkey, Cyprus and Italy. You can usually change travellers' cheques in exchange bureaux, some but not all banks, major post offices and some hotels, but not usually in guest houses and other small establishments. Always keep a note of the numbers of your travellers cheques in a separate place. You can also draw cash with major credit cards through ATM machines outside certain banks (none in Syria). It is advisable to buy a small amount of local currency before setting out; there is no limit on the amount in notes that you can change back into sterling when you return, but some countries have a limit on the amount of local currency you can take in and out; except in Malta, it is usually high enough

9

not to bother the ordinary traveller.

Health

Travellers from the UK should obtain a copy of the booklet T5 *Health Advice for Travellers* from major post offices, follow its advice, and complete the form E111 which is included in it; then have it stamped and signed by the post office, and keep it with their passport. Greece and Italy are within the European Economic Area; Malta has a reciprocal agreement with the UK. Any **medicines** or other health needs which may be required should be taken with you, together with a doctor's note authorizing you to carry them and naming them in case you need replacements. If you have a delicate stomach you are advised to buy bottled water. **Travel insurance** is essential to cover the cost of medical emergencies, which can be high. Consult your physician for the latest information on **immunization**.

Language

See the section on 'Learn a phrase a day' on pp. 232–34 for Greek and Turkish. Maltese is a Semitic language derived from ancient Phoenician; Arabic is spoken in Syria and Palestine (and Lebanon but there French is also widely used), and Hebrew in Israel. But in all countries there are many people who speak English.

Opening times and admission charges

Every effort has been made to give opening times correct at the time of writing, but they can change without notice. Most places for which opening times are given charge for admission but, because they are liable to change, admission charges are not listed.

Photography

Always carry sufficient film in case it is not available locally. Remember Muslim women often dislike being photographed.

Poste restante

Letters or packages marked 'Poste restante' ('Fermo posta' in Italy), and with the family name of the recipient clearly printed and underlined, will be kept at main post offices (Merkez postahane in Turkey) for up to four weeks; a passport must be shown when collecting them. In Malta it is necessary to write in advance to the postmaster at Valletta requesting to use this service. There is no poste restante in Lebanon.

Radio reception

The **BBC World Service** can be received on 198 kHz, 648 kHz, 6195 kHz, 9410 kHz, 12095 kHz, 15485 kHz and 17640 kHz in Europe; 1507 kHz, 6050 kHz, and 9410 kHz in Greece; 1323 kHz, 11760 kHz, 15575 kHz and 17640 kHz in the Middle East. It is also broadcast on FM 104.4 and 98.4 in Crete, 94.4 and 100.4 in Athens, 102.2 on Samos, 102.7 in Rome, 101.8 in Malta, 1323 kHz MW in Cyprus, 227 kHz MW in Israel, and 720 kHz MW in Lebanon. Further details from BBC World Service Shop, Bush House, Strand, P.O. Box 76, London WC2B 4PH, Telephone 020 7257 2576, Fax 020 7240 4811 email worldservice.shop@bbc.co.uk Internet http://www.bbc.co.uk/worldservice

Cyprus has the British Forces Broadcasting Services on 89.7, 89.9, 91.9, 92.1, 95.3, and 99.6 FM in different parts of the island.

Maltese television and radio have some programmes in English

The Voice of America can be received on 17.73 MHz, 15.25 MHz, 9.760 MHz, 6.040 MHz, 1.548 MHz, 1.197 MHz and 0.792 MHz; 1260 kHz; 3985 kHz; 5995 kHz; 6010 kHz; 7170 kHz; and 11965 kHz; also 11.84 MHz medium wave.

Canadian and Australian stations can also be received in most areas.

With a WorldSpace receiver it is possible to receive BBC World Service, CNN and other news and music stations with digital clarity wherever there is no obstruction between the antenna and the satellite over the equator. Consult http://www.worldspace.com

BBC, CNN, NBC and SKY satellite television is available in many hotels.

Security

You are advised to keep your purse or handbag (firmly closed), cameras, travel documents and passport attached to your person so as not to leave them behind anywhere; never put down an open purse or bag. It is a good idea to make two photocopies of your passport and visas, insurance documents, credit cards, driving licence and tickets, and leave one at home and keep the other with you but in a separate place from the originals when travelling, in case of loss. Also note the telephone numbers to call if your credit cards are stolen. If this happens, cancel them immediately; it may take several days to have new cards flown out by courier, during which time you may have to cast yourself on the mercy of your hotel or tour operator. If you have two credit cards carry them separately.

Shop hours

(enquire locally about public and religious holidays)

Greece: 08.00–13.30 and 17.30–20.30 on Tuesday, Thursday and Friday, and 08.00–14.30 on Monday, Wednesday and Saturday.

Turkey: Monday to Saturday 09.00–13.00 and 14.00–19.00.

Cyprus: 08.30–13.00, 16.00–19.30 Monday to Saturday from 1 June to 14 September; shops close at 18.00 from 1 November to 31 March, and at 19.00 in the spring and autumn. Early closing is on Wednesday and Saturday at 14.00, and there may be no lunch break in country areas.

Turkish North Cyprus: 07.30–14.00 in summer, 08.00–13.00 and 14.00–17.00 in winter, Monday to Friday, with late opening on Monday 15.30–18.00.

Israel and the Palestinian Territories: 08.00–13.00 and 16.00–19.00 Monday to Thursday, 08.00–14.00 Friday, everything shuts for the sabbath from sunset on Friday to sunset on Saturday in Israeli areas, or all day Friday in Muslim areas.

Italy: 08.30 or 09.00 to 12.30 or 13.00, and 15.30 or 16.00 to 19.30 or 20.00 Monday to Saturday.

Lebanon: 09.00–18.00 Monday to Saturday; many shops close at about 15.00 in summer.

Malta: 09.00–13.00 and 15.30 or 16.00–19.00; note the long closure at lunchtime.

Syria: 08.00–14.00, 16.00–18.00, closed on Fridays.

Telephones

Check the availability for local and long-distance calls, and phone cards, of Telephone company offices, post offices and public call boxes; the situation varies from country to country.

For international calls, dial 00, then the country code, then (except to USA and Canada) omit the first 0. Country Codes: Australia 61; Cyprus 357; North Cyprus 90392; Greece and Crete 30; Israel 972; Italy 39; Lebanon 961; Malta 356; Syria 963; Turkey 90; UK 44; USA and Canada 1.

In Italy dial 170 for a reversed charge call; reversed charge calls cannot be made from Lebanon or Syria.

For international operators call: Greece 161; Italy 15; Malta 194; Turkey 115. In other countries, unless you can direct dial, it is usually necessary to make your call from a main post office.

GSM900 mobile phones are used in Europe, Australia and New Zealand, but are not compatible with the GSM1900 used in USA and Canada. Check with your service provider about using your mobile phone in different countries, and beware of local calls being expensively routed to your home country and back again. Or hire a mobile phone locally.

Temperatures

Temperatures are measured in degrees Celsius or Centigrade: 0°C=32°F; 10°C=50°F; 20°C=68°F; 50°C=122°F; 100°C=212°F. To convert Celsius into Fahrenheit

Conversion table			
From	**To**	**Multiply by**	
Inches	Centimetres	2.54	0.3937
Feet	Metres	0.3048	3.2808
Yards	Metres	0.9144	1.0936
Miles	Kilometres	1.6090	0.6214
Acres	Hectares	0.4057	2.4649
Imperial Gallons	Litres	4.5460	0.2200
US Gallons	Litres	3.79	0.26
Ounces	Grams	28.35	0.0353
Pounds	Grams	453.6	0.0022
Pounds	Kilograms	0.4536	2.2046
Tons	Tonnes	1.0160	0.9843
To	**From**		**Multiply by**

multiply by 9, divide by 5 and add 32.

Time

European time, including Italy and Malta, is one hour in advance of Britain; Greece, Turkey, Cyprus, Israel, Lebanon and Syria are two hours ahead; though daylight saving time is not always introduced on the same date as British Summer Time.

Toilets

In most of the countries mentioned here you are asked to put toilet paper not into the toilet but into a waste bin. Many toilets other than those in hotels are of the squatting type. Paper may not be provided so carry your own.

Visiting Christians in other countries

It is good to encourage the tiny Christian minority in Turkey by your prayers and by discreet visits, but not too openly, for they avoid trouble by maintaining a low profile. Much the same could be said of Messianic Jews; the dwindling number of Arab Christians in Israel need all the encouragement they can get. In Greece, although you may also wish to visit the evangelical Christians, remember that the Orthodox see themselves as the original Christian Church founded by the apostles, with even Roman Catholics as a rebellious breakaway, and Protestants as a schism from that group. They have a long tradition of prayer, teaching and witness, and there are discreet movements of reform.

Weights and measures

Many countries using the metric system indicate decimals with commas and thousands with points, so what in Britain or the USA would be written 2,600.30 may elsewhere be 2.600,30, etc. (See the conversion table above.)

A Middle East Time Line

BC (or BCE)	
5000	Stone and Copper Age; first Mesopotamian civilization
3100	Upper and Lower Egypt united; Sumerians in Mesopotamia
3000–1100	Cycladic civilization in Greek Islands; Minoan civilization in Crete
2600–1900	Old Bronze Age
2400–2200	Akkadian civilization in Mesopotamia, founded by Sargon
1900–1300	Hittite empire in Turkey
1900–1100	Mycenaean Age in Greece
c.1900	Abraham migrates to Canaan
c.1700–1250	Jews enslaved in Egypt
c.1450	Major volcanic eruption on Santorini island, Greek Cyclades
1200	Dorians bring Iron-Age technology to Greece. Civilizations in Turkey: Phrygian, Mysian, Hellenistic (Midas and Croesus), kingdoms of Ionia, Lycia, Lydia, Caria and Pamphylia
c.1250	Jewish exodus from Egypt
c.1200	The Trojan wars; Mycenaean Greeks besiege Troy
c.850	Homer's *Iliad* and *Odyssey* composed
c.850–700	Prophets in Israel: Elijah, Elisha, Amos, Hosea, Isaiah, Micah
800–480	Archaic Age; city states in Greece
753	Legendary foundation of Rome by Romulus
722	Fall of Samaria to the Assyrians
c.700	Rise of Medes in Persia
700–509	Etruscan kings rule Rome
587 or 586	Fall of Jerusalem to Persians
550	Cyrus defeats Medes in Persia, allows Israel to return from exile in Babylon, invades Anatolia
509	Roman republic founded, governed by two consuls elected for a year, and the senate
500–320	Greek democracy in Athens
490	Athenians defeat Persians at the Battle of Marathon, then Persians defeat Spartan king Leonidas at Thermopylae and burn Athens, then Greek navy defeats Persian navy
480–338	Classical Age in Greece
461–429	Pericles building in Athens

431–421	First Peloponnesian war: Sparta supports Corinth against Athens, ending in truce
416	Alcibiades of Athens besieges Syracuse in Sicily, then joins Sparta against the Athenians
413–404	Second Peloponnesian war: Sparta under Lysander, with Persian help, defeats Athens
399	Enforced suicide of Socrates in Athens
338–146	Hellenistic period begins when Philip of Macedon conquers Greece
334–323	Philip's son Alexander the Great conquers, and spreads Greek culture in, Asia Minor (Turkey), Persia, Syria, Egypt and parts of India
323	On Alexander's death his empire is divided between Ptolemies in Egypt, Seleucids in Antioch-on-the-Orontes, and Antigonids in Greece and Asia Minor who are soon defeated by the Seleucids
281–272	Romans defeat Pyrrhus, king of Epirus, to conquer southern Italy
279	Celts set up Galatia
264–261	First Punic War, Rome captures Sicily from Carthage
218	Second Punic War, Hannibal crosses the Alps and defeats Rome
210	Scipio fights Carthage in Spain, 204 in Africa, 202 defeats Hannibal
168	Romans defeat Macedon. The Romans begin to take over the Greek empire, but Greek remains the common language
166	Jewish revolt against Seleucid Greeks led by Judas Maccabeus.
166–63	The reign of the Hasmonean kings in Israel
146	Destruction of Carthage
129	Romans establish province of Asia with capital at Ephesus
70	Pompey and Crassus are consuls of Rome
64	Pompey annexes Syria, ending the Seleucid dynasty
63	Pompey captures Jerusalem for the Romans
60	Triumvirate of Pompey, Crassus and Julius Caesar
59	Julius Caesar becomes consul
49	Julius Caesar crosses the Rubicon and drives Pompey from Rome
44	Julius Caesar assassinated
43	Triumvirate of Octavius, Antony and Lepidus
42	Antony and Octavius defeat Cassius and Brutus at Philippi

37–4	The reign of Herod the Great
37BC–AD70	The 'Second Temple' period in Jerusalem; actually Herod the Great built the third temple on the site
30	Antony defeated at Actium and commits suicide
27	Octavius renamed Augustus and declared to be a god
Around 6 BC	Birth of Jesus

AD (or CE)

14–37	Tiberius is Roman emperor
c.28	Saul is student of Gamaliel at Jerusalem
30	Crucifixion and resurrection of Jesus
33–41	Ministry of Peter and Philip
33	Martyrdom of Stephen (Acts 7, 8) and conversion of St Paul (Acts 9:4–19)
34	Paul in Arabia (Galatians 1:17)
36	Pontius Pilate resigns as procurator
34–37	Paul in Damascus (Galatians 1:17)
37–39	Aretas ruling Damascus, Paul's flight (2 Corinthians 11:33; Acts 19:20)
37–41	Caligula is Roman emperor
35–37	Paul visits Jerusalem (Galatians 1:18; Acts 9:26) and returns to Tarsus in Cilicia (Acts 9:30) and Syria (Galatians 1:21)
39	Herod Antipas exiled by Emperor Caligula
41–54	Claudius is Roman emperor
41 or 49	Expulsion of Jews from Jerusalem by Emperor Claudius (Acts 17:2)
44	Martyrdom of James the son of Zebedee. Peter freed from prison, goes to Caesarea (Acts 12)
44	Death of Herod Agrippa I (Acts 12:23)
45–46	Paul called by Barnabas to supervise the church in Antioch-on-the-Orontes (Acts 11:26)
46	Paul and Barnabas take famine relief to Jerusalem and collect Mark (according to Acts 11:30, 12:25, though this visit is apparently not mentioned in Galatians)
46	First missionary journey: Paul, Barnabas and John Mark sent from Antioch to Cyprus and Galatia: Perga (John Mark leaves them), Antioch-of-Pisidia, Iconium, Lystra and Derbe, and back through Attalia to Antioch-on-the-Orontes (Acts 13, 14)
48	The Council in Jerusalem agrees that gentile (non-

	Jewish) Christians need not be circumcised (Acts 15:1–35; not mentioned in Galatians)
49–50	Second missionary journey: Paul and Silas to Syria and Cilicia, Derbe and Lystra (Timothy joins them), Phrygia and Galatia, Troas (Luke joins them), Neapolis, Philippi, Thessalonica, Berea, and Athens (Acts 15:36—16:40)
50–51	In Corinth (Acts 17:1) Paul writes two letters to the Thessalonians
51–52	Hearing before Gallio in Corinth (Acts 17:12; this is a fixed date because an inscription discovered in Delphi shows that this was the year when Gallio was proconsul). Return via Ephesus (where Paul leaves Priscilla and Aquila) to Jerusalem (Acts 17:22; Galatians 2)
52–60	Felix procurator of Judea
52	Paul in Antioch-on-the-Orontes (Acts 17:22) argues with Peter (Galatians 2:11–14)
52	Apollos in Corinth (Acts 17:24–28)
52	Third missionary journey begins: Paul from Antioch-on-the-Orontes to Galatia and Phrygia (Acts 17:23)
52–54	Paul in Ephesus. (Acts 19:1—20:1) Around this time he writes his letter to the Galatians, a lost 'previous letter' to the Corinthians, then Paul's first letter to the Corinthians, then the 'sorrowful letter'. Possibly he makes a visit to Corinth (2 Corinthians 12:14, 13:1–2, not mentioned in Acts). In prison in Ephesus (not mentioned in Acts) Paul writes the 'captivity epistles' (Philippians, Colossians and Philemon) though some put them later, in Caesarea or Rome
54–68	Emperor Nero succeeds Claudius
54	Riot in Ephesus (Acts 19:21–41)
54–55	Paul, with his companions (Acts 20:4) to Macedonia (Acts 20:1; where he wrote his second letter to the Corinthians 1–9 and later 10–13); and maybe Troas (2 Corinthians 2:12–13) and Illyricum (Romans 15:19)
55–57	Paul in Corinth (where he wrote his letter to the Romans; Acts 20:2), back to Philippi, Troas, Assos, Miletus, Patara, Tyre, Ptolemais, Caesarea-on-Sea, Jerusalem (Acts 20, 21:1–26)
57–61	Paul's arrest in Jerusalem, imprisonment in Caesarea (Acts 21:27—23:35). Trial before Felix (Acts 24)

59–60	Festus succeeds Felix as procurator of Judea. Trial before Festus, appeal to Caesar (Acts 25). Appearance before Agrippa II (Acts 26)
61–62	Departure for Rome, shipwreck, winter on Malta (Acts 27, 28:1–15)
62–64	Arrival and house-arrest in Rome (Acts 27:16–31). Paul writes Ephesians if authentic, possibly Luke writes his Gospel and Acts of the Apostles
64	Paul released (some say executed), travels to Spain and/or revisits Asia Minor
64	The fire of Rome and persecution under Nero
66	Death of James the Just in Jerusalem (mentioned in Josephus' *Antiquities*)
66	Paul arrested (2 Timothy 1:12, 4:13)
67	Peter and Paul martyred in Rome (according to Eusebius, writing in the fourth century)
68–69	Galla, Otho and Vitellius are Roman emperors
68 or 95	The Revelation to John written in Patmos
69–79	Vespasian is Roman emperor
70	Destruction of Jerusalem
79–81	Titus is Roman emperor
81–96	Domitian is Roman emperor
96–162	Antonine emperors of Rome: Nerva, Trajan, Hadrian, Antoninus, Marcus Aurelius
193–275	Severus dynasty in Rome
284–305	Diocletian is Roman emperor, persecution of Christians
306–37	Constantine is Roman emperor
313	Edict of Milan promises religious freedom
324–1453	Byzantine period
330	Constantine makes Byzantium capital of the Roman empire and renames it Constantinople
379–95	Emperor Theodosius, a great church builder
395	Division of the Roman empire into eastern and western empires
455	Sack of Rome by Vandals
527–65	Emperor Justinian
570–632	Life of Muhammad
614	Persians destroy churches in the Holy Land
644	Division of Muslims into Sunnis and Shi'ites, Umayyad Arab dynasty in Damascus
750	Abbasid Arabs topple Umayyads, make Baghdad their capital
800	Charlemagne proclaimed emperor by the pope
962	Otto I founds the Holy Roman Empire

1037–1109	Abbasid Arabs overthrown by their mercenary guards the Seljuk Turks. Seljuk empire centred in Iran
1095	First crusade to protect pilgrim routes to Jerusalem from the Turks
1099	Crusaders destroy Jerusalem, killing Jewish, Muslim and Christian inhabitants
1187	Saladin drives the crusaders from Jerusalem
1204	Crusaders sack Constantinople
1210	Venetians occupy Crete
1250	Saladin's successors are ousted by their Mamluk guards
1282	Sicilian Vespers: massacre of French settlers in Sicily
1288	Ottoman empire founded, takes control of countries abandoned by the collapsing Byzantine empire
1291	Mamluks drive the crusaders from Acre
1453	Ottoman Turks conquer Constantinople
1517	Ottomans defeat Mamluks at Aleppo
1520–66	Suleiman the Magnificent rules from the gates of Venice to North Africa
1669	Crete surrenders to the Turks
1796–98	Napoleon in Italy and Egypt
1821–29	Greek wars of independence from the Turks
1870	Italy united
1916	Arab revolt against the Turks, supported by Lawrence of Arabia for Britain
1917	British cabinet promise Zionists a home in Palestine: the Balfour Declaration
1918	French mandate in Syria and Lebanon, British mandate in Egypt, Palestine, Transjordan and Iraq
1923	Exchange of minority populations between Greece and Turkey. Turkish Republic under Atatürk and Greek Republic formed
1938	Death of Atatürk
1946–49	Greek Civil War
1948 and 1967	Arab–Israeli wars
1967–74	Military rule in Greece
1974	Partition of Cyprus

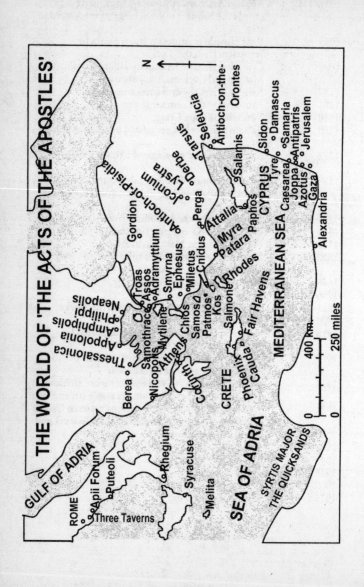

THE WORLD OF 'THE ACTS OF THE APOSTLES'

N

GULF OF ADRIA

ROME
Apii Forum
Puteoli
Three Taverns
Rhegium
Syracuse
Melita

SEA OF ADRIA

SYRTIS MAJOR
THE QUICKSANDS

Berea
Thessalonica
Nicopolis
Apollonia
Amphipolis
Philippi
Neapolis
Samothrace
Mytilene
Athens
Corinth
Chios
Samos
Patmos
Kos

CRETE
Phoenix
Cauda
Fair Havens
Salmone

Troas
Assos
Adramyttium
Smyrna
Ephesus
Miletus
Cnidus
Rhodes

Gordion
Antioch-of-Pisidia
Iconium
Lystra
Derbe
Perga
Attalia
Myra
Patara
Paphos

Tarsus
Seleucia
Antioch-on-the-Orontes

Salamis
CYPRUS

MEDITERRANEAN SEA

Sidon
Damascus
Tyre
Caesarea
Joppa
Samaria
Antipatris
Azotus
Jerusalem
Gaza

Alexandria

0   250 miles

0   400 Km.

The World of the Apostles

THE ACTS OF THE APOSTLES

The book we know as the Acts of the Apostles claims to be a continuation of what we know as the Gospel of Luke (Acts 1:1). The Gospel, though not claiming to be by an eyewitness, states that it has compared the reports of those who were, to produce an orderly account for somebody called 'Your excellency Theophilus' (Luke 1:1). There are a number of questions we should ask before reading Luke and Acts, and different people will give different answers. These different opinions do not change the spiritual message of the books, but they will affect the way we approach them. The following is an attempt to lay out the alternatives, so that readers can make their own decisions.

When were Luke and Acts written?

A century or more ago there were some, mostly in Germany, who said that all the books of the New Testament were written years after the events they describe, often well into the second century AD. Most people now recognize that such scepticism has no basis.

Today it is more common to find writers describing the Gospels and Acts as coming from the 80s and 90s of the first century. This is because they

seem to describe a well-organized church, suffering persecution which, they say, corresponds to the conditions at that time. Moreover, they point to the predictions Jesus made of the destruction of Jerusalem in e.g. Luke 21:20–24 and Mark 13:14–20, and suggest these could only have been written after it was destroyed by the Romans in AD 70.

There are some who return to the traditional dating before AD 70. They refer to the availability of living eyewitnesses (Luke 1:2–3); and the descriptions of persecution from the Jews, not the Romans, in the 60s that St Paul mentions in his letters. Anyone with any political acumen, leaving aside the gift of prophecy, they say, could have foreseen that Jewish rebelliousness would bring the Romans down upon them sooner or later. And Jerusalem was destroyed by fire, yet none of the predictions mention this, as they would have done if they had been written after the event.

Who wrote them?

Those who accept a late date say they were written by an unknown author who may have incorporated short passages which give genuine reminiscences of eyewitnesses. There are passages in Acts where descriptions of what 'they' did suddenly change into what 'we' did: Acts 16:10–17; 20:5–16; 21:1–18; and 27:1–16. These could have been extracted from genuine memoirs, or they could have been invented to give an impression of genuineness.

Traditionally the author is regarded as Luke, 'the beloved physician' (Colossians 4:14; Philemon 24; 2 Timothy 4:11), a Greek companion of St Paul, but not referred to as an apostle and not one of the Twelve (for the usage of these terms see below under Legends of the Twelve). Lukas is a Greek name, commonly given to slaves, and many people who practised the then somewhat primitive art of medicine were slaves who hoped eventually to buy their freedom.

Then the 'we' passages would describe the times when Luke was actually present. It is hard to see why a skilled editor would have put some of the story in the first person without changing the whole of it. And if later Christians had been going to invent an author for an anonymous work, we would have expected them to choose someone much more important.

Why does Acts end before the trial of Paul in Rome?

It could be because its purpose was to describe the spread of Christianity from Jerusalem 'to the ends of the earth' (Acts 1:8), and Rome, being the centre of

the empire, was the climax of this process. The readers, it is assumed, already knew what happened next.

It could be that the author intended to write a sequel, or even wrote one which has been lost.

Or maybe the story ends there because that is when Luke wrote it down, while Paul was under house arrest awaiting trial. This raises the possibility that Luke and Acts were both written as part of the defence documents connected with the trial. Luke copies extensively from Mark's Gospel, however, so this theory would bring into question the reasons why most scholars assume a late date for Mark.

Who was Theophilus?

Theophilus is Greek for 'lover of God', so it could be a general term suggesting that the books were suitable for any religious person wanting to know more about the lives of Jesus and his followers.

Or they could have been intended for a real individual, and Theophilus could have been his real name or a pseudonym.

Theophilus could have been the defence attorney, or even the judge, in Paul's trial.

Why were Luke and Acts written?

They present Jesus, Peter and Paul as being friendly towards non-Jews (usually called 'Gentiles' which means 'the nations') and as being well-treated by them. It seems to be suggested that Christianity is no threat to the Roman empire, and that Gentiles may be included in the people of God.

Some claim to detect an ongoing battle between Peter and Paul (Galatians 2:11) and see these books as presenting Paul's side of the argument.

The books present the death and resurrection of Jesus as part of God's plan of salvation, and use the metaphor of sacrifice to describe how this leads to forgiveness of sins, eternal life and the beginning of the kingdom of God. They appeal to the reader to believe in Jesus and accept the offer of salvation.

What is the Western Text?

A group of manuscripts of Acts from the early church in the western part of the Roman empire, which give different readings and additional information in many passages, and could possibly be nearer the original than the Alexandrian text followed in most Bibles.

Alternatively, they could be entirely the invention of a later copyist.

Is the Acts of the Apostles true?

Most writers, even up until the Renaissance, did not understand the concept of scientific history, and regarded legendary stories as a valuable

way of pointing out the true meaning of events. It was normal practice to invent speeches to put into the mouths of historical characters to represent what was believed to be their opinion. It may have been that the author of Acts made no clear distinction between fact and fiction.

He does claim, however, to be making an accurate record (Luke 1:3–4), and he seems to model himself on Greek historians such as Herodotus. Visits to the places he mentions confirm the accuracy of his descriptions, and inscriptions (foundation stones, memorials and gravestones, etc.) show that his naming of the officials in various towns is correct in every detail.

There are a few points at which the lists of contemporary rulers in e.g. Luke 2:1–3 seem to be at variance with what we know from other sources. This could be because the other writers are wrong; or because documents yet to be discovered will explain the discrepancies; or because Luke, with no chance of consulting contemporary documents in a library, made some errors. This need not affect, however, our admiration of his general truthfulness.

There are instances where the events in Acts do not fit exactly with those Paul describes in his letters (see for instance below under Paul's Letter to the Galatians). Normally one would expect that Paul's first-hand account is more accurate, though it is possible that in the heat of dictation he did not remember accurately, or was selective in what he thought appropriate to mention.

Many modern commentators claim that Acts, for theological reasons, represents some of the places that Paul visited in the wrong order, and that he only made two visits to Jerusalem as described in Galatians. Whether or not that is true, this book lists the journeys in the time line and the text as Acts records them.

Conclusions

Discussion of these and other issues for which there is no space in this volume will be found in many commentaries on the Acts of the Apostles. I hope this book will be useful to those whose attitude to the Bible ranges from extreme literalism to extreme scepticism. One's appreciation of its spiritual message need not depend on its historical accuracy. Personally I am very sceptical about later legends, but I believe that although not infallible in its details, the book of Acts is among the most reliable historical documents we have from ancient times. It is my experience that visiting the places Luke wrote about brings his descriptions alive, gives an explanation of the motives of the people he is writing about, makes his accuracy astonishingly impressive, and makes the story he is telling

thrilling and inspiring in its spiritual implications for us today.

Whether or not you agree with me, I hope this book will inspire you to follow in the paths of the apostles, that it will be a useful companion and guidebook on the way, and a reference work after you return; or if you are not able to make such a journey or journeys, that it will help you to read the exciting travelogue which we call the book of Acts with new eyes.

A Summary of Acts

Acts 1–5

Acts of Peter and the other members of the Twelve. At Pentecost the gospel spreads from its Galilean beginnings to include overseas Jews and proselytes (non-Jews who had converted to the Jewish faith and accepted the whole of the Jewish law as binding on them).

Acts 5–8

Appointment of the Seven. Martyrdom of Stephen. Acts of Philip. Inclusion of Greek-speaking Jews, Samaritans, and legally disqualified God-fearers (Gentiles who respected the Jewish religion but had not converted to it).

Acts 9

Conversion of Paul.

Acts 10–12

Peter baptizes the gentile God-fearer Cornelius. The church in Antioch-on-the-Orontes preaches to Gentiles. James is killed and Peter released from prison.

Acts 13—15

Paul's first missionary journey. Sent by the church in Antioch-on-the-Orontes with Barnabas and John Mark to preach in synagogues in Cyprus and Perge. Mark leaves them. They visit Antioch-of-Pisidia (where they 'turn to the Gentiles'), Iconium, Lystra, Derbe, and back again to Antioch-on-the-Orontes. The Council in Jerusalem decides that Gentiles are allowed to become Christians.

Acts 16—17:26

Paul's second missionary journey. Paul and Silas take a letter reporting the decision of the Council in Jerusalem through Tarsus to the Galatian churches he had visited on his first journey, collects Timothy in Lystra, is prevented from going to Ephesus, has a vision in Troas, visits the Macedonian cities of Philippi and Thessalonica, the Greek cities of Athens and Corinth, then returns via Ephesus where he leaves Priscilla and Aquila.

Acts 17:23—21:16

Paul's third missionary journey. Disturbed by reports that 'Judaizers' are demanding that gentile Christians be circumcised, Paul visits Galatia and Phrygia. He spends three years in Ephesus. Driven out by a riot, he revisits Macedonia,

Greece, Macedonia again and Troas. In Miletus he bids farewell to the Ephesian elders.

Acts 21:17—27:31

Paul returns to Jerusalem, is arrested, imprisoned in Caesarea, tried, appeals to Caesar, is shipwrecked in Malta and travels on to Rome, having planted churches in at least nine of the provinces of the Roman empire.

HELLENISTIC AND ROMAN CITIES AT THE TIME OF 'THE ACTS'

In the wake of Alexander the Great's conquest of the Middle East, many cities grew up with a civic life based on the Greek language and Greek learning. In the Roman empire many cities continued to develop on similar lines. Many of the buildings whose remains we can visit today date from after the apostles' time, but they have often been built on the site of earlier similar buildings. Common features of most cities which are mentioned in this book are:

- An *acropolis*. Usually the cities were built near a hill, to which the army and most of the people could retreat and defend themselves in time of attack. In peacetime it housed the *castrum*, the military headquarters, and the *main temple* of the city.
- An *agora* or marketplace, sometimes more than one, from which we get the word

25

PROVINCES
and Districts
OF THE
ROMAN
EMPIRE
AT THE TIME
OF 'THE ACTS'

'agoraphobia'. In Latin it is called the *forum*.

- An *aqueduct* to bring water to a growing population. It often terminated in a *nymphaeum*, which was an elaborate fountain.
- *Baths*, with underfloor heating through a *hypocaust*, and including an *apodyterium* for disrobing, a yard called a *palaestra* or *palestra* for exercise, a pool, a *sudeterium* or steam room, a *caldarium* for hot washing and a *tepidarium* or *frigidarium* for a cold bath, and areas to stroll and chat.
- A *gymnasium*. Although the name comes from 'gymnos' meaning naked – 1 Timothy 4:8 – it was not only used for exercise but also for a complete educational system, supervised and often financed by officials called *gymnasiarchs*.
- Houses, called *domatia* in the towns and *villas* in the countryside. They were often

built round a central courtyard called an *atrium*, open to the sky, often of a *peristyle* design, which means surrounded by pillars. Often the rainwater was channelled into a pool or *impluvium* in the centre of the atrium. The main reception room, off the atrium, was called the *tablinium*; the dining room where diners reclined round a three-sided U-shaped table was called the *triclinium*.
- Large communities of the *diaspora*, or *Jews of the Dispersion*, were found doing business in many of the hellenistic cities, many features of their life organized by the *synagogues*.
- A *necropolis*, which was a cemetery in which bodies were buried in *sarcophagi*, which means flesh-eaters in Greek, or sometimes in cave tombs with niches called *loculi* for bodies, the bones of which were later placed in *ossuaries*.

- Monuments to local heroes called a *heroon*, and many *statues* of men and gods.
- A *stadium* for running races, and an *arena*, *hippodrome* or *amphitheatre* for chariot races and fights between *gladiators*.
- *Streets* laid out on the grid pattern developed by Hippodamus of Miletus, the two main streets at right angles called the *Cardo* and the *Decumanus Maximus*. They were often paved in marble, with stepping stones for pedestrians to cross, and grooves for the chariot wheels. A *colonnade* of pillars might run down each side, sheltering a footpath leading to a row of *tabernae*, which were shops with selling areas and workshops downstairs and living accommodation or store rooms above. The section of dwellings enclosed by one block of streets was called an *insula*. A colonnaded area for strolling or teaching was called a *stoa*.
- *Temples* to many gods, often with a sacred enclosure called the *temenos* and an inner sanctum called the *cella*, and an outer porch of pillars called a *propylon* or *pronaos*. The *priests'* duties included sacrificing animals (they were virtually the only slaughter-houses), examining the entrails for *auguries* of the future, and presiding at feasts, organized by families or *trade guilds* who brought the animals for sacrifice and ate what was left.

- Legal judgements could be given anywhere the governor or magistrate instructed his tribune, praetor or guard to set up his standard; this became the *praetorium* or *tribunal*. Outdoors there would be a bench or platform called the *bema*; halls used for legal business and other assemblies were called *basilicas*, but in the Byzantine period this term was applied to churches built on the same plan.
- *Theatres*. The Greeks were *spectators* and came to watch the chorus singing and dancing in the *orchestra*, the central area in front of the stage, which had a simple '*scene*', from the word 'skene' for a tent, behind it. The Romans, however, built an *auditorium*, also called *cavea*, where they could hear the verse speakers on the stage ('audire' is the Latin verb 'to hear', 'spectare' is the Latin verb and 'theasthai' is the Greek verb 'to watch', 'orcheisthai' is the Greek word for 'to dance'). In the Roman theatre the 'scene' has turned into a building of two or more storeys with elaborate carvings. The stage area in front of the scene was known as the '*proscenium*'. When the theatre was used for gladiators and fights with wild beasts, an extra parapet had to be built to protect those in the front seats. When the audience are seated all round a sand-strewn

'*arena*' (the Latin word for 'sand') it becomes an *amphitheatre*.

- A small theatre called an *odeon* (concert hall, for the singing of odes) or *bouleuterion* (council chamber – sometimes the same building doubled as both). The government of the town might include the *demos*, the assembly of the people, the *boule* (pronounced boo–lee) or council presided over by *archons*, assisted by a *grammateus* or secretary; and the *senate* of elders. The military governor was the *strategos*.

- *Walls*, features of which were *revetments*, a retaining wall or facing of masonry, *ashlars* or shaped stones, *casemate* or hollow walls, *glissades* or smoothed areas to hinder those who wished to climb or ride up to the walls, and triple *gates* which meant that attackers who broke through the first gate could be fired on by bowmen on the walls. Attackers used a combination of *undermining*, *ramps*, *battering rams* and *catapults*.

Places in the Holy Land Mentioned in Acts

JERUSALEM

See the note above under Practical Details: Israel, concerning the Intifada. Guidance is offered here for visiting pilgrimage sites in the Holy Land, ready for when the situation returns to relative stability. At all times the warnings of experienced local guides should be heeded.

The Holy Land in Acts

In Acts 1–5 Luke recounts the acts of Peter and the other members of the Twelve. At Pentecost the gospel spreads from its Galilean beginnings to include overseas Jews and proselytes. In chapters 5–9 the Seven, all Greek-speaking Jews, are appointed to help the Twelve, and one of them, Stephen, is martyred. Another member of the Seven, Philip, by his preaching brings about the inclusion within the church of Samaritans, and legally disqualified God-fearers. Chapters 10–12 tell how Peter baptizes the gentile God-fearer Cornelius; the church in Antioch-on-the-Orontes preaches to Gentiles; James is killed and Peter released from prison. The first twelve chapters of Acts show the first Christians, who were almost all Jews, grappling with the problem of what to do when Gentiles wanted to join the Christian community; in particular the question of how much of the Jewish law must they observe?

John Mark's Mother's House (Acts 12:12–17)

As soon as he realized this, Peter went to the house of Mary, the mother of John whose other name was Mark, where many had gathered and were praying. When he knocked at the outer gate, a maid named Rhoda came to answer. On recognizing Peter's voice, she was so overjoyed that, instead of opening the gate, she ran in and announced that Peter was standing at the gate. They said to her, 'You are out of your mind!' But she insisted that it was so. They said, 'It is his angel.' Meanwhile Peter continued knocking; and when they opened the gate, they saw him and were amazed. He motioned to them with his hand to be silent, and described for them how the Lord had brought him out of the prison. And he added, 'Tell this to James and to the believers.' Then he left and went to another place.

The first church in Jerusalem

Traditionally the place where the disciples were meeting on the Day of Pentecost when the Holy Spirit came upon them (Acts 2:1) has been held to be the same upper room (Acts 1:13) where Jesus held the last supper with his disciples; (although if 3,000 people heard the disciples at Pentecost the assembly may have moved to Solomon's portico, see below). Probably this upper room was also the place where the church first gathered in Jerusalem, for soon afterwards, when Peter was released from prison after being questioned by the Sanhedrin, he found where the other Christians were praying for him in their usual meeting place:

Is the Cenacle the right place?

Since John Mark's mother but not his father is mentioned she must have been a widow: it is nice to speculate that John Mark, the nephew of Barnabas from Cyprus (Acts 12:25), was the young man carrying a water pot (usually women's work) in Luke 22:10 (and parallel passages in the other Gospels) to help his mother out at a busy time. The room shown as the site of the upper room today is called the Cenacle. It was built by crusaders, but it is directly above the entrance hall to what has been called since the tenth century AD 'David's Tomb'.

A combination of evidence from Herodian stones in the walls, coins found under the floor, and ancient maps, confirms that this was the site of a synagogue-church, with a niche in the eastern wall, used by first-century Jewish Christians. The church built on this site in the fourth century was known as 'The Upper Church of the Apostles', and in the fifth century as 'Sion, the mother of all the churches'. It is unfortunate that the plan of the Cenacle is one of the most complex sites described in this book, because so many buildings were built over the remains of earlier ones.

How to find the Cenacle

Going out of the old city of Jerusalem by the Sion Gate to the south, go straight ahead along the top of the car park, and down a narrow alley, forking left at the wall of the Dormition Abbey, following the sign which reads 'Coenaculum'. Enter a door on the left, climb the stairs, pass through one room and across a roof to find the vaulted chamber. To return to the tomb of David turn left on coming out of the door, enter a covered passageway in front of you and take the first turn to the left. (see map)

Opening Times
The Cenacle 08.00–12.00 and 15.00–16.00, closed on Friday afternoons
David's Tomb 08.00–12.00 and 15.00–18.00, closed on Friday afternoons

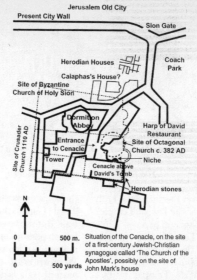

Situation of the Cenacle, on the site of a first-century Jewish-Christian synagogue called 'The Church of the Apostles', possibly on the site of John Mark's house

Luke's account of Pentecost

The coming of the Holy Spirit on the first Christians was proof to them that God was working through them to spread the good news of his love. The people from many countries who are listed in the Acts as being present at the festival of Pentecost (from the Greek word for 'fifty') were probably Jews of the Dispersion returning to their mother country for the harvest festival, fifty days after Passover; so for many of them Hebrew was not their main language. Speaking in tongues is a common form of ecstatic utterance produced by the Holy Spirit at times of heightened religious feeling, but on this occasion Luke emphasizes that the experience was understood by people speaking many different languages. He wanted his readers to understand that the experience of the Spirit is for everybody, and could be a unifying influence in the linguistically divided Roman empire.

THE JERUSALEM TEMPLE

The Temple in Jerusalem, rebuilt by King Herod the Great, was one of the most impressive buildings of the ancient world; pilgrims today can visit the **Haram ash-Sharif** in the old city of Jerusalem, an area controlled by Muslim authorities, which occupies the area where the temple stood. The **Al-Aqsa mosque** is one of the holiest sites of Islam, and there is some evidence that the **Dome of the**

31

The Temple in the time of the apostles

Rock is over the site of the Holy of Holies of the Jewish Temple. There are several parts of **Herod's Temple** now visible, including the south-eastern corner, popularly called 'the pinnacle of the Temple', and the steps up to the former Triple Gate in the southern wall. But the largest area, where Jewish people concentrate their prayers, is what is known as the **Western Wall** – the old name 'wailing wall' is no longer used.

The Beautiful Gate and Solomon's Portico (Acts 3:1–11)

One day Peter and John were going up to the temple at the hour of prayer, at three o'clock in the afternoon. And a man lame from birth was being carried in. People would lay him daily at the gate of the temple called the Beautiful Gate so that he could ask for alms from those entering the temple. When he saw Peter and John about to go into the temple, he asked them for alms. Peter looked intently at him, as did John, and said, 'Look at us.' And he fixed his attention on them, expecting to receive something from them. But Peter said, 'I have no silver or gold, but what I have I give you; in the name of Jesus Christ of Nazareth, stand up and walk.' And he took him by the right hand and raised him up; and immediately his feet and ankles were made strong. Jumping up, he stood and began to walk, and he entered the temple with them, walking and leaping and praising God. All the people saw him walking and praising God, and they recognized him as the one who used to sit and ask for alms at the Beautiful Gate of the temple; and they were filled with wonder and amazement at what had happened to him. While he clung to Peter and John, all the people ran together to them in the portico called Solomon's Portico, utterly astonished.

Visiting the Temple Mount

Observant Jews do not wish to and are not welcome to visit the Haram ash-Sharif area, but others can do so with the assistance of an Arabic-speaking guide. You will be expected to remove your shoes when visiting the mosque and the Dome of the Rock, and you must be modestly dressed. Jesus taught in Solomon's Portico (John 10:23) and it was a regular meeting place for the apostles (Acts 3:11, 5:12). Porticoes ran all round the Temple courtyard, and Solomon's Portico is likely to have been the one under the rooftop Hall of the Sanhedrin, where the Al-Aqsa mosque now stands. The Beautiful Gate, which is not mentioned outside the Acts of the Apostles, was probably the same as the Nicanor Gate, between the Court of the Gentiles and the Court of the Women, which was made of fine Corinthian bronze.

Opening Times

Haram ash-Sharif Telephone (02) 283313, Saturday to Thursday 08.00–15.00, closed 11.30–12.30 in winter, 12.30–13.30 in summer. During Ramadan open 07.30–10.00 only. Closed on Fridays and Muslim holidays

THE PLACE OF OF ST STEPHEN'S MARTYRDOM

Seven Greek-speaking disciples were appointed to help the original leaders, and one of them, Stephen, became involved in disputes with non-Christian Jews. After giving a speech (Acts 6–7) which subtly attacks those traditionalist Jews who had often rejected God's plan for them, Stephen was stoned to death outside the city of Jerusalem, nobody knows exactly where.

The appointment of the Seven

Two words sometimes confused in the New Testament are 'Hellenes', meaning Greeks, and 'Hellenists' meaning Greek-speaking Jews. Jews brought up in Galilee and Judea spoke Aramaic, a language derived from the Hebrew of the Old Testament, and resisted the introduction of Greek culture; Jews brought up in the rest of the Roman empire, known as the dispersion or the diaspora, were more liberal and mostly spoke Greek and read the Old Testament in the Greek Septuagint translation. Acts 6 tells us that there was a dispute between the Christians who spoke Aramaic and those who spoke Greek. The solution was to appoint seven men to help the Twelve, the original leaders of the church, with the distribution of charity. The Twelve were all Aramaic-speaking, but the Seven all have Greek names such as 'Stephen', and one of them, Nicolaus, was a Gentile, or non-Jew, who had earlier been admitted to the Jewish religion. For these converts the word 'proselyte' was used; they were expected to keep the whole of the Jewish law. The Seven are often

The appointment of the Seven, and the Synagogue of the Freed Slaves (Acts 6:7–15)

The word of God continued to spread; the number of the disciples increased greatly in Jerusalem, and a great many of the priests became obedient to the faith. Stephen, full of grace and power, did great wonders and signs among the people. Then some of those who belonged to the synagogue of the Freedmen (as it was called), Cyrenians, Alexandrians, and others of those from Cilicia and Asia, stood up and argued with Stephen. But they could not withstand the wisdom and the Spirit with which he spoke. Then they secretly instigated some men to say, 'We have heard him speak blasphemous words against Moses and God.' They stirred up the people as well as the elders and the scribes; then they suddenly confronted him, seized him, and brought him before the council. They set up false witnesses who said, 'This man never stops saying things against this holy place and the law; for we have heard him say that this Jesus of Nazareth will destroy this place and will change the customs that Moses handed on to us.' And all who sat in the council looked intently at him, and they saw that his face was like the face of an angel.

Stephen's martyrdom (Acts 7:58–60)

Then they dragged him out of the city and began to stone him; and the witnesses laid their coats at the feet of a young man named Saul. While they were stoning Stephen, he prayed, 'Lord Jesus, receive my spirit.' Then he knelt down and cried out in a loud voice, 'Lord, do not hold this sin against them.' When he had said this, he died.

referred to as deacons, but not in the pages of the New Testament.

A tablet dug up near the Pool of Siloam

The Synagogue of the Freedmen may have been made up of descendants of Jewish captives taken into slavery in Rome by Pompey in 63 BC, and later set free. If they were Greek-speaking, they were suspected of being much more 'liberal' than the Hebrew-speaking congregations. So many of them would have wanted to distance themselves from those of their members who became Christians. The Christians appeared to reject the importance of the Temple and much of the Jewish law. One of those from Cilicia who argued with Stephen may have been the Greek-speaking rabbi Saul from Tarsus. A tablet inscribed in Greek was

---

The tablet from Siloam

Theodotus, son of Vettenus, priest and ruler of the synagogue, son and grandson of rulers of the synagogue, built this synagogue for reading the Law and teaching the commandments, and the guest house, rooms and water supply as an inn to meet the needs of those who come from abroad; it was founded by his fathers and the elders and Simonides.

---

unearthed near the Pool of Siloam, south of the present-day walls of Jerusalem, referring to the officials of a synagogue who must have been Jews of the Dispersion, as they had Greek-sounding names, which they may have adopted from the slave owners who set them free.

The place of Stephen's martyrdom

Although the **Lion Gate** near the northeast of the old city is often called Saint Stephen's Gate, that is a late attribution; originally the name was applied to the **Damascus Gate** in the north, where the Roman gateway survives underneath the present gate. The Byzantine **Chapel of St Stephen** in the grounds of the French Dominican École Biblique, in Derekh Shekhem, which runs north from the Damascus Gate, is where the first martyr's bones are believed to have been buried.

Saul of Tarsus, later called St Paul, would have been one who remembered exactly where it

happened, for whatever thoughts were going through his head at that moment, they led to a complete change in his life; this was the beginning of a long process of learning new ideas and reassessing the old ones. As a zealous Pharisee (Acts 26:5) he will have seen it as his duty to bring all Israel into obedience to the law, which was the condition for God to fulfil his covenant. When this happened, he believed God would enable his people to drive out the Romans under the leadership of a military Messiah, and this would be followed by the resurrection of loyal Jews who had died. So Saul set out to destroy the heretic followers of Jesus of Nazareth. In Saul's vision (Acts 26:14), 'the Christ' (which means the Messiah or anointed king) compared Saul to an ox kicking against the goad which is being used to turn it into the right path. Saul, astonished to find that the resurrection had already taken place, then surrendered to the risen Lord whom Stephen had spoken of at his death.

Philip and Peter Move Outwards

Samaria, lying north of Jerusalem on the ridge of hills which runs down the spine of the country, and Gaza at the south west corner, are in the Occupied Territories; Azotus, Lydda, Joppa and Caesarea are on the coastal plain of Israel. Acts 8 tells how, following the martyrdom of Stephen, a period of persecution fell on the church, led by Saul of Tarsus. Forced to flee Jerusalem, Philip the evangelist, one of the Seven, not to be confused with the Philip who was one of the original Twelve whom Jesus chose, took the gospel to Samaria, Gaza and Azotus, while Simon Peter travelled to Lydda, Joppa and Caesarea-on-Sea. Thus, almost without planning it, they began the growth of the church out from its Jewish heartlands to areas of mixed population.

SAMARIA

Acts 8:4–24 recounts how Philip preached, healed and made converts in Samaria. The witness of the Samaritan woman whom Jesus spoke to at the well (John 4:4–42) must have prepared the way for Philip's mission. The Jews hated the Samaritans, who were descended from the people of mixed race who were brought in to populate the land while the Jews were in exile, and were sufficiently like the Jews and yet sufficiently different in their beliefs to be regarded as a threat. For Jesus to talk to a Samaritan woman at the well was remarkable, for 'Jews have no dealings with Samaritans' (John 4:9; compare Luke 9:51–56; 17:11–19), and the Parable of the Good Samaritan (Luke 10:25–37) is a challenge about race relations. So for the apostles to go there and lay their hands on the heads of those who had been baptized could be considered a bold gesture of tolerance. Were these the first non-Jews to be baptized, and is this why Luke tells the story at the beginning of his defence of the apostle to the Gentiles? A magician called Simon, seeing that the new converts received the Holy Spirit, offered the apostles money in return for the gift of imparting the Holy Spirit. So he gave his name to 'simony', which is the crime of making a personal profit out of one's spiritual position, especially selling promotion in the church.

The city of Samaria was renamed Sebaste by King Herod the Great and is now called Sebastiya or Shomron; the remains, from the days of King Ahab up until Byzantine times, may be visited on route 60. It is some 15 kilometres (9 miles) north of Nablus, a word derived from Neapolis, which was the name in New Testament times for the Old Testament city of Shechem, near to which, at Sychar, Jesus spoke with the Samaritan woman at the well.

Opening Times
National Parks site Tel. (02) 242 235, daily 08.00–17.00 from April to September; 08.00–16.00 from October to March, closing one hour earlier on Fridays and the eve of Jewish holy days. Closed on Yom Kippur
Jacob's Well at Nablus Tel. (05) 375123, daily 08.30–12.00, 14.30–17.00. Toilets near the entrance

GAZA

Gaza was one of the cities of the Philistines (Judges 16:21, etc.) on the coastal plain. After it was destroyed in 93 BC a new town was built nearer the sea and the ruins of the old town were called 'Desert Gaza'; there is no 'Desert Road' so it must have been on the road from Jerusalem to Desert Gaza that Philip baptized the unnamed Ethiopian official. As far as we know he was the first African to be baptized; he was probably a God-fearer if he was reading the scroll of Isaiah, but the most significant factor about his admission to the Christian church is that as a eunuch he would not have been admitted to the Jewish religion (Deuteronomy 23:1). The story

is told in Acts 8:26–40; notice that verse 37 is relegated to a footnote in most Bibles because it is not in all the manuscripts; possibly someone, even Luke himself, added it at a later stage when they realized that you cannot have a baptism without a statement of faith. The political situation in the Gaza Strip changes so much that you must seek up to date advice before considering paying it a visit.

AZOTUS

(Acts 7:40) where Philip reappeared, is the old Philistine city of Ashdod (1 Samuel 5:1, etc.) on route 4, the coastal highway from Gaza to Tel Aviv-Jaffa; the city is now entirely modern with a major harbour.

LYDDA

Lydda is not in the hill-country where the pure Jewish population was to be found, but on the coastal plain where the Jews lived alongside, and in some cases had intermarried with, Phoenician and Greek Gentiles. When Peter arrived at Lydda he found a congregation of believers. He healed one of them, a paralysed man with the Greek name of Aeneas (Acts 9:32–5), and the news spread through the Plain of Sharon, which lies between Mount Carmel and the coast. Lydda is now called Lod, and lies on route 40 between Ramla and where Lod (Ben Gurion) airport, the main airport of

---

St George

St George, devotion to whom was brought to England by the crusaders, was probably a martyr of Lydda in the second or third centuries AD. In the Eastern Church and in Islam he is associated with fertility. The story of his slaying a dragon which was threatening a young woman is first mentioned in the twelfth century; it may be derived from the legend of Perseus, who slew the Kraken, a sea monster, near Joppa, where the entrance to the harbour is marked by Andromeda's rock. This in turn should be compared to the Canaanite myth of the creation of the world by a hero who slew a sea monster called Tiamat, echoes of which may be found in references to Leviathan in the Bible.

Israel, is situated, 51 kilometres (32 miles) from Jerusalem on route 1.

ANTIPATRIS

Also off route 40, to the north of Lod airport, is Rosh Haayin, the site of biblical Antipatris, where Paul's armed escort left him on the way to Caesarea (Acts 23:31). On the site of the biblical Aphek (1 Samuel 29:1) King Herod the Great had built a city which he named after his father Antipater. On the large mound there stands today the ruin of a **crusader castle**.

JOPPA

From Lydda Peter moved to Joppa (Acts 9:38–43), a Phoenician port, supposed to be named after Noah's son Japheth (Genesis 6:10), from which the prophet Jonah had set sail (Jonah 1:3). There he raised Tabitha, also known as Dorcas, from the dead, and stayed at the house of Simon the tanner, an occupation which was technically unclean in the eyes of orthodox Jews. It was here that he had his vision of a great sheet full of kosher and non-kosher animals which he was told to eat; he recognized this as an instruction to baptize the 'unclean' God-fearer Cornelius, a member of the hated occupying Roman army.

Joppa is now called Yafo or Jaffa. Tel Aviv, which was founded by Jewish pioneers on the sand dunes in 1909, has grown to absorb Yafo, of which it was originally a suburb. Yafo, on the Mediterranean coast south of the centre of Tel Aviv, is a quaint harbour town with narrow alleys winding through the artists' quarter down to the sea. **St Peter's Church** was built in 1654 on the foundations of the crusader fortress; in the square next to it is an **underground visitors' centre**. At the end of an alley next to the lighthouse at the south end of the town is the doorway of what is shown as the **house of Simon the tanner**.

Opening Times
Yafo Visitors' Centre Sunday to Thursday 09.00–22.00, Friday 09.00–14.00
Simon the Tanner's house daily 08.00–19.00

Caesarea Aqueduct

CAESAREA

Caesarea-Maritima, which I translate as Caesarea-on-Sea, so called to distinguish it from many other towns named after the imperial family, was the port town where the Roman governor of the province of Syria resided except when official duties took him to Jerusalem. It was built by King Herod the Great in the twelve years beginning in 22 BC, and named in honour of Caesar Augustus. Pilgrims today reach it from route 2, the main coast road of Israel, and can still see the magnificent **theatre**, with a **stone** naming Pontius Pilate, and the **aqueduct**. The foundations of the fine palace which Herod built and where the Roman governors sat in judgement on St Paul have been uncovered near the **harbour**,

and there are **Roman stones** in the clear waters there, which reveal the standard of underwater engineering involved in building the original jetties. The restaurant at the end of the harbour quay today stands over what is traditionally called **Paul's Prison**. The **Church of St Peter** in the harbour area is said to have been built on the site of the house of Cornelius the centurion.

Caesarea in the New Testament

Caesarea is mentioned in many verses of the Acts of the Apostles. Philip the evangelist was the first to proclaim the gospel there (Acts 8:40), and he entertained Paul and Luke in his house there (Acts 21:8–16); he could well have then given Luke the information which he

Pontius Pilate inscription, Caesarea

used in the early chapters of Acts. Paul used Caesarea as his port of arrival or departure from the Holy Land (Acts 9:30, 17:22), and Peter escaped there when Jerusalem became too dangerous (Acts 12:19). Most importantly, it was where the Roman centurion Cornelius was stationed, and when Peter heard God in a vision telling him not to reject what God had accepted, he visited Cornelius there, saw that he and his companions had received the Holy Spirit, and was forced to change his mind about baptizing Gentiles as Christians (Acts 10:1—11:18). And it was in Caesarea that Paul, on trial before the governor Felix and his successor Festus, made his appeal as a Roman citizen to exercise his right to be tried by the emperor's court in Rome (Acts 23:23—26:32).

Opening Times
National Parks site in the Crusader harbour Tel. (06) 36 1358 or (06) 36 1060, daily 08.00–17.00 April to September, 09.00–16.00 October to March. Closes an hour earlier on Fridays and the eve of Jewish holidays; the same admission ticket or green card gives admission to the Roman theatre. Toilets at the eastern end of the shops to the north of the tourist area

AKKO (PTOLEMAIS)

Akko is a town on the Mediterranean coast of Israel 22 kilometres (14 miles) north of Haifa. It is likely that pilgrims will visit it after seeing Caesarea, which is 35 kilometres (21 miles) south of Haifa. So although it is not mentioned until later in Acts, it is appropriate to describe it here. The harbour of Ptolemais was where Paul landed on his last journey to Jerusalem (Acts 21:7).

Named after himself by King Ptolemy II, the Greek ruler of Egypt, Ptolemais became the crusader city of Saint Jean

Akko Harbour

d'Acre and is now called Akko or Acco. The crusaders built a great fortress in 1104, but were driven out by Saladin in 1187. King Richard the Lionheart of England won it back in 1191. In 1219 Saint Francis of Assisi stayed here in the course of an attempt to preach the gospel of love to the Saracens. The Muslims listened courteously, but were not converted, and the tragic history of the crusades has made dialogue between Christians and Muslims almost impossible ever since, though with notable exceptions.

The loss of Acre in 1191 was the crusaders' last battle and the **crusader city** was buried under a great mound of earth. The eighteenth-century **citadel** was built over the top, so that the crusader halls appear to be an underground crypt, and can only be partially cleared; they are not for the claustrophobic. The entrance to the underground crusader city is next to the beautiful **Al-Jazzar Mosque,** the green dome of which dominates the skyline as you pass through the eighteenth-century walls into the old city. The mosque, and its colonnaded cloister, contain many granite and marble **pillars** which were taken from the remains of Roman Caesarea, and will have been seen and touched by Paul, Luke, Peter, Philip and the centurion, Cornelius. The old city also has interesting **khans** (inns or caravanserais), and the **old harbour** of Ptolemais is a busy fishing port. Akko is conveniently reached by train as well as Highway 4 from Haifa.

Opening Times
Al-Jazzar Mosque No admission during Muslim times of prayer
Crusader fortress ('Underground City') Sunday to Thursday 08.30–18.30, Friday 08.30–14.30, Saturday 09.00–18.00. Toilets opposite the Knights' Halls
Khans always open

The Beginning of Paul's Ministry

DAMASCUS (SYRIA)

Damascus, the capital of Syria, claims to be the oldest continuously inhabited city in the world, since before 5000 BC. It was a natural oasis on the banks of the Barada River, where it is crossed by the Way of the Sea, along which trade passed between the Nile and the Euphrates. Now, at the centre of the busy metropolis lies the old city, enclosed by walls, with graceful Muslim architecture adjacent to a maze of dark shopping alleys (souqs) roofed in corrugated iron; through the centre runs 'The Street called Straight'.

St Paul's Gate, Damascus

The history of Damascus

The early inhabitants of Damascus were Canaanites, then Amorites; it was conquered by Assyrians, Babylonians, Persians and Greeks. The Nabatean population came under control of the Romans in 64 BC. The Jewish population was very large; the first-century AD Jewish general and historian Josephus writes that 18,000 Jews were massacred there during the Jewish revolt in the years leading up to AD 70. The road which St Paul travelled from Jerusalem, on his way to stamp out an outbreak of the Christian heresy in the synagogue in Damascus, will have led him for 240 kilometres (150 miles), taking him at least six days. When the cold air from the Golan heights meets the hot air from the desert there are frequent electrical storms. Was it in one of these that 'a light from heaven flashed around' Saul, and he heard the voice of Jesus?

Who was Paul?

In Acts 22:3, Philippians 3:5, etc. Paul tells us he was born a Jew, named Saul, of the tribe of Benjamin – the same tribe as King Saul, after whom he may have been named – born in Tarsus and a Pharisee. Growing up in the Greek university town and Roman provincial capital of Tarsus he must have been fluent in both Latin and Greek and admired both cultures; the

The conversion of St Paul (Acts 9:1–21)

Meanwhile Saul, still breathing threats and murder against the
disciples of the Lord, went to the high priest and asked him for
letters to the synagogues at Damascus, so that if he found any
who belonged to the Way, men or women, he might bring them
bound to Jerusalem. Now as he was going along and approaching
Damascus, suddenly a light from heaven flashed around him. He
fell to the ground and heard a voice saying to him, 'Saul, Saul,
why do you persecute me?' He asked, 'Who are you, Lord?' The
reply came, 'I am Jesus, whom you are persecuting. But get up
and enter the city, and you will be told what you are to do.'

The men who were travelling with him stood speechless because
they heard the voice but saw no one. Saul got up from the
ground, and though his eyes were open, he could see nothing; so
they led him by the hand and brought him into Damascus. For
three days he was without sight, and neither ate nor drank. Now
there was a disciple in Damascus named Ananias. The Lord said
to him in a vision, 'Ananias.' He answered, 'Here I am, Lord.'
The Lord said to him, 'Get up and go to the street called
Straight, and at the house of Judas look for a man of Tarsus
named Saul. At this moment he is praying, and he has seen in a
vision a man named Ananias come in and lay his hands on him so
that he might regain his sight.' But Ananias answered, 'Lord, I
have heard from many about this man, how much evil he has
done to your saints in Jerusalem; and here he has authority from
the chief priests to bind all who invoke your name.' But the Lord
said to him, 'Go, for he is an instrument whom I have chosen to
bring my name before Gentiles and kings and before the people
of Israel; I myself will show him how much he must suffer for the
sake of my name.'

So Ananias went and entered the house. He laid his hands on
Saul and said, 'Brother Saul, the Lord Jesus, who appeared to
you on your way here, has sent me so that you may regain your
sight and be filled with the Holy Spirit.' And immediately
something like scales fell from his eyes, and his sight was
restored. Then he got up and was baptized, and after taking some
food, he regained his strength. For several days he was with the
disciples in Damascus, and immediately he began to proclaim
Jesus in the synagogues, saying, 'He is the Son of God.' All who
heard him were amazed and said, 'Is not this the man who made
havoc in Jerusalem among those who invoked this name? And has
he not come here for the purpose of bringing them bound before
the chief priests?'

failure of the noble Roman aim to unify the world in their empire probably gave him his vision of a world united by the Christian faith. Yet he completed his education as a Jewish rabbi in Jerusalem as a pupil of Gamaliel (Acts 5:34, 22:3) and his thinking was always essentially Jewish. He was trained, as every Jewish boy had to be, in 'his Father's business', to be a tent-maker, but if he had inherited citizenship of Tarsus (Acts 21:39) and Roman citizenship (Acts 22:25) from his father his family were probably prosperous merchants trading in the tent cloth made from the dark-haired Cilician goats.

The word Pharisee means 'separated', and comes from the same root as 'parsin' in Daniel 5:24. They separated themselves from the Jews who wanted to adopt a hellenistic Greek lifestyle; eventually they claimed to be separated by their tradition from those who were less diligent in their obedience to the law of scripture, both cultural and ceremonial. For their legalism and hypocrisy (which means play-acting) they were condemned by Jesus, yet they were the most religious people of their day. Because Saul's nephew had access to the secrets of the priestly household (Acts 23:16), it may be that he was related to the high priest's family, the Sadducees. The Dead Sea Scrolls have shown that there was no monolithic Jewish orthodoxy in the first century but a melting pot of different opinions, many of them opposed to the Temple and the priesthood. One can speculate on the mixture of attraction and revulsion Saul felt towards the faith proclaimed by Stephen, before he gave way and was converted on the road to Damascus.

Getting to Damascus

Highway 7 proceeds from the disputed territory of the Golan Heights northeast to Damascus, called Ash Sham or Dimashq, the capital of Syria. Damascus airport (Tel. 543 0201/9) is 25 kilometres (16 miles) by motorway southeast of the city. The Hejaz railway leads south to Amman in Jordan, and another line, like the Motorway 5, leads north to Homs (Emesa, 161 kilometres or 100 miles from Damascus) and Halab (Aleppo, 355 kilometres or 222 miles from Damascus). Other sites in Syria of interest to historians include Bosra, Palmyra, Doura-Europos, Ebla, Serjilla, the fifth-century AD Church of Saint Simeon Stylites the Elder, the pillar saint, Ugarit, and Krac des Chevaliers. From Aleppo Highway 5 leads to the border with Turkey and the towns of Antakya (Antioch-on-the-Orontes) and İskenderun (Alexandretta). (For entry regulations, etc. see above under Practical Details – Syria.)

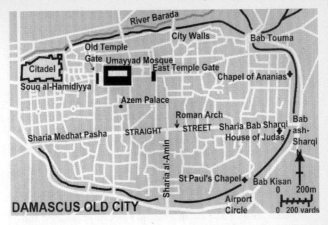

Map labels:
River Barada
City Walls
Bab Touma
Old Temple Gate
Umayyad Mosque
East Temple Gate
Chapel of Ananias
Citadel
Souq al-Hamidiyya
Azem Palace
Roman Arch
Bab ash-Sharqi
Sharia Medhat Pasha
STRAIGHT
STREET
Sharia Bab Sharqi
House of Judas
Sharia al-Amin
St Paul's Chapel
Bab Kisan
Airport Circle
DAMASCUS OLD CITY
0   200m
0   200 yards

Damascus today

An empty Orthodox church on the Kaukab Hill, 10 kilometres (six miles) south-west of Damascus on the edge of the Golan desert, is claimed as the **site of St Paul's conversion**; but so is a sacred rock in the cemetery.

The old city of Damascus is dominated at the northwest corner by the **citadel** overlooking the River Barada; it is on the site of a Roman fort.

Making your way from there along the colourful **Souq al-Hamidiyya**, and resisting the temptation to spend the day bargaining, you reach the five enormous Corinthian columns of the gateway to the third-century AD **Temple of Jupiter**. This may also be the site of the House of Rimmon mentioned in 2 Kings 5:18. The great

Umayyad mosque is built on the site of the inner courtyard of this temple, and there are more pillars in the small archaeological garden by the north wall. The mosque is one of Islam's holiest sites and an architectural gem comparable to Jerusalem's Dome of the Rock. All visitors should remove their shoes; female visitors may be required to wear the wrap-around black cloak and head-covering provided. The three minarets are built on Roman towers; the tallest, at the southeast, is called the Medinet Isa (Minaret of Jesus) because Muslims believe that this is where the prophet Jesus will enter the world at the Last Judgement. A green-domed shrine in the southern prayer hall is one of several places which claim to contain the head of John the Baptist; in

45

A 'Damascus Road' conversion

Some people have a dramatic and sudden conversion to
Christianity like St Paul, others grow into faith more gradually.
Even for the second type, there sometimes come moments when
we have to completely reassess our attitudes and our priorities.
Saul was persecuting the disciples of Jesus, the Christian
church, yet Jesus asked him, 'Why are you persecuting me?' It is
possible to see here the beginning of Paul's close identification
of Jesus with individual Christians and with the Christian
community. The church is the body of Christ; those who attack
his followers are attacking Jesus himself, who said in Luke
10:16, 'Whoever rejects you rejects me, and whoever rejects me
rejects the One who sent me.' Paul must have found something
Christlike in the character of Ananias, who was brave enough to
forgive – and baptize – one whom he had regarded as his enemy.
Yet conversion is only the first step in a process of salvation and
sanctification which lasts for the rest of our earthly life. Paul's
theology did not come ready-made to Saul on his conversion,
nor was it fully worked out during his retreat in Arabia. It is
fascinating to try to discern how his thinking developed in
response to the different experiences he had in the places he
visited.

Byzantine times the site was
occupied by a basilica dedicated
to St John the Baptist. To the
east of the mosque are the
remains of the triple eastern
gateway of the **Temple of
Jupiter**.

South of the Ummayyad
Mosque is the beautiful
eighteenth-century AD **Azem
Palace**.

Walking on to the south one
reaches the central portion of
the **'Street called Straight'**.
This is the east–west axis of the
old city of Damascus and is a
busy market. Travelling east
along it the first half is called
Sharia Medhat Pasha, then at a

Roman arch from 64 BC it
changes its name to Sharia Bab
Sharqi. In Roman times it was
15 metres (50 feet) wide, and
some of the columns originally
bordering it can be found in the
shops of the bazaar, together
with traces of a Roman theatre.

A small mosque stands behind a
projecting balcony in a lane just
off the east end of Straight
Street. Originally it was a Greek
church dedicated to St Judas,
and it is said to be on the site of
the **house of Judas**, where Paul
stayed and was healed.

The Old City of Damascus has
walls today which follow the
line of the Roman walls, and at

the east end of Straight Street, at Bab ash-Sharqi, the **Roman East Gate** still stands.

To the north of Bab ash-Sharqi is the fourth-century **House of Ananias** (Kineesat Hanania), an underground chapel maintained by Franciscans, said to be the home of the disciple who restored Paul's sight. It is on the level of the Roman street, and later a pagan temple and then a mosque were built over it.

To the south-west of Bab ash-Sharqi, **St Paul's Chapel** on Ibn 'Assaker Avenue is within a medieval gate (Bab Kisan) in the wall of the city, which may be the point where Paul was lowered in a basket, an indignity which must have still smarted when he described it in 2 Corinthians 11:33, blaming it on the ethnarch of Damascus under the Nabatean King Aretas IV (9 BC – AD 40). The present gate dates from the period of the Ottoman empire, and the chapel is underneath it, where remains of the Roman Gate of Saturn may be seen, as well as a single pillar from the original Christian church.

The National Museum is off Sharia Choukri al-Quwatli to the west of the old city.

Readers of the story of Naaman the Syrian in 2 Kings 5:1–14 will remember Abana and Pharpar, the rivers of Damascus so proudly referred to by Naaman the Syrian, which were probably the **River Barada**, which passes through the city, and the **Nehr el-Awaj** which passes through the plain 16 kilometres (10 miles) to the south.

Opening Times
Ummayad mosque daily from dawn until after evening prayers, but closed during noon prayers 12.30–14.00
House of Ananias Wednesday to Monday 09.00–13.00 and 15.00–18.00
Azem Palace Wednesday to Monday 09.00–18.00 in summer; 09.00–16.00 in winter; closed from 12.30–14.30 on Fridays
National Museum Wednesday to Monday 09.00–18.00 in summer; 09.00–16.00 in winter; closed from 11.15–13.00 on Fridays

TARSUS (TURKEY)

The south-eastern Mediterranean coast of Turkey is less often visited than other areas, but the cities of Tarsus and Antakya are full of historical and biblical interest. They are also quite safe, though it is sometimes not possible to travel further east without special permission, because of the Kurdish conflict. Tarsus, the home town of Saint Paul, was founded around 2000 BC. It is about 15 kilometres (10 miles) from the sea; Tarsus lies on the Cilician plain, and was an important staging post on the road which connected Greece and Rome with the East. For many centuries it had been a strategic point for defending that road where it passed by a narrow gorge, known as the Cilician Gates, through the Taurus Mountains, north of Tarsus. The hair of the black goats of the Taurus Mountains was woven into cloaks (2 Timothy 4:13) and tents; flax was grown on the fertile plain for making into linen and canvas. In 65 BC Pompey made Cilicia a province with Tarsus as its capital. The Roman orator Cicero became the governor of Cilicia in about 50 BC. Up the River Cydnus (Tarsus Suyu or Tarsus Irmaği), which in biblical times flowed through the middle of the city of Tarsus, ships from the Mediterranean could approach as close as Lake Rhegma, 8 kilometres (5 miles) away; and Cleopatra's barge could come right into the city for her famous meeting with Mark Antony in 41 BC, at which time he gave it the status of a 'free city'.

Tarsus in the Bible

After Paul's conversion, and some time spent in Arabia and Damascus, we have two different accounts of his return to his home district:

Acts 9:30: When the believers [in Jerusalem] learned of [Paul's conversion], they brought him down to Caesarea and sent him off to Tarsus.

Galatians 1:18–22: Then after three years I did go up to Jerusalem to visit Cephas and stayed with him fifteen days; but I did not see any other apostle except James, the Lord's brother. In what I am writing to you, before

God, I do not lie! Then I went into the regions of Syria and Cilicia, and I was still unknown by sight to the churches of Judea that are in Christ; they only heard it said, 'The one who formerly was persecuting us is now proclaiming the faith he once tried to destroy.'

But when the church in Antioch discovered that non-Jews were beginning to show an interest in Christianity, they needed help from a Jew with experience of the gentile world:

Acts 11:25: Then Barnabas went to Tarsus to look for Saul.

Later he must have passed through Tarsus on his second and probably third missionary journeys:

Acts 15:41: He went through Syria and Cilicia, strengthening the churches.

Acts 18:23: After spending some time [in Antioch] he departed and went from place to place through the region of Galatia and Phrygia, strengthening all the disciples.

Paul always referred proudly to his home town when telling his life story:

Acts 21:39: Paul replied, 'I am a Jew, from Tarsus in Cilicia, a citizen of an important city; I beg you, let me speak to the people.'

Acts 22:3: 'I am a Jew, born in Tarsus in Cilicia, but

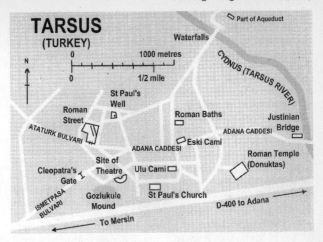

TARSUS
(TURKEY)

N

0   1000 metres

0   1/2 mile

Part of Aqueduct

Waterfalls

CYDNUS (TARSUS RIVER)

St Paul's Well

Roman Street

ATATURK BULVARI

Roman Baths

Justinian Bridge

ADANA CADDESI

Eski Cami

ADANA CADDESI

Roman Temple (Donuktas)

Cleopatra's Gate

Site of Theatre

Ulu Cami

ISMETPASA BULVARI

Gozlukule Mound

St Paul's Church

D-400 to Adana

To Mersin

brought up in this city [Jerusalem] at the feet of Gamaliel, educated strictly according to our ancestral law, being zealous for God, just as all of you are today.'

Getting to Tarsus

Tarsus lies on the south coast of Turkey on route D-400. The Cilician Gates (Tekirbeli Geçit or Gülek Boğazi, 1260 metres (4134 feet) above sea level) are just over 50 kilometres (30 miles) north of Tarsus. The railway from Ankara serves Adana, Tarsus and Mersin. There is an airport at Adana.

Tarsus today

The city which St Paul knew is buried deep beneath the present rather scruffy town. There is a monumental arch (Kancik Kapisi) on the road into the town from Mersin; it is the old Sea Gate of the town and is called **Cleopatra's Gate**; it may be on the site of one which young Saul of Tarsus knew, but in its present form it is made up of fragments from the second century AD, the Byzantine period, the Middle Ages, and the restoration in 1994.

Walking from there towards the Government House (Hükümet Konaği) you see two signs pointing left; one leads to the **Old City** (Antik Şehir), the other sign is to **St Paul's Well** (Senpol or Sin Pol Kuyusu). In the Old City an impressive stretch of the **Cardo**, the main road of the Roman city along which young Saul must have walked many times, has been uncovered: it is paved with large dark basalt slabs, and underneath it runs a deep drain; there are pillars, a shop and a number of other buildings beside the road.

49

Then you can walk north for 150 metres (165 yards), or alternatively follow the sign from the main road, to St Paul's Well. Formerly it stood in the courtyard of a house; now the area around it has been excavated and so far nothing dating from earlier than the Middle Ages has been discovered. But it is claimed that the well was in Saul's family home, and it has been regarded as a sacred site for a long time, so that might be so.

Tucked away in the side streets of the town there is some brickwork from an old **Roman bath** (Altından Geçme, second or third centuries AD) and the ruin of a second-century AD **Roman temple** called the 'Dönüktaş'. Near the attractive waterfalls in the north-east of the city is a fragment of the **Roman aqueduct**, and much further south on the same river a **bridge** from the time of the emperor Justinian (527–65 AD), stranded on dry land beside the modern bridge like a beached whale.

The **Ulu Cami Mosque** is on the site of a Roman temple and then a Christian church, and some pillars and other stones from the earlier structures are displayed outside. North of this is the **Kilise Cami** (which means Church Mosque, sometimes called the Eski Cami) which was also converted from an early church, and south of it is St Paul's Church, rebuilt in 1862, possibly on the site of the first church in the town to be dedicated to him, which has been left as it was though it is not in use as a church now.

A multi-cultural education

Goat hair, canvas and leather were made into tents and awnings. The heavy stitching took craftsmen who could be found in neither the Cilician rural population, nor among the Romans and Greeks who made up the bulk of the population in the towns. But among the immigrant groups to be found in all Roman towns, the Jews were one of the largest.

It is probable that young Saul, as he was then known, followed in his father's footsteps as a tent-maker (Acts 17:3). As is often the case with immigrant groups who are prevented from taking a part in the political life of a city, the Jews concentrated on trade and became rich. Saul may have inherited enough to support him in those stages of his life, such as imprisonment and house-arrest, when he was unable to work at his craft. His family may also have been able to lend money to the always impoverished Roman provincial authorities, and been rewarded with Roman citizenship, which cost the tribune, who later arrested Paul (Acts 22:28) for instance, a large sum. Paul probably spoke Latin to the Roman administrators in his home town. But Saul's parents were Pharisees, and will have ensured he had a thorough Jewish education in the synagogue, learning much of the Hebrew scriptures by heart.

Yet the conquests of Alexander the Great, three and a half centuries earlier, had spread the Greek language and culture over the whole Mediterranean region. Paul was fluent in Greek, and it was in that language, not in Hebrew or Latin, that the apostles could write and be sure that everyone would understand them.

Tarsus also had a famous university; the Stoic poet Aratus, whom Paul quotes in Athens (Acts 17:28), was born nearby. The Jews of the Dispersion, unlike those in Jerusalem, spoke fluent Greek and were not so afraid of being contaminated by Greek culture. Until he went to Jerusalem to study under Gamaliel (Acts 22:3), and after his conversion until Barnabas came to fetch him, he will probably have joined in the deep philosophical discussions which go on all the time in university towns; his intellectual searching after a union between the thought-worlds of Jew and Greek, and the stoicism with which he faced his suffering may have had their origin here.

Opening Times
Tarsus Old City excavations
Tel. 0324 613 7134, daily
08.00–17.00. Toilets on the left
as you enter
St Paul's Well daily
08.00–17.00

Paul's First Missionary Journey

After his conversion in around AD 33, Saul was for some three years in Damascus and Arabia (Galatians 1:17; Acts 19:20). In about 35 Saul visited Jerusalem (Galatians 1:18; Acts 9:26) and then returned to Tarsus (Acts 9:30). In Galatians 1:21 he mentions visits to Cilicia and Syria during this period. Around AD 45–46 Saul was called by Barnabas to supervise the church in Antioch-on-the-Orontes (Acts 11:26), and in 46 Saul and Barnabas took famine relief to Jerusalem (Acts 11:30, 12:25; Galatians 2:1–16?). Then from about 46 to 48 the church in Antioch-on-the-Orontes sent Saul with Barnabas and Mark on the first missionary journey (Acts 13, 14). First they preached in the synagogues in Barnabas' native Cyprus, where they had a significant meeting with the governor Sergius Paulus and Saul started using the Roman form of his name, Paul. Then they travelled to Asia Minor, modern-day Turkey. In Perga Mark left them, and they travelled inland to Antioch-of-Pisidia (where they 'turned to the Gentiles'), Iconium, Lystra and Derbe, then back through Attalia to Antioch-on-the-Orontes (Acts 14:26—15:2).

ANTIOCH-ON-THE-ORONTES AND SELEUCIA

Antakya, the site of Antioch-on-the-Orontes, is a small but bustling garrison town in the south of Turkey near the Syrian border. Alexander the Great, King of Macedonia, waged a phenomenal campaign across forbidding terrain against the Persian empire in the fourth century BC, finally defeating them in the plain of Issus in 333 BC. The port on the sea coast nearby is known as Alexandretta, or, because the oriental form of Alexander was Iskander, as İskenderun.

When Alexander died his empire was divided between his generals, *the Ptolemies in Egypt and the Seleucids in Syria. The first of the Seleucids was Seleucus Nicator (Seleucus the Conqueror), who founded sixteen cities around the*

Bust of Alexander the Great

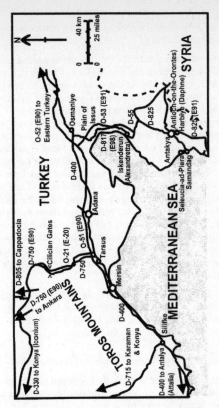

Middle East, all named Antioch in honour of his father, Antiochus. He also named five Laodiceas after his mother and nine Seleucias after himself. To distinguish them they are all given a second name, and the Antioch inland from Alexandretta was long known as Syrian Antioch, although it is now actually in Turkey.

A better name is Antioch-on-the-Orontes; it lies between Mount Silpius and the River Orontes, which rises in the Beqa'a Valley in Lebanon. It lay on a caravan route from the Euphrates valley to the Mediterranean, and was ideally situated for ruling the Seleucid empire which curved around the north-east end of the Mediterranean Sea; it later became the capital of the Roman province of Syria. It quickly grew to become the third greatest city of the Roman empire, after Rome

The gospel preached to Greek-speakers in Antioch-on-the-Orontes (Acts 11:19–26)

Now those who were scattered because of the persecution that took place over Stephen travelled as far as Phoenicia, Cyprus, and Antioch, and they spoke the word to no one except Jews. But among them were some men of Cyprus and Cyrene who, on coming to Antioch, spoke to the Hellenists [some manuscripts read 'Greeks'] also, proclaiming the Lord Jesus. The hand of the Lord was with them, and a great number became believers and turned to the Lord. News of this came to the ears of the church in Jerusalem, and they sent Barnabas to Antioch. When he came and saw the grace of God, he rejoiced, and he exhorted them all to remain faithful to the Lord with steadfast devotion; for he was a good man, full of the Holy Spirit and of faith. And a great many people were brought to the Lord. Then Barnabas went to Tarsus to look for Saul, and when he had found him, he brought him to Antioch. So it was that for an entire year they met with the church and taught a great many people, and it was in Antioch that the disciples were first called 'Christians.'

See also: Acts 11: 27–30 In Antioch, the prophet Agabus predicts a severe famine. Acts 13: 1–3 The Church in Antioch sends Saul on his first missionary journey. Acts 18: 22–3 Paul revisits Antioch between his second and third journeys.

Paul's dispute with Peter in Antioch (Galatians 2:11–14)

But when Cephas came to Antioch, I opposed him to his face, because he stood self-condemned; for until certain people came from James, he used to eat with the Gentiles. But after they came, he drew back and kept himself separate for fear of the circumcision faction. And the other Jews joined him in this hypocrisy, so that even Barnabas was led astray by their hypocrisy. But when I saw that they were not acting consistently with the truth of the gospel, I said to Cephas before them all, 'If you, though a Jew, live like a Gentile and not like a Jew, how can you compel the Gentiles to live like Jews?'

and Alexandria. The ancient city of Antioch was surrounded by a wall built by the emperor Justinian, and the main street was paved in marble by King Herod the Great.

One of its features was the grove of Daphne, an area of waterfalls outside the city, where legend tells of the nymph Daphne, turned into a laurel bush there to escape the attentions of the god Apollo, who was pursuing her. Here grew up an area of extensive pleasure gardens, notorious for immorality, where Cleopatra and Mark Antony were married in 40 BC. Famous games took place in these gardens, and the chariot race in the movie Ben Hur purports to take place here.

The mixed population was a ferment of religions, and as we see from Nicholas of Antioch, a convert to Judaism, one of the Seven mentioned in Acts 6:5, Greek-speaking people were interesting themselves in oriental religions, including Christianity. More than a fifth of the population were Jews, mostly very hellenized. The fact that a Galilean prophet named Yeshua was called the Messiah would mean nothing to Greek speakers, so his followers in Antioch called him Jesus and translated his title from 'the Messiah' to 'the Christ', both words meaning an anointed king; hence their neighbours derisively called them 'Christians'. It is claimed that Saint Matthew's Gospel was written in Antioch.

Ignatius of Antioch (c.AD 30–107)

Soon after the beginning of rhe second century, Ignatius, Bishop of Antioch, was arrested and taken to Rome to be thrown to the lions. In the letters he wrote to different churches during his journey, we see the calm, prayerful way in which the early Christians accepted martyrdom:

> I am writing letters to each of the churches, to reassure them that it is by my own free choice that I am laying down my life for God . . . Please don't make a misguided attempt to be kind to me. Let me be fodder for the wild beasts, for that is the means by which I shall come to God. I am God's wheat, and the animals' teeth will grind me up into flour, ready to be made into a pure loaf for Jesus Christ. Please encourage the lions to become my tomb; don't let any scraps of my body be left behind. That way, when I have fallen asleep my remains will not be a nuisance to nobody. In that way I shall be a real disciple of Jesus . . .

Letter to the Romans 4

Getting to Antioch-on-the-Orontes

Alexandretta or İskenderun, still a busy port on the Mediterranean coast of Eastern Turkey, is about 200 kilometres (125 miles) from Tarsus on the O-51 (E90) and the O-53 (E91) motorways, or the toll-free D-400 and D-817 (E98). From İskenderun, route D-55 winds up the steep Belen Pass, where there are fine views. Turning right at a major road junction onto the D-825, the road then descends to the fertile Amik Plain, and the Orontes Valley, to reach Antakya (Hatay), 60 kilometres (38 miles) from İskenderun.

Church of St Peter, Antakya

Antakya today

Remains of the ancient city of Antioch lie 11 metres (35 feet) underground, but many of the roads follow the line of the Roman streets, which were laid out in the Hippodamus grid pattern by the town planners of the Roman city (see below under Miletus). Emperor Diocletian persecuted the Christians here, but under Constantine the Great, Antioch became the seat of one of the patriarchs, and ten councils of the church were held there. As it is clear from scripture (Galatians 2:11) that Simon Peter came to Antioch, whereas there is no certain proof that he went to Rome, this was at one time used to argue that the church of Antioch was the most important in the world.

There used to be many churches in Antioch, but one of the few remaining from ancient times is the Church of St Peter, where he is said to have preached to Christians meeting in secret in a cave. **St Peter's Grotto** is just off the Kurtuluş

Caddesi, the road to Reyhanli, about 4 kilometres (2½ miles) north-east of the centre of the town. Those who do not accept that St Luke came from Philippi suggest he was a native of Antioch, and gave this cave to the Christian community for a meeting place. Remains of some frescoes and a simple mosaic floor survive from the cave chapel, which was extended into a church (Senpiyer Kilisesi) with a gothic façade in the thirteenth century, and renovated in the nineteenth. On the right of the altar, a small spring is alleged to have healing properties, and to have been used for baptisms, and on the left a tunnel, now blocked off, could have been used as an escape route in times of persecution. A narrow, steep and rocky path leads from the entrance to the church up the hillside to a relief of two human figures carved into the cliff face, the **Charonion**. These are sometimes referred to as Peter and Mary; but a sixth-century historian said it represented Charon the ferryman who carries people across the mythical River Styx to the

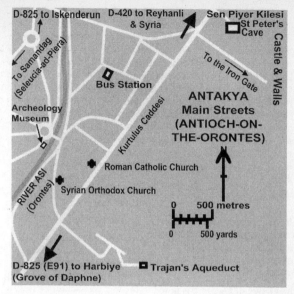

D-825 to Iskenderun D-420 to Reyhanli & Syria Sen Piyer Kilesi / St Peter's Cave Castle & Walls

To Samandağ (Seleucia-ad-Piera)

To the Iron Gate

Bus Station

ANTAKYA
Main Streets
(ANTIOCH-ON-
THE-ORONTES)

Archeology
Museum

Kurtulus Caddesi

Roman Catholic Church

RIVER ASI (Orontes)

Syrian Orthodox Church

0   500 metres

0   500 yards

D-825 (E91) to Harbiye
(Grove of Daphne)   Trajan's Aqueduct

world of the dead. Others say it represents a Syrian goddess of nature.

The ruined **citadel**, and remnants of the **city walls**, on the hilltop above St Peter's Church, were reconstructed by Emperor Justinian on the site of the earlier walls, and were much repaired in the Middle Ages.

South of St Peter's Grotto, up the next lane and then up a narrow mountain path, is the so-called **'Iron Gate'** (Demirkapı), a huge dam built by Emperor Justinian in the sixth century AD on earlier foundations in an effort to prevent the seasonal floods which local people still call 'donkey-drowners'.

Fragments of the **aqueduct** (Memekli Köprü) built by Emperor Trajan in the third century AD are also on this hillside, further south, reached through a series of side streets.

The River Orontes, now called Asi Nehir, runs through the centre of the town. The main street on the east of the river, called Kurtuluş Caddesi, has been shown to follow the course of the **colonnaded street** of Antioch built between 27 BC and AD 37, and covered in marble by King Herod the Great. It was the first street in the world where it was possible to walk for 4 kilometres (two and a half miles) under cover in the colonnades.

The archaeological museum in the Gündüz Caddesi contains many large mosaics from Roman villas of Antioch and Daphne.

The **Grove of Daphne** is now an area of open-air restaurants, pools and rivulets 8 kilometres (5 miles) to the south of Antakya at Harbiye, on the D-825 (E91) road.

Opening Times
Senpiyer Kilisesi Tel. 0326 225 1568, Tuesday to Sunday 08.00–16.30. It is now a museum, but tour groups may hold services there by arrangement with the custodian, or invite the Capuchin fathers (Tel. 0326 215 6703) to say mass there for them. Toilets downstairs in the ticket office
Archaeological museum Tel. 0326 214 6168, Tuesday to Sunday 08.30–12.00 and 13.30–18.00. Toilets beside the ticket office

Seleucia-ad-Piera

An unnumbered road leads south-west from Antakya for 30 kilometres (18 miles) to the beach resort of Samandağ. On the way you can turn left up a steep mountain road which climbs for three kilometres (2 miles) to the ruined monastery on **Wonderful Mountain**, where St Simon Stylites the Younger (AD 384–491) lived for forty years on top of a pillar.

In Acts 13:4 we read that 'being sent out by the Holy Spirit, they went down to Seleucia; and from there they sailed to Cyprus'. The port of **Seleucia-ad-Piera** was founded by and named after Seleucus Nicator at the foot of Mount Piera. Only small remnants of a **harbour** and of the **city walls** remain at Çevlik, 6 kilometres (4 miles) north of Samandağ. A steep, but not too difficult, walk above Çevlik leads to an amazing 1,300 metres (almost a mile) long canal, including a 130 metres (140 yards) long and 7 metres (23 feet) high tunnel, built on the orders of the emperors Titus and Vespasian (Titüs ve Vespasianüs Tüneli) to divert a stream which threatened to flood Seleucia. To walk through the tunnel itself you need a torch and the ability to keep your balance on slippery rocks. It was built by a labour force of slaves, which included Jews deported after the fall of Jerusalem in AD 70. Nearby are some **Roman rock-cut tombs**.

Opening Times
Titüs ve Vespasianüs Tüneli
daily 08.30–18.00. Primitive toilets in the café by the road

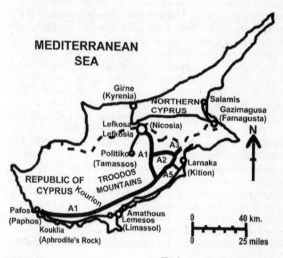

CYPRUS

The island of Cyprus is a pleasant place for a holiday, with a warm Mediterranean climate all year round. Many British people have settled there. In between relaxing on the beaches or cycling in the mountains, tourists may care to visit the places which Paul and Barnabas knew. Unfortunately since 1974, the island has been divided into the Turkish north and the Greek-speaking south. You cannot visit the north except from Turkey, or by day trips from the south, and you cannot visit the south from the north.

Acts 15:39 tells how after quarrelling with Paul in Antioch, Barnabas took Mark and went to Cyprus; Acts 21:3 and 27:4 mention sailing past Cyprus; and Acts 21:16 speaks of Paul staying in Jerusalem at 'the house of Mnason of Cyprus, an early disciple'.

Acts 11: 19–20 also refers to Christians from Cyprus.

Barnabas of Cyprus (Acts 4:36–37)

There was a Levite, a native of Cyprus, Joseph, to whom the
apostles gave the name Barnabas (which means 'son of
encouragement'). He sold a field that belonged to him, then
brought the money, and laid it at the apostles' feet.

Paul and Barnabas preach in Cyprus (Acts 13:4–13)

So, being sent out by the Holy Spirit, they went down to
Seleucia; and from there they sailed to Cyprus. When they
arrived at Salamis, they proclaimed the word of God in the
synagogues of the Jews. And they had John also to assist them.
When they had gone through the whole island as far as Paphos,
they met a certain magician, a Jewish false prophet, named
Bar-Jesus. He was with the proconsul, Sergius Paulus, an
intelligent man, who summoned Barnabas and Saul and wanted
to hear the word of God. But the magician Elymas (for that is
the translation of his name) opposed them and tried to turn the
proconsul away from the faith. But Saul, also known as Paul,
filled with the Holy Spirit, looked intently at him and said, 'You
son of the devil, you enemy of all righteousness, full of all deceit
and villainy, will you not stop making crooked the straight paths
of the Lord? And now listen – the hand of the Lord is against
you, and you will be blind for a while, unable to see the sun.'
Immediately mist and darkness came over him, and he went
about groping for someone to lead him by the hand. When the
proconsul saw what had happened, he believed, for he was
astonished at the teaching about the Lord. Then Paul and his
companions set sail from Paphos and came to Perga in
Pamphylia. John, however, left them and returned to Jerusalem.

The history of Cyprus

Cyprus is dominated by two
mountain ranges, the northern
range called Kyrenia, and the
Troodos mountains in the west.
In Greek mythology Aphrodite
arose from the foam on the coast
of Cyprus. Stone Age
settlements have been found
near Limassol, and pottery from
Cyprus has been found in
Bronze Age layers in Syria,
Palestine and Egypt. Greeks
settled on Cyprus in the
Mycenaean period and left their
pottery at Salamis, Paphos and
several other places. By 1000 BC
the island had come under the
control of the kings of Tyre;
later the Ptolemies claimed the
title of 'Kings of Egypt and of
Cyprus'; and in 52 BC, after
Cyprus had become part of the
Roman empire, Cicero became

its governor. It lies at the crossroads of all the sea routes across the Mediterranean, and was involved in all aspects of trade; but especially it was a source of copper, and kupros is the Greek word for copper. Cyprus has been occupied by Byzantines, Muslims, Crusaders, Venetians and Turks. It came to Britain as a fruit of the Crimean War, became independent under Archbishop Makarios as president in 1960, and in 1974 was divided between the Turkish North Cyprus and Greeks in the rest of the island. Because it was founded by Barnabas, the Orthodox Church in Cyprus claims to be independent of the other patriarchates and elects its own archbishops. The Turkish empire gave the Christians a certain amount of independence under their own leaders, which is why Orthodox bishops have always played a political as well as a spiritual role.

Getting to Cyprus

The South: The Republic of Cyprus

There are air connections from many places through Lárnaka airport in the southern part of the island, and ferries to Haifa in Israel and Piraeus in Greece (sometimes via Patmos and Rhodes, or Crete instead) sail from the port of Limmasol (Lemesós). (See above under Practical Details – Cyprus.)

The North: Turkish North Cyprus

At the time of writing it is only possible to visit the north from the Turkish mainland, coming into Ercan airport (Tel. 231 4703), about 14 kilometres (9 miles) east of Lefkoşa (North Nicosia or Lefkosía), or by ferry from Taşucu near Silifke or from Mersin to the ports of Girne (Kyrenia) or Gazimağusa (Famagusta).

Salamis Agora

Famagusta
North Cyprus

Salamis, where Paul and Barnabas first landed in Cyprus, is about 200 kilometres (130 miles) from Seleucia in Syria, where Paul and his party had embarked. It is on the east coast 9 kilometres (6 miles) north of Famagusta (Gazimağusa). It is signposted to the east side of the Famagusta–Bogazi highway, beside the sea, and the air is filled with the sound of the waves. It would be just possible to make a day trip there from the Republic of Cyprus, with an early start as soon as the border opens at 8 am, travelling from Lefkoşa to Famagusta by minibus and then to Salamis by taxi, and return before the border closes at 5 pm. Famagusta is 58 kilometres (36 miles) from the border crossing point at Lefkoşa (North Nicosia). (See the section in the introduction under Practical Details – Cyprus.)

On your right as you enter the site at Salamis there is a well-preserved **gymnasium complex**, with many pillars standing around the exercise yard, the Palestra. Next to it you can trace the outline of a **stadium**, and then you come to a magnificent **theatre** from the first century BC with a restored seating area capable of holding an audience of more than 15,000. You can then drive round the site and see the less impressive remains of a **Roman villa**, a large **agora** with the **Temple of Zeus**, the father of the Greek gods, at the far end, and **two Christian basilicas**, one of which was the largest building in Cyprus when it was first erected. You are given a clear map of the site with your admission ticket. On the opposite, west, side of the coast road, passing the remains of the seventh and eighth-century BC **royal tombs**, you come to the **Church of Apostolos Varnavas**, an eighteenth-century building containing portions of a fifth-century monastery of St Barnabas. The apocryphal Acts of Barnabas, which probably date from about the fifth century, claim that after another dispute with Bar-Jesus, Barnabas was burnt to death in the hippodrome, leaving his nephew Mark to escape to Alexandria. The monastery church contains a collection of icons, and the monastery buildings have an archaeological collection, mostly early pottery. What is claimed to be the tomb of St Barnabas is in the crypt of a small chapel about a hundred metres (yards) east of the monastery church. The Christian population of Salamis moved to **Famagusta** following the Arab invasion in 647. Shakespeare set his tragedy of Othello in Cyprus, and a tower in the citadel near the harbour in Famagusta is called **Othello's tower**.

Ercan Airport Tel. 231 4703 is about 14 kilometres (8 miles) by expressway east of North Nicosia (Lefkoşa)

Opening Times
Salamis archaeological site
daily 08.00–dusk. About 200 metres (yards) after you enter, you find the toilets on your left, opposite the theatre
Church of Apostolos Varnavas and archaeological museum, **Salamis** Tel. 378 8331, daily 09.00–18.00. Toilets in the corner of the courtyard

Lárnaka
Republic of Cyprus

The Acts of the Apostles tells us that Paul and Barnabas made a preaching tour of all the synagogues from Salamis to Paphos. No first-century synagogues have been found but we can presume there was one in each of the big cities on the island. The Acts of Barnabas says that they visited Lapithos (Lapta), 15 kilometres (9 miles) west of Kyrenia; Lampadistus which was located at a site now called Kalopanayiotes 73 kilometres (46 miles) south-west of Nicosia; Ledra which is the modern Nicosia; Kition and Tamassos. The modern city of Lárnaka, on the south coast, is built over the ruins of ancient **Kition**, which was probably the Kittim referred to in Genesis 10:4, Numbers 24:24, 1 Chronicles 1:7 and Daniel 11:30, and was the birthplace of Zeno, the founder of Stoic philosophy. The only place where they are visible is at a site about 1 kilometre (half a mile) north-west of the city centre, off Leontiou Machaira, where the foundations of a temple dating from around 1200 BC can be seen. Lazarus is supposed to have come to Cyprus as a witness to the resurrection, after Jesus raised him from the dead (John 11). There were plots to kill him (John 12:10-11), and he may have come with those who fled there after the stoning of Stephen (Acts 11:19). Early local traditions tell us that Barnabas made him Bishop of Kition, where he must have given a unique witness to the Christian belief in resurrection. His tomb under the altar in the Church of Agios Lazaros, on the street called Agiou Lazarou in the centre of Lárnaka, is where he was buried after dying a second time; his bones were taken to Constantinople in 890 and then to Marseilles in 1202.

Lárnaka International Airport (Cyprus Airways Tel. (04) 692 700) is 6 kilometres (4 miles) south of the city

Opening Times
Ancient Kition Monday to Friday 09.00–14.30. Toilets at the far east end of the site.
Church of Agios Lazaros, Lárnaka daily 08.00–12.30 and 15.30–18.30. Toilets in the courtyard to the right of the church.

Nicosia

(The part which is in North Cyprus is called **Lefkoşa**; the part in the Republic is known as **Lefkosia**.)
The central area of this divided city is still surrounded by a sixteenth century wall built by the Venetians. The important Cyprus museum is just outside the walls, south of the Ledra Palace Hotel border crossing point, on Leoforos Mouseiou. Starting from the south-western suburb of Lakatameia, a 17 kilometres (11 miles) drive along the E902 is signposted from time to time to **Tamassos** or **Agios Irakleidios**.
Tamassos was a source of

copper mentioned in Homer's *Odyssey*. It once occupied a large area around the modern village of Politikó, but the signposts will lead you to the only easily visible remains, the royal tombs, well-preserved underground burial chambers from the seventh century BC, carved in stone to resemble wooden houses.

Turning left on leaving these brings you to the monastery of Agios Irakleidios. Tradition says that Heracleides was born in Tamassos and guided Paul and Barnabas there. Two of his bones are displayed in a silver case to the left of the altar in the chapel, and there are a number of stone sarcophagi from the Roman period inside and outside the domed mausoleum behind the chapel. Mnason of Cyprus, mentioned in Acts 21:16, is also supposed to have been buried here. He and Heracleides are said to have both been converted by St Paul, and among the first bishops of the church in Cyprus appointed by St Barnabas.

Opening Times
Nicosia Cyprus museum Tel. (02) 865 888, Monday to Saturday 09.00–17.00, Sunday 10.00–13.00. Toilets: follow the signs to 'O-O'
Tamassos royal tombs Tuesday to Friday 09.00–15.00, Saturday and Sunday 10.00–15.00. Toilets on the left side of the ticket office
Agios Irakleidios monastery open all daylight hours, but

mid-May to mid-September closed 12.00–15.00. Toilets on the left of the entrance driveway

Limassol (Lemesós)
Republic of Cyprus

The principal port of the Republic is also a pleasant holiday resort. East of the town the important ancient city of **Amathous** is still being excavated; a clear plan on a pedestal on the site explains the buildings around the agora. To the west are the remains of **Kourion**, with a theatre, the foundations of a large Byzantine church, a stadium and a Temple of Apollo. Limmasol is 82 kilometres (51 miles) from the border crossing point at Nicosia (Lefkosia) via the A1 motorway.

Opening Times
Ancient Amathous daily 09.00–19.30 in summer, 09.00–17.00 in winter. Toilets by the ticket kiosk
Ancient Kourion daily 07.30–19.30 in summer, 07.30–17.00 in winter
Kourion sanctuary of Apollon Ylatis daily 09.00–19.30 in summer, 09.00–17.30 from October to April

Páfos
Republic of Cyprus

Páfos is a pleasant seaside resort with modern hotels and good beaches, but quiet enough to retain a friendly atmosphere. It is at the west end of the island, 72 kilometres (45 miles) from Limmasol (Lemesós), on the A1 motorway, which should be completed in 2001. If you turn

Church of St Paul's Pillar, Páfos

off the A1 onto the B6 before reaching Páfos, however, you come to **Aphrodite's Rock**, the most westerly of a group of rocks on the seashore, called Petra tou Romiou (the Rock of the Greek). The legend is that the goddess, called Venus in Latin, came ashore here in a shower of foam from which she had been born, as in Botticelli's painting. Four kilometres (2 miles) nearer to Páfos are the ruins of the **shrine of Aphrodite** and the **Kouklia museum**. The original settlement of Paphos was here at Kouklia, which is therefore called Palea Paphos. But because there was no harbour at Kouklia, the population of the port city of Nea Paphos, which Paul, Mark and Barnabas visited, soon exceeded it.

The modern town of **Páfos**, 11 kilometres (7 miles) further on, is divided into upper and lower towns, called Ano Páfos and Kato Páfos respectively; the remains of the Roman city of Nea Paphos are mostly in an **archaeological park** near the harbour in Kato Páfos. The

park is being redesigned with an entrance by a new visitors centre beside the port.

There pilgrims can visit the remains of three Roman villas with sumptuous mosaics. To the east is the so-called **House of Dionysos**, protected by a large wooden building. Next, to the west of it, is the small **House of Aion**, with a concrete building over it. Finally the **House of Theseus** is not covered; it is named after a circular mosaic showing Theseus killing the minotaur. This residence was so large it must have been the palace of the proconsul, the Roman governor of Cyprus; although dating from the second century it is probably on the site where Paul preached to Sergius Paulus.

North of the houses with the mosaics, close to the modern lighthouse, is an **odeon** which was restored in 1970. In front of it is the large square **agora** or forum, and an **Asklepion** or healing temple is at the south-west corner of the agora.

Leaving the archaeological park

65

The influence of a governor

Barnabas was a wealthy man, and in his native Cyprus no doubt an important one. That could well have been why Barnabas, who was at that point the senior member of the new mission team setting out from Antioch, decided to go first to Cyprus where he had friends and could wield some influence. Also, some of the Jewish Christians were already wary of this rebellious young preacher Saul who seemed to be as interested in speaking to the pagans as to the Jews. So they could have encouraged Barnabas to take him to a place where he could be kept in the synagogues under careful Jewish supervision. If so, it didn't work, for they were summoned to the house of the Roman governor. Until he met Sergius Paulus, the apostle had been described as 'Saul who was also called Paul'. But from that moment on he is simply known by the Latin name Paul. It is as though his first encounter with a senior Roman official inspired him to play down his Jewishness and plan the conversion of the Roman world. Recently discovered inscriptions have shown that the family of Sergius Paulus came from Antioch-of-Pisidia; maybe he suggested a visit there; and Paul may have started to work out a strategy based on the capitals of the different provinces of the Roman empire.

and travelling north from the port along Leoforos Apostolou Paulou, a turning on the right leads to the **Hrysopolitissa Church**, known as the **Church of St Paul's Pillar**. Here are the foundations of a large fourth-century AD basilica; a small medieval gothic church was built out of the stones on one corner of the site. It belongs to the Cypriot Orthodox Church but they allow Roman Catholics, Anglicans and Lutherans to hold regular services there. To the south of the church is a column, where Paul is supposed to have been whipped with the 'forty lashes less one' (2 Corinthians 11:24–25). It was considered that forty lashes would kill a man, and Paul says he received this punishment many times, but there is no biblical evidence he was punished in Paphos.

Agia Solomoni and the Christian catacomb, a little further north on the Leoforos Apostolou Paulou, is a subterranean Jewish tomb which, like the **Agios Lambrinos** caverns nearby, once had frescoes, now faded or defaced, showing they were used for early Christian worship.

Turning left onto Tafon ton Basileon, and travelling about 2 kilometres (1 mile) north of Kato Páfos, we find, overlooking the sea, the **'Tombs of the Kings'**, in fact some anonymous but very impressive tombs, built below ground to resemble private houses, between the third century BC and the third century AD.

Páfos International Airport (Cyprus Airways Tel. (06) 422 641) is 8 kilometres (5 miles) to the south-east of the modern city

Opening Times
Kouklia museum and Temple of Aphrodite Monday to Saturday 09.00–17.00 and Sunday 10.00–16.00 from September to May; Monday to Saturday 09.00–19.00 and Sunday 09.00–17.00 from June to August. Toilets in the museum
Páfos mosaics Tel. (06) 240217, 08.00–19.30 daily. Toilets in the port area
Páfos 'Tombs of the Kings' daily 08.30–19.30 in summer or 08.30–17.00 October to April

THE GATEWAY TO GALATIA

Turkey is becoming one of the world's most popular holiday destinations, and the majority of tourists go to the beaches on the Aegean coast, in the south-west of the country. Further south is the area known from the colour of the sea as the Turquoise Coast. The more inquisitive may also visit some of the multitude of archaeological sites in this region. Pilgrims will want to look at the places visited by the apostles. Paul

and Barnabas crossed from Cyprus and landed at the port of Perga in the Roman province of Galatia; Perga was several miles inland, but a small boat from Cyprus could have come up the River Kestros to a port nearby for Barnabas and his party to land. On their return journey, however, a larger boat may have been necessary to take them to Antioch, which could only sail from the coastal port of Attalia.

Perga (modern name Perge) was the birthplace of the third–

century BC mathematician
Apollonius, who wrote a famous
book on conic sections, and
believed that the earth moved in
orbit around the sun.

Attalia (modern name Antalya)
was founded in the second century
BC by Attalus II, King of
Pergamon, and in 25 BC it was
made the capital of the Roman
province of Pamphylia. People
from Pamphylia were present on
the day of Pentecost (Acts 2:10)
and Paul and Barnabas may have
found Spirit-filled believers in
Jesus in the synagogue there.

Hadrian's Gate, Antalya

Getting to Perga and Attalia

Modern pilgrims will probably
come from the resorts on the
Aegean coast and travel south
along route D-400, which
begins at Marmaris, the base for
visiting Cnidus (see below
under the Journey to Rome).
Passing Dalaman, where there
is an airport, and Fethiye, the
next biblical site you pass is
Patara, down a turning on the
right a few kilometres beyond
Kinic. The road continues past

Kas to Demre, the ancient
Myra, then past Finike, and on
to Antalya (Attalia). Between
Finike and Antalya, in the
foothills of one of the twenty or
more mountains called Mount
Olympos in the ancient world,
is the **Chimaera**, an area
where, since ancient times,
burning gases have been issuing
from crevices in the rocks.
According to Homer, the
Chimaera was a fire-breathing
monster who was killed by
Bellerophon, riding on the
winged horse Pegasus. Finike is
some 120 kilometres (75 miles)
from Antalya, and 179
kilometres (112 miles) from
Fethiye. Perge (Perga) is 2
kilometres (1½ miles) north of
the town of Aksu, and 18
kilometres (11 miles) north-east
of Antalya, and Aspendos, by
the Köprü Çayi stream, is 50
kilometres (30 miles) east of
Antalya. From Antalya there are
several possible routes to
Antioch-of-Pisidia; or of course
the whole journey may be done
in the opposite direction.
Antalya has a busy airport 10
kilometres (6 miles) to the east,
a new port and a bus station.
(For Patara, see below under
Paul's Third Missionary
Journey, and for Myra, under
the Journey to Rome.)

Antalya today

The modern **Antalya**, which is
a fast-growing tourist resort,
lies on a limestone plateau well
above sea level; Paul will have
needed to climb down to the
harbour. The walls of the old

> *Arriving at Perga on the first missionary journey*
> *(Acts 13:13–14)*
>
> Then Paul and his companions set sail from Paphos and came to
> Perga in Pamphylia. John, however, left them and returned to
> Jerusalem; but they went on from Perga and came to Antioch in
> Pisidia.
>
> *Leaving from Attalia at the end of the first missionary*
> *journey (Acts 14:25–26)*
>
> When they had spoken the word in Perga, they went down to
> Attalia. From there they sailed back to Antioch, where they had
> been commended to the grace of God for the work that they had
> completed.

city follow approximately the line of the walls of the Roman city, but none of the buildings survive from Paul's time. The **Tower of Hıdırlık** (Hıdırlık Kulesi) on the coast south of the harbour is probably a first-century AD mausoleum which may have been used as a lighthouse. North-east of here, the **Kesik Minare** is a truncated minaret on a site which was successively a second-century AD Roman temple, a Byzantine church and a mosque from the period of the Seljuk Turkish empire; parts of the vestibule may be Roman, but the roof and the top of the minaret were burnt in a fire in 1896 and never rebuilt.

East of the old city, the fine triumphal arch known as the **Gate of Hadrian** (Hadrianüs Kapısı) dates from around 130 AD and stands on the site of the old Perga Gate. There is a unique **fluted minaret** (Yivli Minare) on the north of the city,

built by the thirteenth-century Seljuk Sultan Allâeddin Keykubad, on whom the character of Aladdin in the Arabian Nights may be based, and the adjacent mosque is said to have been built on the site of a church. There is a fine **museum** (Antalya Müzesi) 2 kilometres (1½ miles) west of the centre of the town, with beautiful classical marble statues, many of them from the baths at Perga, and Roman tombs.

Perge today

Perge has magnificent remains which have been well-excavated by the Turkish authorities. The first building the modern visitor comes to, beside the road, is a well-preserved Greco-Roman **theatre** seating about 15,000 people; at present it is closed to visitors.

Next, by the coach park, is a second-century AD **stadium**, seating 12,000 people, one of

PERGE (PERGA)

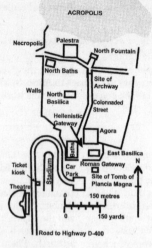

ACROPOLIS

Necropolis · Palestra · North Fountain · North Baths · Site of Archway · Walls · North Basilica · Colonnaded Street · Hellenistic Gateway · Baths · Agora · East Basilica · Ticket kiosk · Stadium · Car Park · Roman Gateway · Theatre · Site of Tomb of Plancia Magna

0 — 150 metres
0 — 150 yards

Road to Highway D-400

the best preserved stadia in the world. The stade was the Roman mile, so a stadium contains a race track; a certain number of times round the track and the runners would have completed a mile; every Roman city had one. (See p. 234 for words ending in -ion or -eum.)

Outside the city gate was the tomb of a remarkable woman called **Plancia Magna**, who was the civic leader of Perga in the second century AD. The **gate** is double: the outside one is Roman, and the inner one is Greek or hellenistic, with two huge round towers. Notice the inscription on a stone inside the hellenistic gate to Plancia

Magna in her role as priestess to the Temple of Artemis in Greek, or Diana in Latin. Inside the gate the road runs north, with the **southern fountain** and **baths** on your left, with

Gateway at Perga

Reconstruction of Stage Building at Aspendos Theatre, G. Niemann 1881

fine under-floor heating by hypocausts, and originally covered in statues; the **gymnasium** or palestra was in front of it. The fourth-century AD market square or **agora** on the right is probably on the site of an earlier one, where St Paul may well have preached. The **colonnaded street** had an attractive stream of water in a raised channel running down the centre for cooling, and coming from a **shrine to Neptune** at the far end. A few ruins on the acropolis may be from the famous **Temple of Artemis** at Perga.

While in the area, pilgrims may take the opportunity to visit **Aspendos**, which, while it is not mentioned in the Bible, has an even finer **theatre**, built in the reign of Emperor Marcus Aurelius (AD 161–80) and restored under Atatürk in 1930. Climb the steep path behind the toilet to view the theatre from the top of the hill and continue to the right, or use the lower path or the road past the car park, to view the impressive **aqueduct**.

Opening Times
Antalya Müzesi Tel. 0242 238 5686, Tuesday to Sunday 09.00–18.30. Toilets on the right in the entrance lobby
Perge archaeological site daily 09.00–19.00. Toilets by the car park
Aspendos daily 09.00–19.00 May to October; 08.00–17.30 November to April. Toilets on the right after you pass the ticket booth

Why did John Mark leave?

Paul and Barnabas now turned towards Phrygia, Pamphylia, Galatia, Bythinia and Asia. People from all these places were present on the day of Pentecost (Acts 2:9–10) but apparently no churches had been established there. At this point on the first missionary journey John Mark left Paul and his uncle Barnabas to continue their journey without him and made his own way home. He may well have been the John Mark whose mother's house was used as a meeting place for the Christians in Acts 12:12; who wrote the Gospel of Mark and identified himself as the young man who ran away naked when Jesus was arrested (Mark 14:51–52); and who was brought from Jerusalem by his uncle in Acts 12:25. Was he just a young man who was homesick? Was he frightened by the prospect of a journey over the rugged mountains to the remote Antioch-of-Pisidia? This was certainly one of the journeys Paul referred to when he said he had been 'in peril from robbers' (2 Corinthians 11:26). The way the Taurus Mountains fall sheer into the sea in places meant that there was no coastal road in Paul's day, only mountain passes at the top of the river valleys, which are beautiful to us but must have been perilous for him. Or did Mark share with Barnabas a disquiet at Paul's increasing interest in a mission to the hated Gentiles, and decide to have nothing more to do with him?

If Paul's letter to the Galatians was written to the southern Galatian towns it may give us a clue (though see below on the North Galatian towns for the contrary view). In Galatians 4:13–14, Saint Paul tells the Galatians that he came to them because of sickness: 'You know that it was because of a physical infirmity that I first announced the gospel to you; though my condition put you to the test, you did not scorn or despise me, but welcomed me as an angel of God, as Christ Jesus.'

This illness may have been the thorn or 'stake in the flesh' referred to in 2 Corinthians 12:7–8, and it has been suggested it was malaria. The trembling caused by malaria might have led him to expect to be despised, and the coastal estuaries were full of mosquitos. It was the Turkish leader Kemal Atatürk (1881–1938) who gave instructions for rows of eucalyptus, which are still prominent, to be planted to drain the swamp. Other suggestions have included epilepsy (Acts 9:4), eye problems (Galatians 4:15, 6:11), a speech defect (Galatians 4:13; 2 Corinthians 10:10, 11:6), a headache or earache, depression or temptation, or the humans who opposed him. Was a desire to get up into the mountains away from the swamps, in spite of the strain on a man travelling when racked with fever, a factor in Paul's decision to go to Antioch-of-Pisidia; and did Barnabas decide to go with him, in spite of Mark's desertion, to keep an eye on his health and his teaching? Maybe it was at this juncture that Paul saw how the suffering of the crucified

Messiah gave meaning to his own and everyone else's suffering, a point which was central to his preaching.

Paul was very angry about Mark's cowardice, and his refusal to take the young man with them on his next journey led to a permanent split between Paul and Mark's uncle Barnabas (Acts 15:37–39). Fortunately Paul does seem to have been reconciled with Mark later (Colossians 4:10; 2 Timothy 4:11; Philemon 24) and Mark also went on to work with the apostle Peter (1 Peter 5:13)

ANTIOCH-OF-PISIDIA (TURKEY)

The ruins of Pisidian Antioch, on the high Anatolian plain near Yalvaç, are quite dramatic, and less visited than their importance to Christians would lead one to expect. The province of Galatia was broken down into regions, and Antioch, where the three regions of Pisidia, Phrygia and Lycaonia met, was called Antioch-of-Pisidia to distinguish it from the other fifteen Antiochs. It had been founded by Seleucus I in about 300 BC, bequeathed to the Romans in 25 BC by Amyntas, the last King of Galatia, and turned by Emperor Augustus into the most important Roman colony in southern Asia Minor. A colony was a town settled by retired Roman soldiers for defensive reasons. Antioch was also a garrison town with a large contingent of the Roman army based there. It stood on the frontier of an area of tribal people, and was intended to bring Roman civilization to them and by good administration keep them under control. Maybe Paul had been inspired by Sergius Paulus to try an experiment of using it to bring the message of Jesus to those on the fringes of the empire. An inscription was found in Antioch mentioning Lucius Sergius Paulus the younger; it has been suggested that this may have been the son of the governor of Cyprus, whose family may therefore have come from Antioch.

Getting to Antioch-of-Pisidia

The remains of Antioch-of-Pisidia are approximately 1.6 kilometres (one mile) north of the modern town of Yalvaç, which lies on route D-320, a turning off the D-330 and D-695. Modern pilgrims approaching Yalvaç from Antalya, 230 kilometres (144 miles) away in the south, are faced with a choice of routes through Beyşehir or Eğirdir shown on the map on p. 78; they all pass through dramatic mountain scenery, but the gradients on the D-695 are not quite so steep as the others. Coming from Konya (Iconium), it is 176 kilometres (110 miles) along route D-330.

Antioch-of-Pisidia today

A tour of the remains of Antioch today starts at the **Triple Gate** dated to AD 212, and includes the well-preserved

ANTIOCH-OF-PISIDIA

main streets around which every Roman town was built: the **Cardo** and the **Decumanus** at right angles. The Decumanus ran through a 60 metres (66 yards) long tunnel underneath the hellenistic **theatre**, enlarged by the Romans to seat 15,000, where Thekla was supposed to have suffered (see below under Iconium). Off the Cardo was a **columned street** leading to the **Square of Tiberius**. A triple-arched **triumphal gateway** separated this from the **Square of Augustus**, the highest point of the city. This held, in early times, a temple to the mother goddess Cybele. Then in hellenistic times she was replaced by the moon goddess Men. In Roman times this in turn gave way to a striking **temple to the emperor Augustus**, the foundations of

which can now be seen. There are carvings of **garlanded bull's heads**: the bull was the symbol of the goddess Men. The outline of a **bouleuterion** and of the **agora** or market place can be seen; the **baths** are huge but not yet fully excavated. A first-century AD aqueduct strides across the hills to bring water to the city, terminating in a first-century AD **nymphaeum**, from which, together with three other fountains, water was distributed though stone, clay and lead pipes to the whole city. Without running or 'living' water no city could survive; if the enemies of the town cut its aqueduct the town was usually abandoned for ever. It would be surprising if Paul did not tell the people of Antioch about our need for Jesus the Living Water.

Paul 'turns to the Gentiles' in Antioch-of-Pisidia (Acts 13:14–15)

They went on from Perga and came to Antioch in Pisidia. And on the sabbath day they went into the synagogue and sat down. After the reading of the law and the prophets, the officials of the synagogue sent them a message, saying, 'Brothers, if you have any word of exhortation for the people, give it.'

Paul preached an electrifying sermon, telling his listeners that the death and resurrection of Jesus was the fulfilment of God's promises to his people, the Israelites. The consequences unfold in verses 42–49:

As Paul and Barnabas were going out, the people urged them to speak about these things again the next sabbath. When the meeting of the synagogue broke up, many Jews and devout converts to Judaism followed Paul and Barnabas, who spoke to them and urged them to continue in the grace of God.

The next sabbath almost the whole city gathered to hear the word of the Lord. But when the Jews saw the crowds, they were filled with jealousy; and blaspheming, they contradicted what was spoken by Paul.

Then both Paul and Barnabas spoke out boldly, saying, 'It was necessary that the word of God should be spoken first to you. Since you reject it and judge yourselves to be unworthy of eternal life, we are now turning to the Gentiles. For so the Lord has commanded us, saying, "I have set you to be a light for the Gentiles, so that you may bring salvation to the ends of the earth."'

When the Gentiles heard this, they were glad and praised the word of the Lord; and as many as had been destined for eternal life became believers. Thus the word of the Lord spread throughout the region.

When the **Byzantine basilica of St Paul** was built in the fourth century AD it was one of the largest churches in the world. The most exciting find of recent times has been the discovery of some foundations protruding from beneath the basilica. Although it cannot be proved, it is claimed that they are those of a **first-century synagogue**. If so, it is the only first-century synagogue to be found outside the Holy Land apart from Delos and Ostia, and the modern pilgrim can read Paul's sermon in the very place where it was delivered. The

Bull carving, Antioch–of–Pisidia

surviving part of the **aqueduct** can be reached from the entrance to the site up a narrow earth road; beware of heavy trucks.

Opening times
Yalvaç archaeological museum Tel. 0246 441 5059, daily 09.00–18.00. Toilets on the left of the ticket booth
Antioch archeological site Tel. 0246 441 6126, always open. Toilets inside the ticket booth, up the slope to the right of the entrance

The importance of Antioch-of-Pisidia

St Paul's sermon in Pisidian Antioch was a turning point in his ministry: he preached first to the Jews, and was at first welcomed by them. But his audience in the synagogue included two other categories of non-Jewish people, whom the Jews referred to as proselytes of the law and proselytes of the porch. The first were those who had accepted the whole structure of the Jewish law, and that meant Jewish culture: they were the 'converts to Judaism'. The second group were those who were attracted by Jewish teaching about one creator God, and by a morality so much higher than that of the pagan people around them, but did not feel able to take on the whole of Jewish cultural tradition. They were always referred to as 'God-fearers'; these are the ones Paul is talking to when he addresses the 'others who fear God'. 'God-fearers' are mentioned ten times in Acts, in Caesarea-on-Sea (Acts 10), Antioch-of-Pisidia (Acts 13), Philippi (Acts 16), Thessalonica and Athens (Acts 17) and Corinth (Acts 18).

St Luke was not present when this sermon was preached; perhaps it was so important that Paul remembered it vividly and gave Luke a full account. Or maybe Luke wrote out what Paul always said when addressing for the first time a synagogue with both Jews and Gentiles present. Like every rabbi's sermon it begins with a summary of the scriptural account of what God had done for his people. What made it so provocative was that, like St Stephen's last sermon which Paul may have heard, it shows how God's promises to Israel were fulfilled in Jesus, yet the people of Israel had rejected him. By Jesus, said Paul, everyone, even non-Jews, could be forgiven for their sins, without keeping the law of Moses.

The God-fearers must have been so excited about this that they told all their friends, and almost the whole population, who had never shown any interest in Jewish religion before, crowded around the tiny synagogue on the next sabbath. This made the Jews furious; if this renegade Jew called Paul was teaching that every Tom, Dick and Harry could be welcomed into God's covenant community, then it seemed as if the Jewish race, who had so faithfully kept the law of the covenant, would be swamped and forgotten. They rejected Paul, and for the first time, Paul openly rejected his fellow-Jews and turned to the Gentiles. If he hadn't, you and I might never have become Christians. This was the first Christian community to be established independently of any Jewish synagogue. (See also **Jews and Gentiles** on p. 87.)

ICONIUM (TURKEY)

One of the loveliest mosques in Turkey is the green-roofed Mevlânâ museum in Konya, formerly the home of the Sufi sect of the whirling dervishes. There was a saying, 'See the world, but above all see Konya.' It is on the site of the town known to Paul and Barnabas as Iconium, which they travelled to when they left Antioch-of-Pisidia. One legend of the origins of the town of Iconium contains interesting parallels with the early chapters of Genesis: there was a great flood, whose waters receded at the command of Zeus, when Prometheus and Athena made images or 'icons' of human beings and breathed life into them to repopulate the world. Another story is that Perseus conquered the area by showing them the Gorgon's head, which turned all who looked at it to stone; but a village presented him with an image or 'icon' of the head, and on that site he founded Iconium. Emperor Claudius gave the town the honour of calling itself Claudiconium during a period of readministration; however it remained a Greek town and was never romanized. The town was not as important as Pisidian Antioch; it was a small town in the district administered by Antioch; now their roles are reversed.

Getting to Konya

Konya is at the hub of a number of roads. In a clockwise direction, due north and then veering west is route D-300 to Afyon, then comes the D-715

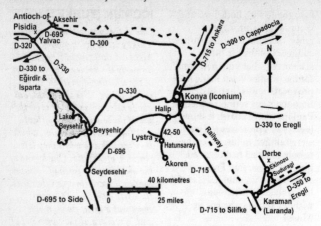

towards Ankara (265 kilometres or 166 miles), the D-300 towards Nevşehir in Cappadocia (217 kilometres or 135 miles), D-330 towards Tarsus and Adana (351 kilometres or 219 miles), D-715 to Silifke (256 kilometres or 160 miles), D-696 to Seydişehir (85 kilometres or 53 miles), and due west the D-330 to Lake Beyşehir and Yalvaç, about 176 kilometres (110 miles) away.

Konya today

Konya is now a piously Muslim town; visitors should dress modestly and not eat in public during the fasting season of Ramadan. Konya has little to show from biblical times, though the hill of **Allaettin Tepesi**, called after Sultan Allâeddin Keykubad, is over the site of the Greek acropolis and later the Seljuk fortress. The beautiful **Mevlânâ** is now officially no longer a mosque but a museum; but it is common courtesy in most eastern countries to remove one's shoes when entering any building, and women should cover their heads and shoulders.

Opening times

Konya Arkeoloji Müzesi, Sahip Ata Caddesi, Tuesday to Sunday 09.00–12.00 and 13.30–17.15
Mevlânâ Müzesi Tel. 0332 351 1215, Tuesday to Sunday 09.00–17.10; Monday 10.00–17.10. Turn right as you come out, and after about a hundred metres (yards) turn right and some toilets are just round the corner

The Acts of Paul and Thekla

There is a book with this name, dating from the late second century. It is probably best to regard it as a response to the desire for new Christian converts to have some Christian fiction, much as many readers

Déjà vu in Iconium on the first missionary journey (Acts 14:1–6)

Driven out of Antioch-of-Pisidia for preaching the good news to Jew and Gentile alike, Paul and Barnabas meet the same reaction in Iconium.

The same thing occurred in Iconium, where Paul and Barnabas went into the Jewish synagogue and spoke in such a way that a great number of both Jews and Greeks became believers. But the unbelieving Jews stirred up the Gentiles and poisoned their minds against the brothers. So they remained for a long time, speaking boldly for the Lord, who testified to the word of his grace by granting signs and wonders to be done through them. But the residents of the city were divided; some sided with the Jews, and some with the apostles. And when an attempt was made by both Gentiles and Jews, with their rulers, to mistreat them and to stone them, the apostles learned of it and fled to Lystra and Derbe, cities of Lycaonia, and to the surrounding country.

See also verses 20–21: Apparently undeterred, Paul and Barnabas returned to Iconium and to Antioch on this journey.

require today. But like many historical novels, it contains a great deal of historical fact, and may include some information which St Luke saw no need to include in the Acts of the Apostles. The story is that an old man called Onesiphorus (compare 2 Timothy 1:16 and 4:19) was told to look out for St Paul on the road from Antioch to Iconium, at the crossroads at Misthia, near modern Beyşehir. He was given a description so that he could recognize the apostle:

> He is a sturdy little bald-headed man, with eyebrows that meet at the centre, rather a large nose, bow-legged, and full of grace, who at times seems to have the face of an angel.

Could this be based on memories passed down for a few generations among the Christians? According to the book, Paul stayed with Onesiphorus and preached in the courtyard of his house, where he was seen by a young woman called Thekla who lived in the house next door. She was converted by what she heard and became one of Paul's most devoted followers. The book continues with an account of her travels; her sufferings under persecution from the enemies of Christianity; and her death at Seleucia-in-Cilicia, the modern **Silifke**, where there are fragmentary remains of a cave dwelling and a monastery.

Sufis

It is worth studying the prayers and poems of the Sufis, who, with their emphasis on personal love of God and the importance of loving our friends, are nearer to Christianity than many other sects. They used to induce a trance by spinning around, winning the title of 'whirling dervishes'; they only perform this now at their annual festival in December. Christians will want to ask themselves whether there is any comparison between this and the physical means we ourselves use to achieve an atmosphere of prayer. Their leading teacher was Mevlânâ Celaleddin Rumi, who wrote:

God, my beloved, only love brings us close to you. Wherever we tread we are the earth under your foot. Is it right that on the road of love I should see the world in your company and not see your face?

LYSTRA AND DERBE (TURKEY)

Only those determined to go everywhere that Paul went will travel to the bare hilltops which represent the sites of these two obscure towns to which Paul and Barnabas fled after they left Iconium, and reading the scriptures in the right place, having successfully identified them, will be their reward. Most ancient towns were located on hills so that they could be defended. Successive generations left layers of domestic rubbish and demolished buildings, forming what archaeologists call a tel. Then if the site was abandoned, neighbouring cities would use any stones left above the surface as a source of shaped stone for new buildings elsewhere – the preservation of heritage sites is a modern idea. Lystra, Derbe, and as we shall see later,

Colossae, have nothing to offer the visitor but a bare and so far unexcavated tel. Apparently this is the first book to give full details of how to find them.

Locating Lystra

The site of Lystra was unknown until an American archaeologist, Professor Sitlington Sterrett in 1885 discovered an altar dedicated to Emperor Caesar Augustus, and a Roman coin, on a mound about a mile north-west of the small Turkish village of Hatunsarai. Both of them preserved the word 'Lustra', the Roman form of the Greek 'Lystra'. For a while the altar stood on the top of the tel, then it and the coin were placed in Konya museum.

From Konya follow the D-696 Seydişehir road to Hatip, then turn left onto the 42-50 towards Akören. After 27 kilometres (17

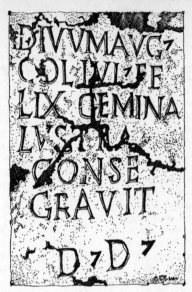

Lystra Altar at Konya Museum

miles) you reach the village of Hatunsarai, but before entering it, at the 27 kilometre signboard, turn right where a sign reads 'Güneydere 10, Gökyurt 16', and another brown sign says 'Lystra 2 km, Klistra (Gökyurt) 16 km'. After less than 1.5 kilometres or one mile on this paved road, an unpaved track turns off left by an olive tree, and the tel of Lystra (Tel Zordula Hüyük) is on the left of the road in front of you to the west. The track leads to the spring known as **St Paul's Well**; from there you can climb the south side of the tel, where the city gate must have been as it is the only side which is not too steep to climb;

a few shaped stones are lying about but that is all.

Locating Derbe

Derbe was only identified in 1956, when a stone was found by M.H. Ballance at Kerti Hüyük, dated to AD 157, inscribed 'by the council and people of Derbe' and mentioning Bishop Sestillianus. It is now in the Konya Archaeological Museum. Then the gravestone of a Bishop Michael of Derbe, dating from somewhere between the fourth and sixth centuries AD, was found in 1958 near Suduraği. It is kept in the forecourt of Karaman Museum.

81

Karaman (ancient Laranda) is 106 kilometres or 66 miles south-east of Konya on the D-715. Driving from Karaman on the D-350 towards Ereğli, there are three turnings to the left, any of which you can choose, at a distance from Karaman respectively of 3 kilometres (2 miles) signposted Ekinözu 20 km; at 12 kilometres (7 miles) signed to Alaçatı 4 km, Suduraği 9 km, and on a yellow sign Canhasan 2 km, Derbe 13 km (on this road you must turn left at Suduraği); and finally by the 18 kilometre signboard (11 miles from Karaman) a sign to Suduraği 9 km, Akçaşehir 30 km. I would recommend the last as it is only 8 kilometres (5 miles) on the minor road with no turnings. All three are paved roads, but on each you go over an uneven railway crossing. Then at Ekinözü you turn right on a good unpaved road which is not signposted (but ignoring the sign which points straight ahead at this point to Beydilli 5 km., Akçaşehir 25 km). After choosing a couple of left forks in the village, this leads you north for about 3 kilometres (2 miles) and over a small bridge to an isolated tel which is Kerti Hüyük or Devri Şehri (which means the city of Derbe). Derbe is about 92 kilometres (57 miles) from Lystra, which would have taken Paul and Barnabas two or three days to travel on foot.

Lystra and Derbe before Paul arrived

The presence of Latin inscriptions shows that Lystra, built on top of a hill, was an important military vantage point, and retired Roman soldiers were settled there by Emperor Augustus in 6 BC to establish a colony. Essentially however both Lystra and Derbe were oriental towns where people spoke the local languages in preference to Latin or Greek, which many of them could hardly understand.

There was a small Jewish community in Lystra, one of whom was Loïs, whose daughter Eunice was married to a Greek, and the mother of Timothy (2 Timothy 1:5). Living so far from other Jewish communities, they must have been slack in their observance of the law. Timothy, having a Jewish mother, was technically a Jew, but they had not even bothered to have him circumcised (Acts 16:3).

Inscriptions show that Zeus (Jove) and Hermes (Mercury) were the principal deities worshipped in this area; carvings in Antioch-of-Pisidia and many other places show bulls with their horns wreathed in flowers ready for sacrifice. The accuracy of Luke as an historian is shown by inscriptions found there showing that the towns were indeed in Lycaonia, contrary to the beliefs of more recent geographers.

On the first missionary journey (Acts 14:6–24)

The apostles learned of [the trouble at Iconium] and fled to Lystra and Derbe, cities of Lycaonia, and to the surrounding country; and there they continued proclaiming the good news.

In Lystra there was a man sitting who could not use his feet and had never walked, for he had been crippled from birth. He listened to Paul as he was speaking. And Paul, looking at him intently and seeing that he had faith to be healed, said in a loud voice, 'Stand upright on your feet.' And the man sprang up and began to walk. When the crowds saw what Paul had done, they shouted in the Lycaonian language, 'The gods have come down to us in human form!' Barnabas they called Zeus, and Paul they called Hermes, because he was the chief speaker. The priest of Zeus, whose temple was just outside the city, brought oxen and garlands to the gates; he and the crowds wanted to offer sacrifice. When the apostles Barnabas and Paul heard of it, they tore their clothes and rushed out into the crowd, shouting, 'Friends, why are you doing this? We are mortals just like you, and we bring you good news, that you should turn from these worthless things to the living God, who made the heaven and the earth and the sea and all that is in them. In past generations he allowed all the nations to follow their own ways; yet he has not left himself without a witness in doing good – giving you rains from heaven and fruitful seasons, and filling you with food and your hearts with joy.' Even with these words, they scarcely restrained the crowds from offering sacrifice to them.

But Jews came there from Antioch and Iconium and won over the crowds. Then they stoned Paul and dragged him out of the city, supposing that he was dead. But when the disciples surrounded him, he got up and went into the city. The next day he went on with Barnabas to Derbe.

On the second missionary journey (Acts 16:1–6)

Paul went on also to Derbe and to Lystra, where there was a disciple named Timothy, the son of a Jewish woman who was a believer; but his father was a Greek. He was well spoken of by the believers in Lystra and Iconium. Paul wanted Timothy to accompany him; and he took him and had him circumcised because of the Jews who were in those places, for they all knew that his father was a Greek. As they went from town to town, they delivered to them for observance the decisions that had been reached by the apostles and elders who were in Jerusalem. So the churches were strengthened in the faith and increased in numbers daily.

Lystra and Derbe, where Paul found colleagues for the work of the gospel

Paul and Barnabas may never have intended to visit these remote and primitive places, but simply used them to escape from Iconium. The danger in Lystra came from misguided popularity; the crowd may have known of the legend, recorded in Ovid's *Metamorphoses*, of Philemon and Baucis, an elderly couple from that area who give hospitality to Zeus and Hermes, while the rest of the population is punished for ignoring them. Paul's reply shows how he adapted the gospel when speaking to entirely pagan audiences. The crowd in Lystra was easily swung from worship to stoning. Yet from these two backward places came two of Paul's companions on the remainder of his journeys. Gaius from Derbe is only mentioned in Acts 20:4, but Timothy from Lystra is described as one of Paul's closest colleagues in nineteen places not including the two personal letters known as First and Second Timothy. These tell us that he was the leader of the church in Ephesus. Paul must have had the gift of recognizing the potential for leadership in a young man from a remote village, more Greek than Jewish and ill-instructed in the Jewish law. It is often the unlikely candidates who play the most important part in God's plans.

Opening Times

Karaman Archaeological Museum Turgut Özal Caddesi, Tel. 0338 213 1536, daily 08.00–12.00 and 13.30–18.30. Toilets downstairs

CAPPADOCIA (TURKEY)

Although Cappadocia was not on St Paul's recorded itinerary, many pilgrims visit the Christian sites and the intriguing landscape there on their way to or from the Galatian towns.

Cappadocia today

Cappadocia is full of fantastic scenery; houses and churches hollowed out of the volcanic ash, and underground cities which may have been used for hiding from persecution. Basil the Great, Bishop of Caesarea-Mazaka (Kayseri) in Cappadocia, his brother Gregory of Nyssa, and Gregory of Nazianzen, who was brought up in Güzelyurt and at university with Basil in Athens, are important for their part in the controversies about the incarnation, for their teaching on prayer (see my book *2000 Years of Prayer*), and the development of monasteries.

On route D–300 between Konya and Cappadocia modern travellers may stop for refreshment at the **Sultanhan Caravanserai** (essential walled protection for caravans travelling though the Ottoman empire), 110 kilometres (68 miles) from Konya, and

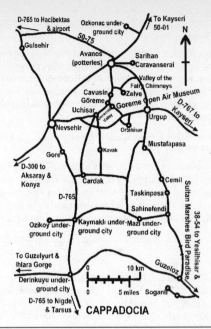

CAPPADOCIA

Icons

The earlier cave churches have simple drawings of Christian symbols, or pictures of Jesus and the saints, on the walls. 'Icon' is the Greek word for picture, but for Christians in the Eastern Church they were always more than just visual aids to remind them of the Christians of earlier ages; the icons are sacraments which convey a sense that the 'great cloud of witnesses' is really present with us every time we worship God; they are windows into eternity. Orthodox Christians will claim that they honour the icons but do not worship them; however between about AD 725 and 842 the emperors ordered the destruction of all icons because they were a hindrance to relations with Muslims, who saw them as idolatrous; and some of the paintings in the cave churches had the faces chiselled out during the 'Iconoclastic Controversy'. When they were permitted again on the first Sunday in Lent in AD 843, amid much rejoicing, that Sunday was named the Feast of Orthodoxy. The painting of icons is always accompanied by strict discipline and prayer.

> ### People from Cappadocia are present on the day of Pentecost (Acts 2:9–11)
>
> 'Parthians, Medes, Elamites, and residents of Mesopotamia, Judea and Cappadocia, Pontus and Asia, Phrygia and Pamphylia, Egypt and the parts of Libya belonging to Cyrene, and visitors from Rome, both Jews and proselytes, Cretans and Arabs – in our own languages we hear them speaking about God's deeds of power.'
>
> ### St Peter includes Cappadocians among those to whom he is writing (1 Peter 1:1–2)
>
> Peter, an apostle of Jesus Christ. To the exiles of the Dispersion in Pontus, Galatia, Cappadocia, Asia, and Bithynia, who have been chosen and destined by God the Father and sanctified by the Spirit to be obedient to Jesus Christ and to be sprinkled with his blood: May grace and peace be yours in abundance.

Aksaray, 42 kilometres (26 miles) further on. In Cappadocia they will probably visit **Üçhisar castle** or **Ortahisar** for the views; **Dove Cote Valley** (Zelve) for the 'Fairy chimneys' (formed when a hard rock protects a column of soft volcanic ash or 'tufa' from the rain which weathers away the surrounding area); **Derinkuyu, Kaymaklı, Özlüce** or **Özkonak** for the underground cities; **Avanos** for the underground potteries; **Göreme, Zelve, Çavuşin, Mustafapaşa, Güzelyurt,** the **Ihlara Gorge,** or the **Soğanli valley** for cave churches. No flash photography is permitted in the cave churches.

Tuzköy airport is 12 kilometres (7 miles) north-west of Gülşehir

Opening Times
Avanos potteries Sirga E.C. San Mer Tel. 0384 511 3686, daily 08.30–19.30. Toilets inside.
Chez Mumtaz Tel. 0384 384 2646, daily 08.00–16.00 in winter; 08.00–18.00 in summer. Toilets inside
Çavuşin church Tel. 0384 532 7168, daily 08.00–18.30. Toilets in the village
Derinkuyu Underground City Tel. 0384 381 3194 and 3184, daily 08.00–18.30. Toilets by the ticket kiosk
Göreme open air museum Tel. 0384 271 2167, daily 08.30–17.30. Toilets on the right as you enter the courtyard, also in the coach park
Güzelyurt Büyük Kilese Camii (Church of St Gregory, now a mosque) always open, no photographs during Friday prayers
Kaymaklı underground city

Tel. 0384 218 2500, daily
08.30–18.00. Toilets opposite
the ticket kiosk
Malı underground city Tel.
0384 365 5083 and 5348, daily
08.00–18.30. Toilets in the
coffee house opposite
Ortahisar fortress Tel. 0384
343 3441, daily 08.00–20.00.
Toilets underneath the curiosity
shop
Özkonac underground City
Tel. 0384 513 5168, daily
08.00–18.00. Portaloos by the
entrance
Özluce underground city Offer
a tip to the guardian
Soğinda Valley churches Tel.
0384 651 6495, daily
08.30–17.30. Telephone and
toilets in the Kappadokya
restaurant near the ticket kiosk
Sultanhanı 07.00–19.00 daily in
summer only. Toilets at the
Sultan restaurant and Kafetyria
opposite
Surıhan Caravanserai Tel. 0384
511 5795 Fax 3199, daily
08.00–17.00. Restaurant, dance
displays and whirling dervishes
when advertised 21.00–21.45.
Toilets inside on the left
Üçhisar Kalesine Tel. 0384 219
2618, daily 08.00–19.30. Toilets
in the hillside, turn sharp right
as you come out
Zelve open air museum Tel.
0384 411 2525, daily
08.00–18.30. Toilets on the left
as you go out of the gate

Jews and Gentiles

After leaving Derbe, Paul and
Barnabas returned through
Lystra, Iconium and Antioch-
of-Pysidia, preached in Perga,
and sailed from Attalia to
Antioch-on-the-Orontes (Acts
14:21–28). There, some Jewish
Christians came from Judea and
insisted that the gentile
Christians could not be saved
unless they were circumcised.
According to Acts, Paul and
Barnabas were sent to
Jerusalem, where a meeting was
held to discuss the problem.

Circumcision

The Jewish nation was formed
by the covenant which God
made with Abraham, the sign of
which was that all male children
were circumcised (Genesis 17).
The story of Stephen shows the
admission of Greek-speaking
Jews to the church on terms of
equality with the original
Aramaic speakers. The
Samaritans were only half-
Jewish; the Ethiopian and
Cornelius were God-fearers
who were already informed
about the Jewish religion. But in
Antioch-on-the-Orontes for the
first time, and later in the
Galatian towns, the Christians
set out to convert Gentiles,
non-Jews who had no prior
knowledge of Judaism. Many
Jews hated and despised the
Gentiles, a feeling which was
often reciprocated. But Jews
had been prepared to admit
Gentiles to the covenant
community provided that the
men were circumcised and
agreed to keep the whole of the
Jewish moral and ritual law. A
fierce debate broke out in the
Christian church as to whether
this was to be required of
Gentile converts to
Christianity.

According to Acts, the leaders were able to persuade the rest of the Jerusalem Christian community to send a letter, claiming that their decision was the opinion of God the Holy Spirit, and acknowledging that observance of Jewish law was not necessary for Christians of gentile origin, because they were not descendants of Abraham and Moses with whom God had made the covenants enshrined in the Jewish legal system. They did however make a few demands; the text is confused, but these appear to be a reinterpretation of the covenant which God made in Genesis 9 with Noah, from whom they believed the Gentiles were all descended.

The letter, which was to be carried to Antioch by leading Jewish Christians, Paul, Barnabas, Judas Barsabbas, and Silas, is a crucial corrective to moralists, then as now, who claim that nobody can be a Christian unless they adhere strictly to patterns of behaviour derived from the Old Testament.

THE NORTH GALATIAN TOWNS

Celtic-speaking Gallic tribes from Gaul gave their name to Galatia, when in the third century BC they settled on the high plateau in the centre of the country. But by the time of St Paul, the Roman province of Galatia covered much of what we know as central Anatolia.

The many different peoples spoke their own languages and worshipped their own gods. Some interpreters consider that where the Gauls settled around **Gordion**, 106 kilometres (66 miles) west of the modern capital of Ankara, was the area to which Paul's Letter to the Galatians was addressed (this is known as the North Galatian theory). **Ankara** was formerly known as Ancyra, or as Angora, the name which was given to the wool from the goats which were bred there. The remains of Gordion, originally the capital of Phrygia and named after its founder, the father of King Midas, are found at the village of Yassıhöyük between Eskişehir and Ankara. Here he set the challenge that whoever could unravel the Gordion knot would win the right to rule Asia, but Alexander the Great cut through it with his sword instead. All the rulers of Gordion were named Gordio or Midas.

Legend says that King Midas was rude about the singing of Apollo, who therefore gave him ears like a donkey. Midas hid them under his hat, but his barber found out and spoke the secret into a hole in the ground. The barley which grew there has whispered ever since: 'King Midas has ass's ears'. (See below under Sardis for the 'Midas touch'.)

A large tumulus at Gordion is called the **Grave of Midas**, and the tomb chamber beneath it,

1. St Paul's Well, Tarsus

2. The harbour, Antalya

3 The Charonion, Antakya

4 White van man: the author's camper van at the site of Derbe

5 'Fairy chimneys', Cappadocia

6 The Sanctuary of the Great Gods, Samothrace

7 Basilica, Philippi

8 Via Egnatia, Kavala

9 Hilltop monastery, Meteora

10 The Tower of the Winds, Athens

11 The Acropolis, Athens

12 Mosaic, Corinth

13 Temple ruins, Corinth

14 Gate to the commercial agora, Ephesus

A letter from the church in Jerusalem to the church in Antioch (Acts 15:22–35)

Then the apostles and the elders, with the consent of the whole church, decided to choose men from among their members and to send them to Antioch with Paul and Barnabas. They sent Judas called Barsabbas, and Silas, leaders among the brothers, with the following letter: 'The brothers, both the apostles and the elders, to the believers of Gentile origin in Antioch and Syria and Cilicia, greetings. Since we have heard that certain persons who have gone out from us, though with no instructions from us, have said things to disturb you and have unsettled your minds, we have decided unanimously to choose representatives and send them to you, along with our beloved Barnabas and Paul, who have risked their lives for the sake of our Lord Jesus Christ. We have therefore sent Judas and Silas, who themselves will tell you the same things by word of mouth. For it has seemed good to the Holy Spirit and to us to impose on you no further burden than these essentials: that you abstain from what has been sacrificed to idols and from blood and from what is strangled and from fornication. If you keep yourselves from these, you will do well. Farewell.'

So they were sent off and went down to Antioch. When they gathered the congregation together, they delivered the letter. When its members read it, they rejoiced at the exhortation. Judas and Silas, who were themselves prophets, said much to encourage and strengthen the believers. After they had been there for some time, they were sent off in peace by the believers to those who had sent them. But Paul and Barnabas remained in Antioch, and there, with many others, they taught and proclaimed the word of the Lord.

dating from around 750 BC, could be the oldest surviving wooden structure in the world. There is also a Galatian tomb in the museum. These parts are close to Phrygia, which is linked to Galatia in Acts 16 and 18. But the Roman province of Galatia included Antioch-of-Pisidia, Iconium, Lystra and Derbe, which Paul visited on his first missionary journey, and many people think it was to these churches that he wrote his Letter to the Galatians.

Opening Times
Midas Tümülüsü and Gordion museum Tel. 0312 638 2188, daily 08.30–17.30. Toilets near the museum entrance and in the car park café

PAUL'S LETTER TO THE GALATIANS

St Paul made converts in the Galatian towns of Antioch-of-Pisidia, Iconium, Lystra, Derbe, and maybe others in North Galatia of whom we are unaware. When he left he was satisfied that he had made it possible for non-Jews to respond to the good news of God's forgiveness in Christ, without having to earn forgiveness by obedience to a code of law. But he was horrified soon after he returned to Antioch-on-the-Orontes to discover that Jewish Christians had followed him to Galatia and told his new gentile converts that in order to be acceptable as Christians they must be circumcised. Circumcision was a sign that they had become part of the people with whom God had made a covenant, and were therefore obliged to keep the whole of the Jewish law. If they had succeeded, Gentile converts would not be admitted to eat with Jewish Christians at the shared meal or agape (pronounced a-gaa-pay) until they had been instructed in Judaism and changed their whole lifestyle. That would have resulted either in two churches who did not share table fellowship, or more likely the death of gentile Christianity and the reduction of the church to a small Jewish sect with an uncertain future. In a fury Paul shot off a letter blazing with passion, as he pleads with the Galatians not to reject the freedom which he had given them, to follow Christ in their own way.

When was it written?

The message of Paul's letter to the Galatians is clear, but it is not easy to decide whether it was written before or after the letter from the church in Jerusalem. According to Acts, the letter from the church in Jerusalem was written on Paul's third visit to Jerusalem after his conversion (Acts 9:26, 11:30, 15:2). But in Galatians, Paul only mentions two visits. That in Galatians 1:18–21 corresponds to Acts 9:26–30. But is Galatians 2:1–10 referring to his visit when he came with famine relief in Acts 11, in which case Paul's letter to the Galatians was written before the letter from the church in Jerusalem? Or do they describe the events when the letter from the Jerusalem church was written, corresponding to Acts 15? Why does Paul not mention the Council of Jerusalem, which decided that gentile Christians did not need to be circumcised? Alternatively the spur which caused Paul to write Galatians may have been his argument with Peter in Antioch (Galatians 2:11–14), which was about whether Jewish Christians could share table fellowship with uncircumcised gentile Christians.

A Summary of the Letter

St Paul's letter to the Galatians begins with a brief introduction (Galatians 1:1–5). Why turn to another gospel? (1:6–10). My gospel is not of human origin.

Phrygia and Galatia linked in the Acts of the Apostles

Acts 16:6–7: They went through the region of Phrygia and Galatia, having been forbidden by the Holy Spirit to speak the word in Asia. When they had come opposite Mysia, they attempted to go into Bithynia, but the Spirit of Jesus did not allow them.

Acts 18:23: After spending some time there he departed and went from place to place through the region of Galatia and Phrygia, strengthening all the disciples.

Paul's relationship with the Jerusalem leaders (1:11—2:14). I have taught justification by faith, not by works of the law (2:15–21). Does the Spirit come by means of the law? (3:1–5). The faith of Abraham (3:6–9). The curse of the cross frees us from the curse on law-breakers, and extends Abraham's blessing to the Gentiles (3:10–14). The analogy with a will (3:15–18). The analogy with a schoolteacher (3:19–29). The freedom of sons and slavery to spirits (4:1–11). Imitate my sincerity, not my opponents' insincerity (4:12–20). The analogy with Hagar and Sarah (4:21–31). The demand for circumcision hinders Christian freedom (5:1–12). But do not abuse your freedom: the works of the flesh and the fruit of the Spirit (5:13–26). Bearing one another's burdens (6:1–6). Sowing what you reap (6:7–10). Personal postscript (6:11–18).

Paul's Second Missionary Journey

After the decision of the church in Jerusalem, from about AD 49 to 50 Paul made his second missionary journey, travelling to Syria (Antioch-on-the-Orontes), Cilicia (Tarsus) and Galatia (Derbe, Lystra, Iconium, and Antioch-of-Pisidia) accompanied by Silas, to tell them of the decision of the Council (Acts 15–16). In Latin the whole of modern Turkey is referred to as Asia Minor, but the Roman province of Asia was the populated area around Ephesus. Paul wanted to go there, and to the province of Bythinia on the Black Sea coast, but the Holy Spirit prevented him. As a result of a vision at Troas, they decided to take the gospel into Europe.

TROAS (TURKEY)

The area around the ancient city of Troy was called the Troad. Many tourists visit the site of Troy, which was already lost underground in St Paul's day; but fewer seek out the nearby ruins of

Alexandria Troas where Paul had his vision. There are impressive remains further south at Assos which are well worth a detour. The ancient city of Troy was also known as Ilium, and the story of the Trojan wars is told in Homer's

Paul's vision at Troas (Acts 16:6–11)

They went through the region of Phrygia and Galatia, having been forbidden by the Holy Spirit to speak the word in Asia. When they had come opposite Mysia, they attempted to go into Bithynia, but the Spirit of Jesus did not allow them; so, passing by Mysia, they went down to Troas. During the night Paul had a vision: there stood a man of Macedonia pleading with him and saying, 'Come over to Macedonia and help us.' When he had seen the vision, we immediately tried to cross over to Macedonia, being convinced that God had called us to proclaim the good news to them. We set sail from Troas and took a straight course to Samothrace.

Paul calls at Troas on his third missionary journey (2 Corinthians 2:12–13)

When I came to Troas to proclaim the good news of Christ, a door was opened for me in the Lord; but my mind could not rest because I did not find my brother Titus there. So I said farewell to them and went on to Macedonia.

Paul heals Eutychus in Troas (Acts 20:4–12)

[Paul] was accompanied by Sopater son of Pyrrhus from Beroea, by Aristarchus and Secundus from Thessalonica, by Gaius from Derbe, and by Timothy, as well as by Tychicus and Trophimus from Asia. They went ahead and were waiting for us in Troas; but we sailed from Philippi after the days of Unleavened Bread, and in five days we joined them in Troas, where we stayed for seven days. On the first day of the week, when we met to break bread, Paul was holding a discussion with them; since he intended to leave the next day, he continued speaking until midnight. There were many lamps in the room upstairs where we were meeting. A young man named Eutychus, who was sitting in the window, began to sink off into a deep sleep while Paul talked still longer. Overcome by sleep, he fell to the ground three floors below and was picked up dead. But Paul went down, and bending over him took him in his arms, and said, 'Do not be alarmed, for his life is in him.' Then Paul went upstairs, and after he had broken bread and eaten, he continued to converse with them until dawn; then he left. Meanwhile they had taken the boy away alive and were not a little comforted.

Paul, in prison, asks Timothy to bring him what he left at Troas (2 Timothy 4:13)

When you come, bring the cloak that I left with Carpus at Troas, also the books, and above all the parchments.

Iliad. *They lasted for around ten years beginning in about 1250 BC, and the principal opponents were Agamemnon of Mycenae and Priam of Troy. Helen, the sister-in-law of Agamemnon, was abducted by Paris, the son of Priam. Odysseus (Ulysses) and Achilles were among the Greek warriors, Hector one of the Trojans, and Troy was only captured by the ruse of the Trojan horse.*

The prosperity of Troy came from ships sheltering in the harbour while waiting for a favourable wind to sail through the Dardanelles. When the harbour of ancient Troy silted up, Alexandria Troas was the port which was developed on the coast nearby in the third century BC and named after Alexander the Great. It was a city of between 30,000 and 40,000 inhabitants with a massive wall 8 kilometres (5 miles) long around it.

In the past it was assumed that Troy, if it ever existed, was located at Troas, until the German archaeologist Heinrich Schliemann (1822–90), using controversial methods, discovered not only the walls of Troy, north-east of Troas, but a hoard of gold jewellery which has had a chequered subsequent history, and is at present distributed between eight locations in seven cities including Moscow and St Petersburg.

When Paul first arrived at the port of Troas, on his second missionary journey, he had a vision of a man from Macedonia calling him to 'come over and help us'. He also called there twice on his third journey; and may have been arrested there when he was sent to Rome for execution in about AD 64 (see 2 Timothy 4:13).

Getting around in the Troad

Starting from the First World War battlefields in the peninsula of **Gallipoli** (Gelibolu) you can cross the narrow straits of the **Dardanelles**, formerly known as the **Hellespont** and now the Çanakkale Boğazi, by a ferry to the town of **Çanakkale**. According to legend, Leander swam the Hellespont each night from Abydos (Çanakkale) to the Temple of Venus at Sestos (Kilitbahir), guided by a torch held by his beloved Hero, a priestess. When the torch blew out Leander drowned and Hero threw herself from her tower in despair. In 1807 Lord Byron was the first in modern times to show that swimming the Hellespont is possible.

Travelling south from Çanakkale on the D–550 (E87) for about 30 kilometres (18 miles) you reach the a signpost to Troia; there the remains of ancient **Troy** (Truva) are found 5 kilometres (3 miles) west of the main road. In spite of splendid new signboards, the site is still somewhat confusing and best visited with a knowledgeable guide. It is thought that level VIIa is the city described by Homer, though this is not undisputed.

About 20 kilometres (13 miles) south of Troy on the D-550 (E87) is the town of Ezine, where you can turn west onto the minor road 17-53, which reaches the coast at the little port of Oduniskelesi or Odunluk Iskelesi. **Alexandria Troas** is scattered over a large area a little way to the south of this, near the village of Dalyan, about 25 kilometres (16 miles) from Ezine and 33 kilometres (21 miles) south of ancient Troy.

From here the 17-52 coast road runs south for about 70 kilometres (44 miles) to **Assos** (Behramkale); then returning east along the 17-52 to the D-550 (E87), it is 63 kilometres (40 miles) east to **Adramyttium** (Edremit).

Pilgrims are likely to visit the Troad on a journey to or from **İstanbul** (Constantinople), which was the small city-state of Byzantium in biblical times. A treasure-house of Muslim architecture, it is also full of memorable Christian remains from the Byzantine empire, and lies across the Bosphorus from **Chalcedon** (Kadıköy) where the definitions of the person of Christ were hammered out. On such a journey Christians will also want to look out for the town of İznik, north-east of Bursa, and famous for its coloured tiles. İznik was formerly known as **Nicea**, and it was the capital of the province of Bythinia. In AD 325 Emperor Constantine, having adopted Christianity as the state religion in the hope that it would unify the empire, called all the bishops to a conference there to produce an agreed statement of what Christians believe: the result was the Nicene Creed. The **Aya Sofya church** in İznik was rebuilt in the sixteenth century, but probably stands on the site where the Council of Nicea was held.

Opening Times
Ancient Troy Tel. 0286 283 0536, daily 08.00–19.00. Toilets off the car park
İstanbul archaeology museum between Gülhane Parkı and Topkapı Sarayı Tel. 0212 520 7740, Tuesday to Sunday 09.00–16.30. Toilets at the end of the courtyard
Aya Sofya church, İznik Tuesday to Sunday 09.00–12.00 and 14.00–17.00, ask for the key at the archaeology museum if it is locked

Alexandria Troas today

The **harbour** of ancient Troas is now a lagoon, but fishing boats still moor at the pier at Oduniskelesi. Very little remains of the ancient city, but the **baths of Herodes Atticus** from the second century AD have handsome arches. It is moving to stand on the beach looking towards Europe and picture Paul's Macedonian vision, the inspiration for so many missionary ventures.

Into Europe

Paul now had a strategy for converting the provinces of the Roman empire, beginning in the area we now call Turkey, where he was born. Like most man-made strategies it went wrong at the very beginning. The next two provinces on his list were 'Asia' and 'Bithynia', and 'the Holy Spirit' or 'the Spirit of Jesus' prevented him. Maybe he heard the Spirit speaking to him while he was at prayer; maybe there was more Jewish opposition; maybe he fell ill again, which is why he needed a physician. Or maybe he could not obtain the necessary papers to travel and recognized that God was at work even in the things he found most frustrating. Some Christians have called this 'negative guidance', when God makes us do the things he wants us to by preventing us from doing something else.

The apostle was staying at the port of Troas when he dreamt that he heard a man from Macedonia calling him to 'come over and help us'. St Luke immediately writes in Acts, 'We sailed to Neapolis and went inland to Philippi'. It is the first of the 'we' passages, in which Luke mentions himself. Luke seems inordinately proud of the town of Philippi in Macedonia; perhaps because he was left behind there on his own to build up the new church (there are no more passages in the first person until Acts 20:5), or

maybe he was himself a Macedonian. Perhaps Paul's dream was about Luke himself, whom he had just met and employed as his personal physician and secretary. Or some have suggested he had a vision of Alexander the Great, whose aim was to unite East and West. Paul decided that, now that he had laid foundations for the kingdom of God in the eastern Roman empire, God was telling him that it was time to begin work in the European part of the empire, though he would not have known it by that name.

ASSOS (TURKEY)

The village known as Behramkale is on the site of ancient Assos, which has been inhabited ever since the third millennium BC. The village is 2 kilometres (1½ miles) from the shore, where the tiny harbour was used for exporting acorns used in dyeing until the 1950s and was reborn as a tourist resort in the 1980s; it is used today by fishing boats. Although it was not until Paul's third missionary journey that Assos is mentioned, it is convenient to describe it here because it is in the Troad and can be visited at the same time as Alexandria Troas. Travelling from Ephesus on his third journey, Paul went to Troas; made a circuit of Macedonia organizing the collection for the poor Christians in Jerusalem; then he travelled into Achaia; through Philippi again, then by sea to Troas. After healing the boy who fell from a

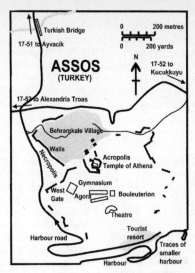

window in Troas, Paul asked his friends to go ahead by sea while he walked to Assos.

The history of Assos

By the sixth century BC, when a large Temple to Athena was built on its acropolis, Assos had become the most important city in the region. It declined under Persian occupation, but its golden age was in the fourth century when the philosopher Aristotle, disappointed not to succeed Plato as head of the Academy, was invited to Assos by the ruler Hermeias, a former pupil of Plato's, and married his niece. Aristotle taught there for three years, and when Hermeias was crucified by the Persians, Aristotle composed a poem in his memory. Cleanthes the Stoic, from whose 'Hymn to Zeus' Paul may have quoted on

Mars Hill the words 'for we are all his offspring' (Acts 17:28), was born in Assos in about 330 BC. In 133 the Romans took possession of Assos and left many inscriptions.

Getting to Assos

The village of Behramkale lies on a crossroads. A secondary road, the 17-52, comes from Kücükkuyu on the D-550 (E87) to the east and leads 60 kilometres (37 miles) to Alexandria Troas to the north-west. Another, the 17-51, comes from Ayvacık, 18 kilometres (11 miles) to the north, past an attractive Turkish bridge, and forms a steep and narrow road to the harbour; before taking a vehicle down this road think of the problems of turning it round and bringing it back up. Behramkale is about 30

97

Paul walks to Assos (Acts 20:13–15)

We went ahead to the ship and set sail for Assos, intending to take Paul on board there; for he had made this arrangement, intending to go by land himself. When he met us in Assos, we took him on board and went to Mitylene. We sailed from there, and on the following day we arrived opposite Chios. The next day we touched at Samos, and the day after that we came to Miletus.

---

kilometres (19 miles) east of Cape Baba (Baba Burnu), the most westerly point in Asia Minor.

Assos today

Just south of the crossroads a turning to the east leads into the **old village** of Behramkale. Walking up through the alleys leads towards the **fourteenth-century mosque**, next to which is the ticket booth for the acropolis. At the top of this are the Doric pillars of the **Temple of Athena** dating from 530 BC. There is a spectacular view across the strait to the island of Lesbos (Mitylene).

A few hundred metres (yards) further south down the road to the harbour is the lower ticket booth, which is usually unoccupied. From here you walk past an extensive **necropolis** with different types of tombs and **sarcophagi**. There are also sarcophagi elsewhere on the site; the word means 'flesh eaters' and they were made of caustic stone, said to be able to consume the flesh from a dead body in as little as forty days. This leads to the

towering remains of the **west gate**, rising to over 15 metres (50 feet) high, which is one of the largest remaining Greek fortifications in the world. Walking through the gate you pass the foundations of a **gymnasium** before coming to the **agora**, at the end of which is the **bouleuterion**, all of which are fragmentary and date from the hellenistic period.

Around 800 metres (half a mile) down the road to the harbour you can see the **theatre** from the Roman period, which is being reconstructed. There are traces of **two harbours**, from either of which Paul could have embarked.

Most impressive to the Christian pilgrim is that long stretches of the **Roman road** from Troas to Assos are clearly visible, looking not much different from when St Paul strode along it 2,000 years ago. The most accessible sections are on the right of the road towards Alexandria Troas, 6 kilometres (just under 4 miles) and 12 kilometres (7½ miles) from Assos crossroads.

The loneliness of the long-distance apostle

Assos is some 48 kilometres (30 miles) from Troas by sea, and against the prevailing wind it would have taken as long to travel in a boat as by land. Paul may have been lent a mule to ride on, but if he decided to walk a distance of some 35 kilometres (22 miles) alone, it was quite an achievement for a man whose health must already be suffering from the many beatings he had received. Was this because he wanted to spend a little longer comforting the family of the boy who fell from the window in Troas, or just because he wanted to be alone and think? He had achieved so much already; what was to be his next step?

Opening Times
Assos ruins daily 08.30–19.00. Toilets in the village 100 metres (yards) down from the ticket booth. Further information on http://www.assos.de

Adramyttium

There is no record in the Acts of the Apostles of St Paul visiting Adramyttium, but on his journey to Rome he embarked at Caesarea on a ship which came from there (Acts 27:2). It was a port in Mysia, south of Troas and east of Assos. It was founded in the fourth century BC near Mount Ida (Kaz Daği), and is mentioned in Homer's *Iliad*. Its modern name is Edremit and it lies on the D-550 (E87) about 140 kilometres (87 miles) south-east of Çanakkale.

PHILIPPI (GREECE)

Visitors to Greece can visit the extensive ruins at Philippi, but nobody lives there now. Kavala, on the other hand, which Paul knew as Neapolis, the port for Philippi, is an attractive and busy city today. The first church which Paul founded in Greece was in the Roman colony of Philippi. His letter to the Philippians shows how proud he was of this new congregation. Paul sailed from Troas, probably stopping for a night in Samothrace and landing at Neapolis, on the coast of the province of Macedonia.

Paul's Prison, Philippi

Samothrace Σαμοθράκη

Samothrace (Samothraki) is a Greek island midway between the mouth of the Dardanelles and the Greek town of Alexandroupolis; it is accessible by ferry from Alexandroupolis or Kavala (see above under National Tourist Offices: Greece, for websites with information on Greek island ferries). Six kilometres (4 miles) north-east of the port of Kamariotissa is the village of Paleopolis; buses run there in the summer. Nearby is the site of the Sanctuary of the Great Gods (Το Ιερό των Μεγάλων Θεών). As it is less visited than most sites, and lies beside a stream between the mountains and the sea, at times it can be so still that the imagination takes wing. Paul will not have been admitted, it was only for those who had been initiated into the secrets and given spiritual rebirth. This may have been one influence on Christian language about baptism. In the museum is a plaster cast of the great statue of Victory found there; the original is in the Louvre in Paris.

Opening Times
The Louvre, Paris Tel. 01 40 20 53 17, Thursday to Sunday 09.00–18.00, Mondays and Wednesdays 09.00–21.45
Sanctuary of the Great Gods, Samothraki Tel. 0551 41474, daily 08.30–20.30; museum daily 08.30–15.00. Toilets by the path between the museum and the site

Neapolis Καβάλα

Neapolis is now called Kavala, (sometimes spelt Kavalla) a corruption of the Latin word meaning a horse, because in Roman and Ottoman times it was the starting point for the 'pony express' mail service along the Egnatian Way through Greece to Rome.

Beside the road coming into Kavala from Philippi and Drama, after the junction with the old road to Thessaloniki as you climb the hill, just before reaching the top you can catch a glimpse of the old Via Egnatia on the right of the modern road; there is no convenient stopping place or access. There is an imposing **aqueduct** in Kavala which may be of Roman origin but was rebuilt in the sixteenth century AD. It crosses the road towards Xanthi, and in front of it is a signpost on the right pointing to the old town on a high promontory, reading 'Panagia and the castle'. Opposite this on the left is the **church of Saint Nicolas**, and a rocky outcrop, between two doors outside on the side nearest the harbour, is shown as the place where Paul first set foot in Europe, and a recently erected memorial shows him doing just that. Paul also sailed from 'Philippi', which means from Neapolis, at the end of his third missionary journey, as reported in Acts 20:6.

Getting to Kavala and Philippi

Kavala lies on the southern coast of the northern Greek province of Macedonia, facing the Aegean Sea; it is on the main national road 2 (E90), the coastal highway linking Thessaloniki to İstanbul, 163 kilometres (102 miles) east of Thessaloniki. Khristoupolis airport is 29 kilometres (18 miles) south-east of Kavala, and the railway station at Drama is 30 kilometres (22 miles) from Kavala on national road 12 to the north-west. There are buses from Kavala to Thessaloniki and İstanbul, and ferries to Thassos all year round, but only in summer to Samothrace. In summer there is also a weekly ferry from Kavala which stops among other places at Samos, Patmos, Cos and Rhodes.

The ancient site of the city called Philippoi (Φιλίπποι) in Greek, is 15 kilometres (9 miles) inland from Kavala on national road 2 from Kavala to Drama; there are frequent buses from Kavala to Drama, and you can ask to be put down after about 20 minutes at Philippoi.

Paul's arrival at Philippi on his second missionary journey (Acts 16:11–40)

We set sail from Troas and took a straight course to Samothrace, the following day to Neapolis, and from there to Philippi, which is a leading city of the district of Macedonia and a Roman colony. We remained in this city for some days. On the sabbath day we went outside the gate by the river, where we supposed there was a place of prayer; and we sat down and spoke to the women who had gathered there. A certain woman named Lydia, a worshipper of God, was listening to us; she was from the city of Thyatira and a dealer in purple cloth. The Lord opened her heart to listen eagerly to what was said by Paul. When she and her household were baptized, she urged us, saying, 'If you have judged me to be faithful to the Lord, come and stay at my home.' And she prevailed upon us.

One day, as we were going to the place of prayer, we met a slave girl who had a spirit of divination and brought her owners a great deal of money by fortune-telling. While she followed Paul and us, she would cry out, 'These men are slaves of the Most High God, who proclaim to you a way of salvation.' She kept doing this for many days. But Paul, very much annoyed, turned and said to the spirit, 'I order you in the name of Jesus Christ to come out of her.' And it came out that very hour. But when her owners saw that their hope of making money was gone, they seized Paul and Silas and dragged them into the marketplace before the authorities. When they had brought them before the magistrates, they said, 'These men are disturbing our city; they are Jews and are advocating customs that are not lawful for us as Romans to adopt or observe.' The crowd joined in attacking them, and the magistrates had them stripped of their clothing and ordered them to be beaten with rods. After they had given them a severe flogging, they threw them into prison and ordered the jailer to keep them securely.

Following these instructions, he put them in the innermost cell and fastened their feet in the stocks. About midnight Paul and Silas were praying and singing hymns to God, and the prisoners were listening to them. Suddenly there was an earthquake, so violent that the foundations of the prison were shaken; and immediately all the doors were opened and everyone's chains were unfastened. When the jailer woke up and saw the prison doors wide open, he drew his sword and was about to kill himself, since he supposed that the prisoners had escaped. But Paul shouted in a loud voice, 'Do not harm yourself, for we are all here.' The jailer called for lights, and rushing in, he fell down trembling before Paul and Silas. Then he brought them outside and said, 'Sirs, what must I do to be saved?' They answered, 'Believe on the Lord Jesus, and you will be saved, you and your household.' They spoke the word of the Lord to him and to all who were in his house. At the same hour of the night he took them and washed their wounds; then he and his entire family were baptized without delay. He brought them up into the house and set food before them; and he and his entire household rejoiced that he had become a believer in God.

When morning came, the magistrates sent the police, saying, 'Let those men go.' And the jailer reported the message to Paul, saying, 'The magistrates sent word to let you go; therefore come out now and go in peace.' But Paul replied, 'They have beaten us in public, uncondemned, men who are Roman citizens, and have thrown us into prison; and now are they going to discharge us in secret? Certainly not! Let them come and take us out themselves.' The police reported these words to the magistrates, and they were afraid when they heard that they were Roman citizens; so they came and apologized to them. And they took them out and asked them to leave the city. After leaving the prison they went to Lydia's home; and when they had seen and encouraged the brothers and sisters there, they departed.

Paul also visited Philippi on his third missionary journey on his way to Achaia (Southern Greece – Acts 20:1) and on his way back (Acts 20:6).

The history of Philippi

A conical hill rising out of the Macedonian plain was fortified by King Philip II of Macedon, the father of Alexander the Great, in 356 BC, to protect the goldfields of Mount Pangeion; he named it after himself, and built the theatre which still

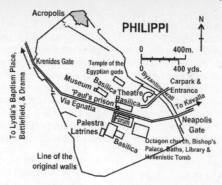

stands. 'Phil-hippos' means a horse-lover (a hippo-drome is for horse-racing; a hippo-potamus is a river-horse). The two main gates, where the Egnatian Way enters and leaves the town, are the Neapolis Gate (towards Kavala) and the Krenides Gate – 'krenides' means wells, and refers to the gold-mines towards which it leads. The Romans captured the city in 148 BC.

In 42 BC the battle of Philippi was fought on the plain west of the city, following the murder of Julius Caesar, between Octavian, later to become Emperor Augustus, with Mark Antony, against Brutus and Cassius, as described in Shakespeare's play *Julius Caesar*. Brutus and Cassius committed suicide, and Cassius was buried on Samothrace. When Octavian triumphed he settled retired Roman soldiers at Philippi and thus turned it into what was known as a 'colony'. They were given land, they dressed like Romans and

often spoke Latin. They were available to defend the city if necessary. They were proud of their Roman citizenship, so it is significant that it is to the Philippians that Paul writes 'our citizenship is in heaven' (Philippians 3:20). Discipline was kept by lictors, whose bundle of rods (Acts 16:22; the Latin term is 'fasces', from which we get the word 'fascist') with an axe in it, for corporal and capital punishment, appears on many monuments. After the Turkish conquest the city was abandoned.

Philippi today

Philippi, Athens and Corinth are the most impressive New Testament sites in Greece. The entrance to Philippi is from the car park, and leads to the **theatre**, founded by Philip II of Macedonia in 356 BC, but enlarged in the second century AD to become one of the largest in the ancient world. Passing a number of small shrines you come to the first of three

Christian Basilicas in Philippi, all of them destroyed by earthquakes. **Basilica A**, as it is called, dates from the fifth century AD. At the west end of this, almost under an earlier **Heroon**, is a cistern from Roman times which is called **Paul's Prison**. The Roman architect Vitruvius tells us that prisons were always near the forum, and the prevalence of earthquakes at Philippi confirms the likelihood of the description of Paul's release. When this cave was discovered in 1876 there were mural paintings of Paul and his companions in prison.

Crossing the modern road carefully, you find that beneath it are paving stones from the Roman **Via Egnatia**, rutted by the wheels of carts and chariots. You are now by the **tribunal**, marked by a series of steps, where Paul's trial would have been held. This is in the centre of the north side of the large (100 metres by 50 metres or about 110 yards by 55 yards) **Roman forum**, paved with marble slabs on which a number of board games have been scratched, which was surrounded by colonnades. On the west were a **temple** dedicated to Antoninus Pius, of whom a headless statue remains, and administrative buildings, including a set of standard measures cut into a stone. To the south a row of shops formed part of the **commercial agora**, there was a large **palestra** (exercise area), and **Basilica B** from the sixth century AD. Four large brick pillars of this still stand; they were meant to support a dome but that collapsed before it was finished; the narthex was rebuilt in the tenth century with the fine Corinthian pillars which still stand. South-west of this there is an elaborate **latrine**.

East of the forum was a **public library**, and then a complex of buildings around an **octagonal church** of the fifth century. It incorporated an earlier church dedicated, as a mosaic pavement shows, to St Paul by Bishop Porphirios in the fourth century, and beneath it has been found a hellenistic tomb. The **bishop's palace**, some **public baths** and **private houses** surround it.

Further west along the modern road is the entrance to the **museum**, next to the remains of the sixth-century AD **Basilica C**, and to the north of this was a **Temple to the Egyptian gods** Isis, Serapis and so on, and at the extreme north of the site the **acropolis** has traces of the walls built by Philip of Macedon.

The place of Lydia's baptism is an attractive riverside spot, with a grove of trees beside a small church, about a kilometre (half a mile) north of the town. Pilgrims can give thanks for their own baptism, renew their baptism promises here, using whatever words are customary in baptism services in the church from which they come, splash a little water on each other, and buy an icon of St Lydia.

Opening Times
The site of ancient Philippi Tel. 051-51 6470 and the **museum** Tel. 051-51 6251 are normally both open Tuesday to Sunday 08.30–15.00, but the museum is closed for restoration at the time of writing. The **octagon complex** can only be visited with an official guide, contact the booth where pedestrians cross the road. Toilets near the car park

The first church in Greece

Philippi was the starting point for the expansion of St Paul's mission into Europe. His team consisted of Silas the prophet from Antioch, Timothy the young man from Lystra, and Luke the physician. The Roman town had few Jewish inhabitants: when Paul arrived in Philippi there were not even ten Jewish men, the number necessary to form a synagogue.

Finding no synagogue in Philippi, Paul had to discover new ways of proclaiming the gospel and finding leaders for the church. Knowing that water was used in Jewish purification ceremonies before they prayed (John 2:6), Paul went out to the banks of the River Gangites, and found there a small group of Jews and God-fearers; among the latter was a woman called Lydia.

There is no mention of Lydia's husband, so she was probably a widow. She appears to have been the head of her household and of a large international trading company dealing in expensive and fashionable purple cloth, dyed with the purple murex shell from Tyre. Jesus told a story about a rich man dressed in 'purple and fine linen' (Luke 16:19), and he was himself wrapped in a soldier's purple cloak at the crucifixion (Mark 15:17 and parallel passages in the other Gospels). Emperor Nero tried unsuccessfully to restrict the highest quality purple cloth for imperial use only; it will have been in demand among the ex-soldiers of a Roman colony.

Lydia came from Thyatira, where there was a guild of purple-dyers, though it is possible that there instead of the murex they used the madder root. Lydia would have been a natural leader; the first Christians would have broken bread in her large house, and the church may have been organized in the same way as her business, with supervisors (*episkopoi*) and servants (*diakonoi*). So when Paul a few years later writes to the church of Philippi, with its bishops and deacons (Philippians 1:1), the first time the word *episkopoi* is used in the New Testament, one could speculate whether the first bishop in Europe was a woman.

In Philippi Paul was arrested

because he had exorcized a slave girl who was believed to be possessed by a Pythoness spirit. The god Apollo was supposed to be embodied in a snake at Delphi, and the slave girl was thought to be able to foretell the future when inspired by Apollo in a trance, like the priest of the oracle at Delphi. The exorcism robbed her owners of the fees they received from her fortune-telling, so they dragged Paul and Silas from the agora to the bema, the seat of the 'duoviri', the two senior officials in charge of a colony. Only those religions which had been shown to be no threat to the empire were licensed under Roman law; the Jewish faith was one, and those born as Jews were excused from making the sacrifices to the emperor as a god which were demanded from everybody else as a proof of loyalty.

The slave-girl's owners complained that what Paul and Silas were teaching was not a *religio licita* (see below under Smyrna), and they were put in prison. There they sang hymns, and the jailer was impressed by their Christian cheerfulness under adversity. They were released when the prison was damaged by an earthquake, and the jailer gave them their opportunity when he cried, 'What must I do to be saved?' They proclaimed the good news of God's love in Jesus, told him to repent and believe, and baptized him 'with his whole household' (including the children?).

Groups of pilgrims today may like to re-enact Paul's trial, imprisonment and release, beside the Egnatian Way along which he travelled. Paul and his companions were driven out of many cities by persecution, but the result was that they were able to found churches in many more cities than if they had remained a long time in one place. We see at Philippi new directions in his evangelism, including all social classes, women, and Gentiles, among those to whom he took the gospel.

PAUL'S LETTER TO THE PHILIPPIANS

Paul's letter to the church at Philippi was written while he was in prison (see 1:13 and 4:22) in either Ephesus, Corinth or most likely Rome, yet its keynote is joy.

A Summary of the Letter

Paul begins in 1:13 by expressing his love for the church he had founded. Although he would prefer to die, to be with Jesus, he recognizes he may have to stay alive to continue his work (1:21). He reassures them in their troubles of God's love (1:28) and exhorts them to unity (2:2). In 2:5 Paul quotes what appears to be an early Christian hymn, about Jesus 'emptying himself' of his glory to come to earth; could this have been the hymn that he and Silas sang in prison in Philippi (Acts 16:25)? He warns them to beware of Judaizers who say that gentile

Christians must be circumcised; yet the effort to live a moral life is compared to the runners in a stadium (3:12). The Philippians were proud to be a Roman colony, but he reminds them that they are a colony of heaven. He appeals to his friends to stop quarrelling (4:2); uses the conventional word for 'farewell', which was 'rejoice', but for once in its literal meaning (4:4), and tells them to concentrate their thoughts on good things (4:8). Finally he thanks the Philippians for the gift they had sent to him in prison.

AMPHIPOLIS AND APOLLONIA (GREECE)

St Paul passed along the Via Egnatia (roughly on the route of the modern National Road 2 [E90]) from Philippi to Thessalonica through Amphipolis and Apollonia.

Amphipolis Αμφίπολις

Amphipolis, 60 kilometres (37 miles) from Philippi was a gold-mining town colonized by the Athenians. It was captured by Philip of Macedon, and Amphipolis (not Philippi as Luke appears to suggest in Acts 16:12) was the capital of the first district of Macedonia under the Romans. A huge fourth-century BC **marble lion**, which Paul would have seen, stands where the modern road towards Amphipolis crosses the River Strymon. Archaeological discoveries there include **walls**, **houses** and a **gymnasium**.

Lion Statue, Amphipolis

Apollonia Απολλόνια

Small signs in the village of Apollonia (not Nea Apollonia which is some distance away) point to ΒΗΜΑ ΑΠ. ΠΑΥΛΟΥ (Apostle Paul's Pulpit). These lead northwards a short distance down a narrow road to a field on the edge of the village, described as **Apollonia archaeological site**, where a **tablet** on a large rock claims that this is where Paul preached. It is 48 kilometres (30 miles) from Amphipolis; a further 60 kilometres (37 miles) took Paul to Thessalonica.

Opening Times
Amphipolis archaeological museum Tuesday to Sunday 08.30–15.00. Toilets on the left of the entrance

> ### Paul arrives at Thessalonica on his second missionary journey (Acts 17:1–9)
>
> After Paul and Silas had passed through Amphipolis and Apollonia, they came to Thessalonica, where there was a synagogue of the Jews. And Paul went in, as was his custom, and on three sabbath days argued with them from the scriptures, explaining and proving that it was necessary for the Messiah to suffer and to rise from the dead, and saying, 'This is the Messiah, Jesus whom I am proclaiming to you.' Some of them were persuaded and joined Paul and Silas, as did a great many of the devout Greeks and not a few of the leading women. But the Jews became jealous, and with the help of some ruffians in the marketplaces they formed a mob and set the city in an uproar. While they were searching for Paul and Silas to bring them out to the assembly, they attacked Jason's house. When they could not find them, they dragged Jason and some believers before the city authorities, shouting, 'These people who have been turning the world upside down have come here also, and Jason has entertained them as guests. They are all acting contrary to the decrees of the emperor, saying that there is another king named Jesus.' The people and the city officials were disturbed when they heard this, and after they had taken bail from Jason and the others, they let them go.

THESSALONICA (GREECE)

Thessaloniki is the second city of modern Greece, and the capital of the prefecture of Macedonia. It is a bustling modern city, and a succession of earthquakes and fires have left it with few ancient buildings. It lies on the isthmus leading to the popular holiday resorts of Halkidiki. Thessalonica was founded in 315 BC by Cassander, one of Alexander the Great's generals, and named after his wife Thessalonike, who was a half-sister of Alexander. Thessalonike means 'Victory in Thessaly'.

After the Roman conquest in 168

BC they made Thessalonica the capital of the province of Macedonia, because of its strategic position on the Egnatian Way at the head of the largest gulf in the Aegean, originally called after the hot springs found there 'The Gulf of Thermae'. The proconsul of the province was based there, and it was ruled by five officials called 'politarchs', the word Luke correctly uses in Acts 17:6, but which was otherwise unknown until it was found on the Arch of Galerius.

Continuing his policy of founding churches in the capital cities of Roman provinces, Paul moved on to Thessalonica. He was only there a short while before he was

THESSALONIKI (not all streets are shown)

Kastra
Vlatadon Monastery
Osios David
Agia Ekaterini
Athinas
Dodeka Apostoli
Nicolaos Orfanos
Agios Dimitrios
Olympou
Filippou
Roman Agora
Agiou Dimitriou
Egnatia
Panagia Ahiropiitos
Rotonda
Arch of Galerius
Route 92 & Athens
Agia Sophia
Tsimiski
Palace of Galerius
Archeology Museum
Port
N
Nikis
White Tower
Towards Kavala
Ramparts
Byzantine Museum
Airport

0   200m.
0   200 yards

again driven out by rioting mobs, but he had time to establish a strong Christian church, to whom he wrote two of his earliest surviving letters.

Getting to Thessalonica
Θεσσαλονίκη

Thessalonica was known as Salonica during the Ottoman empire; now it is called Thessaloniki. Accommodation is hard to come by during the festival months of September and October. It lies at the junction of National Roads 1 (E75), 2 (E86), 2 (E90), 4 (E90) and 12 (E79). Trains arrive at the main station on Monastiriou (Tel. 51 7000) and buses at the terminals nearby. The airport (Tel. 42 5011) is 16 kilometres (10 miles) to the south-east. Ferries and hydrofoils sail from the harbour to many of the nearby islands.

Thessaloniki today

The **white tower** on the waterfront dates from 1536 but is probably on hellenistic foundations. From there it is a short walk to the fascinating collection at the **archaeological museum**, at the junction of Tsimiski and Angeliki streets, but the discoveries from the tomb of Philip II which were displayed there have now been moved to a new museum at Vergina where they were discovered.

The **Arch of Galerius** was erected a little before AD 305, probably on the site of an earlier arch, across the Egnatian Way, to commemorate the victories of Emperor Galerius, son-in-law of Diocletian. In the Plateia Navarinou three streets south of this are the ruins of the **Palace of Galerius**, and north of it the **Rotunda of St George** was probably intended by Galerius as his tomb, but he died elsewhere and it was turned into a church with fine Byzantine mosaics.

Nothing was visible of the

109

Thessalonica which Saint Paul knew until recent excavations of the **Roman forum**, in the square called Plateia Dikastirion; this is where the riot broke out because of Paul's teaching. In its present form the forum dates from the second century AD, and contains an odeon and a portico with shops underneath. North of here, the **Basilica of St Demetrios** commemorates an army officer who became a Christian during the reign of Emperor Galerius in the fourth century. He was speared to death in the public baths, the remains of which are now contained in the crypt of the church. The **Church of Osios David**, up a steep path on the north of the old town, is said to have been built by Galerius as a baths for his daughter Theodora, unaware that she was a Christian, and when he found she had turned it into a church he had her killed. An early mosaic there, with a beardless Christ, is said by some to have been installed on the instructions of Theodora herself.

Emperor Theodosius in the fourth century AD was converted to Christianity in Thessalonica, and made it the base for his war against the Goths. He built most of the **fortifications**, often on Roman and Greek foundations, that we see in Thessaloniki today. A visit to the **walled acropolis** gives an overview of the Byzantine city.

Opening Times
Archaeological museum Tel. 031 830538, Tuesday to Sunday and holidays 08.30–15.00; and Monday 10.30–17.00. Toilets on the right of the entrance and also by the entrance to the lower exhibition hall
Roman forum and **Palace of Galerius** expected to open in 2002
Basilica of Agios Dimitrios daily 07.30–12.00 and 17.00–20.30; crypt Tuesday to Saturday 08.00–20.00; Mondays 12.30–19.00
Rotunda of St George Tuesday to Sunday 08.30–15.00
Osios David at the discretion of the caretaker, who does not speak English and does not allow photography

Mount Athos Αγιον Ορος *(Holy Mountain)*

For at least a thousand years the peninsula of Mount Athos, one of the three which stretch to the south from near Thessaloniki, has been a centre of Greek Orthodox monasticism. No women are admitted, and men, who must be over 18, should apply well in advance. Ordained clergymen need a letter from their bishop which they take or send to the Ecumenical Patriarch of Constantinople (in Thessaloniki through the Metropolis, Vogatsikou 5, Tel. 031 227 677). Only ten foreigners are allowed to visit each day, so first you need to book a date at the Mount Athos Pilgrims' Office in Thessaloniki, by telephone or fax (Tel. 031

861 611; fax. 031 861 811). You will be required to mail them a photocopy of your passport, and if you are Orthodox of your baptism certificate, and then call to collect your booking confirmation at Leoforos Karamanli 14, Thessaloniki, just west of the archaeology museum, between 08.30–13.30 and 18.00–20.00 Monday, Tuesday, Thursday or Friday.

PAUL'S LETTERS TO THE THESSALONIANS

On his second missionary journey in about AD 50 Paul, with Silas and Timothy, had visited Thessalonica, and converted Jews, proselytes and influential women. Then he had left because of the rioting, but when he reached Athens he sent Timothy back to encourage the new Thessalonian Christians. Timothy rejoined Paul in Corinth, and reported that they had understood they would all live to see 'the day of the Lord' and were puzzled that some had died already. Although he wanted the new communities to develop their own leadership, Paul realized they needed continuing supervision, and wrote his first letter to the Thessalonians. Soon afterwards, hearing that the first letter had been misunderstood, and some had stopped work thinking the 'day of the Lord' had passed already, he wrote a second letter to the Thessalonians. These letters show Paul's early apocalyptic thinking (see the introduction to the book of Revelation below).

A Summary of the Letter

In his first letter, after greetings and thanksgiving (1 Thessalonians 1:1–10), Paul turns to self-defence (2:1–13). The Christians of Thessalonica had suffered persecution from their fellow-countrymen, just as Paul and Jesus had from theirs (2:14–16). Paul longed to see them again, but could not, so he sent Timothy from Athens to encourage them (2:17—3:5). Timothy has reported their faithfulness (3:6–13). So Paul urges them to live a life pleasing to God, to avoid fornication, and to love their fellow-Christians (4:1–12). Do not worry about Christians who have died; at the 'coming of the Lord' they and we will rise together to be with the Lord forever (4:13–18). We do not know when 'the day of the Lord' will come, so we must be ready at all times (5:1–11). Paul ends with exhortations and prayers: obey your leaders; do not be idle; discriminate between, but do not quench, spiritual gifts (5:12–28).

In his second letter also, Paul begins with greetings and thanksgiving (2 Thessalonians 1:1–4). When Jesus is revealed from heaven, God will reward the afflicted and punish those who afflict them with eternal destruction (1:5–12). The day of the Lord has not yet come; it is delayed until the 'man of lawlessness' is revealed. He is being held back by 'the restraining power'; when that is removed Jesus will destroy him (2:1–12). So stand firm (2:13–17). A request for prayer (3:1–5) and a rebuke to idlers (3:6–15) are followed by Paul's final greetings (3:16–18).

OTHER STOPPING PLACES IN GREECE

Pilgrims will probably visit Macedonia in the north of Greece before or after a visit to Athens in the south. If this journey is done by coach or car it may be less strenuous than the way the apostle travelled, by small boat, horse and cart, donkey, or on foot, but a number of stopping places will be called for, such as Veria, Meteora, Thermopylae and Marathon, or Nicopolis and Delphi if you have a powerful vehicle.

Berea (Greece) Βέροια

The modern town called Veria, or sometimes Beroia or Veroia, and pronouced VEER-ia, west of Thessaloniki, is the centre of a peach-growing and wine-making area. In the New Testament it is called Berea or Beroea, and there Paul had a short, but fruitful, ministry (Acts 17:10–15). There is nothing to see from biblical times in the town, apart from remains of walls and towers. The Jews of Berea had supported Alexander the Great in his campaigns, which may have resulted in better relations with the Gentiles there than elsewhere, and a more open atmosphere for Paul's preaching. Sopater was one of those whom Paul converted in Berea (Acts 20:4; Romans 16:21).

Visiting Veria today

Veria is 75 kilometres (46 miles) travelling from Thessaloniki on National Road 4, which runs parallel to a new motorway, part of the E90. Coming from the west on National Road 4 you have to cross a steep pass. At the uphill end of the town is a square called Plateia Raktiran, or more often Plateia Orologiou. A sign there points to 'St Paul's Altar', but you immediately take a right fork into ΟΔΟΣ ΜΑΥΡΟΜΙΚΑΛΗ. About 50 meters (yards) up on the left, past the school on the corner, two flights of steps lead to a terrace with fine modern **mosaics** of Paul's conversion and his vision in Troas. It contains three reconstructed steps of a Roman **bema** from which Paul is said to have preached; some say it is on the site of the ancient synagogue. Beside Odos Mitropoleos, which leads into the same square, are some **paving stones** from the old road, scored with wheel marks. There are said to be over seventy churches in the older part of the town, and some old Turkish houses at present undergoing restoration.

Meteora and Kalambaka Μετέωρα και Καλαμπάκα

A night may be spent at Kalambaka, on National Road 6 (E92) some 350 kilometres (194

Visiting Berea on the second missionary journey (Acts 17:10–14)

That very night the believers sent Paul and Silas off to Beroea; and when they arrived, they went to the Jewish synagogue. These Jews were more receptive than those in Thessalonica, for they welcomed the message very eagerly and examined the scriptures every day to see whether these things were so. Many of them therefore believed, including not a few Greek women and men of high standing. But when the Jews of Thessalonica learned that the word of God had been proclaimed by Paul in Beroea as well, they came there too, to stir up and incite the crowds. Then the believers immediately sent Paul away to the coast, but Silas and Timothy remained behind.

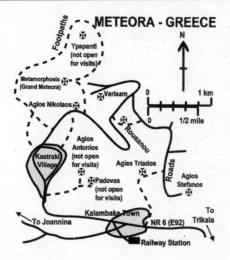

miles) north of Athens, and 188 kilometres (162 miles) from Veria, to visit the spectacular **mountain monasteries** of Meteora nearby. Women must wear skirts below the knee, men must have long trousers and arms must be covered to visit the monasteries. These amazing places stand each on a pinnacle of rock, like the bridge on a surreal ocean liner. They are approached now by steep flights of steps; in earlier days people and supplies had to be hauled up by rope. An inscription by one of these pulley systems can be translated as 'set your mind on things that are above' (Colossians 3:1). The bearded monks wear stove-pipe hats, the nuns are dressed entirely in black. (See 'Visiting Christians in other countries' under General Information above.)

Opening Times
The monasteries of Meteora are normally open 09.00–18.00, but closed for a long lunch break, so check with local guides

Nicopolis

A visit of Paul to Nicopolis is mentioned, in what even those who doubt the authenticity of the whole letter consider may well be a genuine fragment of Paul's writing, in Titus 3:12–15, presumably between his first and second imprisonments in Rome. Nicopolis is near the modern village of Nikopole (Νικόπολη) near the Amvrakikos Gulf on National Road 21 from Preveza to Arta in Epiros, northern Greece. The name means 'City of Victory', it was built by Octavian (soon to be named Emperor Augustus) in thanksgiving for his victory at Actium in 31 BC, to control western Greece. There are remnants of a **theatre**, **temples**, an **aqueduct**, **baths** and an **odeon** on the sprawling site, but the walls and most other remains are Byzantine and it is hardly worth the journey unless you are in the area. The road between Nicopolis and Athens passes the atmospheric site of the Oracle of **Delphi** (Δελφοί), 'the navel of the world', 178 kilometres (110 miles) north-west of Athens on the slopes of **Mount Parnassus** (Παρνασσός). The road between Nicopolis and Meteora crosses the steep and spectacular Katara Pass.

Opening Times
The site of Nicopolis and archaeology museum: Tel. 0682 41 336 Tuesday to Sunday 08.30–15.00
Ancient Delphi and the Sanctuary of Apollo in summer: Monday to Friday 07.30–19.15; Saturday and Sunday 08.30–14.45; in winter daily 08.30–14.45. Toilets on the right after the entrance to the site
Delphi museum Tel. 0265 82 312, in summer: Tuesday to Friday 07.30–19.15; Monday 12.00–18.15; Saturday, Sunday and Public Holidays 08.30–14.45; in winter daily 08.30–14.45. Toilets in front of the museum

Thermopylae and Marathon

The battle of Marathon against the Persians was won in 490 BC at a site 42 kilometres (26 miles) north-east of Athens on National Road 83. The running of a 'marathon' is based on the story that a messenger ran to Athens to carry the news of the victory. Some 200 kilometres (125 miles) north-west of Athens and just south of the town of Lamia beside National Road 1 (E75) there is a statue of Leonidas, the Greek general who died heroically at Thermopylae in 480 BC. Herodotus tells the story of the

The Parthenon, Athens

gallant battle that he fought and lost there.

ATHENS (GREECE)

The sight of the Acropolis is still today, as it was in Paul's day, one of the most unforgettable memories of a visit to Greece, as the graceful temples rise above the pollution and traffic of the modern city. The National Archaeological Museum contains one of the world's great collections of art and artefacts. According to legend, Athena daughter of Zeus defeated Poseidon at this place and gave her name to the city. Between 1'000 and 800 BC Theseus gathered a federation of states with Athens as the head. Between 700 and 500 BC, Athens was the home of Greek philosophy and of the earliest form of democracy, where every free man had a vote on every issue. The century 500–400 BC was the height of Athenian culture under Pericles and others; this was a time of great philosophers and great buildings. In around 400 BC Athens fought the Peloponnesian Wars against the Spartans. It was then ruled by the Macedonians and, from 27 BC to AD 350, by Rome, and more fine buildings were erected. Athens had no political power at this time but was known as a university city.

The Epicurean philosophers, followers of Epicurus (341–270 BC) taught that everything happens by chance, the gods are too remote to be interested in us, and death is the end of everything, so we should devote ourselves to seeking happiness – though this was to be an intellectual rather than a sensual happiness. The Stoics followed Zeno (336–264 BC) who taught that everything is a part of God, so everything happens because it is fated to; the cycle of history ends in flames and begins again; so we should bear our suffering bravely.

Paul in Athens

Paul arrived alone at Athens during the course of his second missionary journey, and immediately began debating with the philosophers for whom the city was famous. In his speech Paul quotes the words 'in whom we live and move' from the Cretan poet

Paul in debate with the philosophers (Acts 17:15–34)

Those who conducted Paul brought him as far as Athens; and after receiving instructions to have Silas and Timothy join him as soon as possible, they left him. While Paul was waiting for them in Athens, he was deeply distressed to see that the city was full of idols. So he argued in the synagogue with the Jews and the devout persons, and also in the marketplace every day with those who happened to be there. Also some Epicurean and Stoic philosophers debated with him. Some said, 'What does this babbler want to say?' Others said, 'He seems to be a proclaimer of foreign divinities.' (This was because he was telling the good news about Jesus and the resurrection.) So they took him and brought him to the Areopagus and asked him, 'May we know what this new teaching is that you are presenting? It sounds rather strange to us, so we would like to know what it means.' Now all the Athenians and the foreigners living there would spend their time in nothing but telling or hearing something new.

Then Paul stood in front of the Areopagus and said, 'Athenians, I see how extremely religious you are in every way. For as I went through the city and looked carefully at the objects of your worship, I found among them an altar with the inscription, "To an unknown god". What therefore you worship as unknown, this I proclaim to you. The God who made the world and everything in it, he who is Lord of heaven and earth, does not live in shrines made by human hands, nor is he served by human hands, as though he needed anything, since he himself gives to all mortals life and breath and all things. From one ancestor he made all nations to inhabit the whole earth, and he allotted the times of their existence and the boundaries of the places where they would live, so that they would search for God and perhaps grope for him and find him – though indeed he is not far from each one of us. For "In him we live and move and have our being"; as even some of your own poets have said, "For we too are his offspring". Since we are God's offspring, we ought not to think that the deity is like gold, or silver, or stone, an image formed by the art and imagination of mortals. While God has overlooked the times of human ignorance, now he commands all people everywhere to repent, because he has fixed a day on which he will have the world judged in righteousness by a man whom he has appointed, and of this he has given assurance to all by raising him from the dead.'

When they heard of the resurrection of the dead, some scoffed; but others said, 'We will hear you again about this.' At that point Paul left them. But some of them joined him and became believers, including Dionysius the Areopagite and a woman named Damaris, and others with them.

Epimenides (also quoted in Titus 1:12); 'we are his offspring' is from the Stoic poet Aratas of Cilicia, the district where Paul himself was born; another Stoic, Cleanthes, has a similar verse. Luke quotes Paul's speech knowing that it will appeal to Theophilus for whom he is writing (Acts 1:1).

Paul probably arrived by sea, landing at **Piraeus** (Pireas, Πιράιος), though there is a church associated with him at **Glyfada**. He will have walked the **Panathenaic Way** and crossed the **agora** or market place, where people met to discuss the issues or gossip of the day. He will have seen the temples on top of the **Acropolis** dominating the city. The **Areopagus**, which the King James Version of the Bible translates as Mars Hill, actually on the slopes of the Acropolis, was named after the god Ares who was supposed to have been tried here by the council of the gods for the murder of Halirrhothios, the son of Poseidon. From the seventh century BC the Council of the Areopagus, a court of thirty men, met in the Stoa Basileios at the foot of the hill to conduct murder trials, later they dealt with other crimes and religious disputes, so Paul was asked to explain, probably to the crowd swarming there rather than to the court, this new god and goddess, 'Jesus' and 'Resurrection', that he appeared to be preaching. There is a story that in an attempt to stop a plague in Athens in 600 BC, some sheep were released on the Areopagus. Each was then sacrificed to the god nearest to whose shrine it lay down. If there was no temple nearby, a new altar was erected on the spot 'To the Unknown God'. Paul used this as the starting point of his address to the court.

Getting to Athens

Ellinikon Airport is 9 kilometres (5½ miles) south-east of Athens; the West Terminal for Olympic Airways (Tel. 01 936 3363) is 1½ kilometres (1 mile) from the East Terminal which serves all other airlines (Tel. 01 969 9466/7). Trains for northern Greece and Europe leave from Larissis Station, Odos Deligianni; those for the Peloponnese go from the nearby Pelloponnisou Station, Peloponissou 3. Information and advance booking from OSE, Filellinon 17, Tel. 01 323 6747. National Road 1 (E75) leads north from the city, and National Road 8A (E94) travels west to the Peloponnese. Although St Paul endured many forms of suffering while travelling, the traffic jams of Athens are one that has been invented since his day.

Athens today

(numbers correspond to the plan of Central Athens)

Pilgrims will want to climb, from the entrance on the west side of the hill, to the top of the **Acropolis** (1). But first, turn

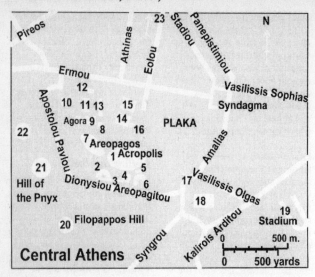

Central Athens

right off the steps up the hill to visit the south slope, containing the **theatre of Herod Atticus (2)** (second century AD), the **Stoa of Eumenes (3)** (second century BC), the **asklepion (4)** (fifth century BC), and the **Panagia Chrysospilliotissa (5)** (a grotto of 320 BC converted into a Christian chapel – Panagia ('All-holy') is the usual Greek word for the Virgin Mary) standing above the ancient **theatre of Dionysos (6)** (fourth century BC). Then return to the steps and climb the ancient staircase to the huge entrance portal called the **Propylaia** on top of the hill, then turning right you can see the little **Temple of Athena Nike**. Walk along the **Panathenaic Way** passing the pedestals on which great statues formerly stood, one of them a 9 metres (30 foot) high statue of Athena which was visible from far out at sea. This leads you to the **Parthenon**, the largest Doric temple in Greece, dedicated to the virgin (*parthenos*) goddess Athena. Continuing around the northern portico, the **Erechtheion** is on your left, with its southern portico supported by the statues of the six maidens known as the **Caryatids**. The originals are in the **Acropolis museum**, which is to the south–east of the Parthenon. The temples on the Acropolis were built by Pericles, who ruled from 461 to 429 BC.

Come down the staircase from the Propylaia again and turn right at the ticket office. The **Areopagus Hill (7)** (Areios Pagos) is a bare rocky slope on the west side of the Acropolis, with slippery steps to the summit. Pilgrims may sit in the shadow of some rocks on Mars Hill and read the speech which Paul made to the court of the Areopagus; in Paul's days the hill will have been covered in buildings including the one where the Court of the Areopagus met. His speech there is reproduced in full in Greek on a bronze tablet beside the steps to the top of the hill. Descend the path through a gate to the right of this.

At the foot of the hill is the **Ancient Agora (9)**, the market-place where Saint Paul debated daily. Just past the ticket office you find the **Church of the Holy Apostles (8)** which was built in the eleventh century AD to commemorate Saint Paul's teaching in the agora. Among the few remaining buildings in the Agora is the **Temple of Hephaestus (10)** (fifth century BC); the foundations of the **colonnade (Stoa) of Zeus Eleutherios (11)** where Socrates taught in the middle of the fourth century BC; and the **Stoa Poikile (12)** (painted colonnade) where, at the end of the same century, Zeno developed the philosophy of Stoicism; the philosophy took its name from the place where he taught. The restored **Stoa of Attalos (13)** (second century BC) houses a museum.

To the east of the Ancient Agora, and north of the Acropolis, is the **Roman agora (14)**, with the **Library of Hadrian (15)** which is not at present open to visitors. Beside it stands the octagonal **Tower of the Winds (16)**, so called from the sculptures of the eight winds on its walls; it was a hydraulic clock designed by Andronikos Kyrrhestes in the first century BC, which Paul will certainly have seen.

About 30 minutes' walk north of the centre, or quicker by trolleybus 5 or 15, the **National Archaeological Museum (23)** is at 1 Tossitsa Street where it turns off the street called 28 Oktovriou-Patission; it is signposted from the Omonia metro station. Its collection is one of the finest in the world.

To the east of the Acropolis, on Amalias, was the **Lyceum** where the peripatetic philosophers, followers of Aristotle, taught; followers of Plato taught while strolling through the **Groves of Academy**, which have been identified near the Church of Agios Tryphon on Odos Alexandrias to the north-west.

To the south-east of the Acropolis, the **Arch of Hadrian (17)** led to the city of Hadrian, though now the entrance is in Vasilissis Olgas. The area is dominated by the huge **Temple of Olympian**

St Paul and the philosophers

'What has Athens to do with Jerusalem?', asked Justin Martyr (c. AD 100–65), implying that philosophy and religion cannot mix. But Paul's speech at Athens, the centre of European culture, is a fascinating insight into how he took on this new challenge. Although Luke was not present, the speech is probably typical of Paul's approach to a Greek audience, which Luke must have heard him use in many places. The intriguing thing is that he starts where they are. From the altar he had seen on Mars Hill he took the idea that they worshipped 'the unknown God'. 'What you worship, without knowing him, is the God we are proclaiming,' said Paul. Not a new God, but the same one they had worshipped all along. However, Paul knew something about God that they didn't.

For a start, 'God does not live in temples made by human hands'. This seems a fairly obvious statement until you imagine it spoken on Mars Hill, with the Parthenon towering above. The greatest achievement of Greek architecture, the centre of worship and the city's pride, but it's uninhabited, says Paul. That was challenging the Greeks where it hurt, and must have taken some courage. Instead, the loving character of the invisible God is revealed by Jesus, who brought us the resurrection. Some were converted, including Dionysius or Denis and a woman called Damaris, who must have become leaders of the new Christian congregation in Athens. Most people only wanted to debate novelties without committing themselves, and told the apostle to come back another day. Nevertheless, in the next century, Aristides and Athenagoras were Athenian philosophers who wrote in defence of the Christian belief in resurrection.

Zeus (18), completed in AD 131. Beyond it to the east is the restored **Roman Stadium (19)**, used for the first Olympic Games of modern times.

South-west of the Parthenon, the **Monument of Filopappos (20)** was built in AD 114–16 on top of Filopappos Hill, also known as the Hill of the Muses, and on a clear day there is a view of the plain of Attica and the Saronic Gulf. A little to the north of this is the **Hill of the Pnyx (21)**, where the democratic assembly of Athens (Ecclesia tou Demou) met in the fifth century BC, and the observatory stands on top of the **Hill of the Nymphs (22)**.

Opening Times
The Acropolis archaeological site Tel. 01 321 0219, Monday to Friday 08.00–17.00; Saturdays, Sundays and holidays 08.30–14.30. Toilets on the path to the right of the steps up to the entrance

The Acropolis museum as above except that on Mondays it is only open 11.00–17.00. Toilets outside on the left

The Ancient Agora site and museum Tel. 01 321 0185, Tuesday to Sunday 08.30–15.00. Toilets at the far end of the museum

The National Archaeological Museum Tel. 01 821 7717/24, April to October: Tuesday to Friday 08.00–19.00; Saturday, Sunday and holidays 08.30–15:00 and Monday 12.30–19.00; November to March: Tuesday to Friday 08.00–17.00; Saturday, Sunday and holidays 08.30–15:00 and Monday 12.30–17.00 (But like most places in Greece, closed on March 25). Toilets down the steps behind the ticket desk

The Roman agora site and the Tower of the Winds Tel. 01 324 5220, Tuesday to Sunday 08.30–15.00

The Olympeion (Temple of Olympian Zeus) Tel. 01 922 6330, Tuesday to Sunday 08.30–15.00

The Temple of Apollo and Acropolis, Corinth

CORINTH (GREECE)

The large peninsula known as the Peloponnese is joined to southern Greece, or Achaia, by a narrow isthmus, between the Aegean and the Adriatic seas. Now the isthmus is crossed by a spectacular modern ship canal, near to the modern city of Korinthos (Κόρινθος). In ancient times, however, to save a long and dangerous sail around the peninsula, cargo was taken out of boats in the Saronic Gulf on the east and carried by slaves over the ridge to be put in different boats in the Corinthian Gulf on the west,

or vice versa. Small boats were actually hauled over the isthmus on a 'stone tramway' (diolkos) built in the sixth century BC.

In the ancient city, whose impressive ruins stand at the foot of the steep hill called Acrocorinth, south of the modern town, approximately 90% of the population were slaves. The Isthmian Games held on the Isthmus of Corinth were second only to the Olympic Games in importance, and Paul may be referring to them in 1 Corinthians 9:24–26. The city was destroyed

121

by the Romans in 146 BC, apart from the Temple of Apollo (sixth century BC), and rebuilt by Julius Caesar in 44 BC. Corinth was the capital of the Roman province of Achaia, governed by a proconsul, and a typical port city with all its vices. One ancient writer tells us there were a thousand official prostitutes at the shrine of Aphrodite, male and female. Contemporary literature describes the people of Corinth as coming from many cultures and languages, immoral, unruly, pretending to be interested in philosophy, proud, argumentative, and frequently torn apart by controversies, and Paul's letters to the Corinthians show that some of this character had infiltrated the church there. After leaving Athens, Paul spent eighteen months in Corinth, an ideal hub for communication with the neighbouring provinces, preaching and making converts.

Getting to Corinth

Leaving Athens towards Korinthos on National Route 8, after 10 kilometres (6 miles) you reach, on the south (left) side of the road, the Byzantine **Moni Daphniou** monastery, with some of Greece's finest mosaics. Turning off the road 22 kilometres (13 miles) from Athens, on the north (right) side of the road is the town of **Elefsina** (Ελευσίνα). Taking a side street called Odos Demetriou at a set of traffic lights in the town, you reach the site of the Eleusinian Mystery Religion. The archaeology is

confusing, and it is best to start with the museum on top of the hill at the far end of the site. Soon afterwards you are presented with a choice between the 8A (E94) motorway which is a toll road, and the old National Road 8. Both roads travel west for 77 kilometres (48 miles) from Athens to the Corinth canal.

Procrustes was a legendary giant who lived near this road. He would offer hospitality to travellers, then force them to lie on an iron bed. If they were shorter or taller than the bed, he would stretch them on a rack or lop off their limbs until they fitted; so we describe as 'procrustean' any attempts to achieve unity by imposing uniformity.

Work was begun by Emperor Nero for a **Corinth ship canal** cutting across the isthmus, but it was not finally built until 1893; it is over 6 kilometres (4 miles) long. Portions of the **Diolkos**, a paved road for dragging boats across the isthmus have been excavated near the west end of the modern canal on either side of the swing bridge on the road from Korinthos to Loutraki. **Ancient Corinth** is some 7 kilometres (4 miles) south-west of the modern city of Korinthos, approached from either the Patras to Korinthos 8A (E65) or the Korinthos to Tripoli 7 (E65) toll-motorways, or on the old road following signs for Patra and Archeocorinthos. Unless you have a powerful car or take a taxi, the top of **Acrocorinth** is a vigorous 1½ hour walk from Ancient Corinth. There are buses from Athens to Korinthos, and buses from Korinthos to Ancient Corinth. Pilgrims travelling by sea between Italy and Greece will use the port of Patras (Πάτρα) and pay the toll to travel the 8A (E65) motorway between there and Korinthos. And you can travel by train between Patras, Korinthos and Athens.

Paul's ministry in Corinth during his second missionary journey (Acts 18:1–18)

After this Paul left Athens and went to Corinth. There he found a Jew named Aquila, a native of Pontus, who had recently come from Italy with his wife Priscilla, because Claudius had ordered all Jews to leave Rome. Paul went to see them, and, because he was of the same trade, he stayed with them, and they worked together – by trade they were tent-makers. Every sabbath he would argue in the synagogue and would try to convince Jews and Greeks.

When Silas and Timothy arrived from Macedonia, Paul was occupied with proclaiming the word, testifying to the Jews that the Messiah was Jesus. When they opposed and reviled him, in protest he shook the dust from his clothes and said to them, 'Your blood be on your own heads! I am innocent. From now on I will go to the Gentiles.' Then he left the synagogue and went to the house of a man named Titius Justus, a worshipper of God; his house was next door to the synagogue. Crispus, the official of the synagogue, became a believer in the Lord, together with all his household; and many of the Corinthians who heard Paul became believers and were baptized. One night the Lord said to Paul in a vision, 'Do not be afraid, but speak and do not be silent; for I am with you, and no one will lay a hand on you to harm you, for there are many in this city who are my people.' He stayed there a year and six months, teaching the word of God among them.

But when Gallio was proconsul of Achaia, the Jews made a united attack on Paul and brought him before the tribunal. They said, 'This man is persuading people to worship God in ways that are contrary to the law.' Just as Paul was about to speak, Gallio said to the Jews, 'If it were a matter of crime or serious villainy, I would be justified in accepting the complaint of you Jews; but since it is a matter of questions about words and names and your own law, see to it yourselves; I do not wish to be a judge of these matters.' And he dismissed them from the tribunal. Then all of them seized Sosthenes, the official of the synagogue, and beat him in front of the tribunal. But Gallio paid no attention to any of these things. After staying there for a considerable time, Paul said farewell to the believers and sailed for Syria, accompanied by Priscilla and Aquila. At Cenchreae he had his hair cut, for he was under a vow.

The ministry of Apollos in Corinth (Acts 18:24—19:1)

Now there came to Ephesus a Jew named Apollos, a native of Alexandria. He was an eloquent man, well-versed in the scriptures. He had been instructed in the Way of the Lord; and he spoke with burning enthusiasm and taught accurately the things concerning Jesus, though he knew only the baptism of John. He began to speak boldly in the synagogue; but when Priscilla and Aquila heard him, they took him aside and explained the Way of God to him more accurately. And when he wished to cross over to Achaia, the believers encouraged him and wrote to the disciples to welcome him. On his arrival he greatly helped those who through grace had become believers, for he powerfully refuted the Jews in public, showing by the scriptures that the Messiah is Jesus. While Apollos was in Corinth, Paul passed through the interior regions and came to Ephesus.

Paul also spent three months in Greece at the end of his third missionary journey (Acts 20:2–3).

Opening Times

Ancient Corinth site and museum Tel. 0741 31 207, April to October daily 08.00–19.00; November to February daily 08.00–17.00; March daily 08.00–18.00. Toilets in the museum

Acrocorinth site Tel. 0741 31 443, 08.00–19.00 Tuesday to Sunday in summer; 08.00–14.30 Tuesday to Sunday in winter

Elefsina site and museum Tel. 01 554 3470, Tuesday to Sunday 08.30–15.00. Toilets behind the ticket office

Moni Daphniou monastery Tel. 01 581 1558, Tuesday to Friday 08.00–19.00, Saturday and Sunday 08.30–15.00; closed for restoration at the time of writing

Ancient Corinth today

Entering the site at the ticket office by the car park, on the right are the remains of a temple in honour of the Caesars, called the **Temple of Octavia**, and on the left the **museum**, in the courtyard of which is a stone which reads 'Synagogue of the Hebrews'. Mosaics in the museum show how rich some of the households in Corinth were; if they made their atrium available for the Christian shared meal, it is not surprising that there were inequalities (1 Corinthians 11:21).

Turning left and left again you see the seven columns of the archaic **Temple of Apollo**; each is made out of a single piece of stone and they measure

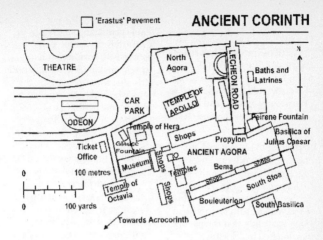

ANCIENT CORINTH

1.8 metres (6 feet) in diameter. Nearby is the **Glauce Fountain** cut from the solid rock.

At the centre of the site is the **ancient agora**. In the agora was the **bema**, a rostrum which formed the magistrate's bench or tribunal, where Paul appeared before Gallio. Being careful not to inconvenience other visitors, groups of pilgrims can read or act out Acts 18:12–17 in the place where it happened. Around the agora are temples, shops, basilicas and porches. The five main types of **capitals** at the top of pillars in classical architecture can be distinguished: Tuscan and Doric, which were quite plain (though the Doric columns were fluted), Ionic with what look like rams' horns, Corinthian with acanthus leaves, and Composite. At the

far end of the agora is the **Peirene Fountain**, a natural spring supplying water tanks behind six arches. A propylon

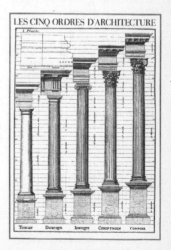

Five orders of Architecture, Perrault 1683

125

and some steps lead to the **Lecheon Road**, the main highway to the port of Lecheon, on the Gulf of Corinth. The road is impressive, 7.6 metres (25 feet) wide. It is lined with shops, one of which could have belonged to Priscilla and Aquila, and leads past temples, markets and the **public latrines**.

Returning to the car park, to one side is the **odeon**, and a rough path leads down the hill to the remains of the **theatre**. At the north-east corner of this is a pavement with an inscribed stone recording that the paving was donated by 'Erastus, procurator and aedile', who may well have been the man mentioned in Acts 19:22, Romans 16:23 and 2 Timothy 4:20.

Acro-Corinth, the citadel into which the population could withdraw when attacked, rises up behind ancient Corinth; there are **ramparts** from various ages and scant remains of the **Temple of Aphrodite** on the summit, with a magnificent view. An ancient myth told how Sisyphus, King of Corinth, was punished for gossiping about one of Zeus' seductions by endlessly having to push a rock up Acrocorinth until it rolled down from the top and he had to start over again. In more recent times Corinth was a centre for the export of the small dried grapes we call currants, a word derived from the French for 'grapes of Corinth'.

Paul in Corinth

Paul spent eighteen months in Corinth from winter AD 49 to summer 51, earning his living by tent-making with Aquila and Priscilla, who were among the Jews who had been expelled from Rome by Emperor Claudius in 41 or 49. Paul started his mission, as usual, in the Jewish synagogue. The 'leader of the synagogue' called Crispus, and several of the non-Jewish 'God-fearers' who attended the services because they were attracted by the Jewish religion, were among Paul's first converts there. Paul moved into the house of Titius Justus, one of the gentile God-fearers, and while he was in Corinth wrote his letters to the Thessalonians. The trial of Paul in Corinth can be dated to AD 51 because an inscription at Delphi records the arrival of the proconsul Gallio in that year. Gallio, whose brother Seneca spoke highly of his kindness and fairness, refused to adjudicate. Paul, however, decided that the time had come for him to move on, with Priscilla and Aquila, whom he took to Ephesus.

Epidauros Επίδαυρος

Epidauros (today pronounced Eppeedavros) is not mentioned in the Bible, but it is possible to go there from Corinth to catch an idea of the longing for healing in the ancient world. This was a famous healing centre, dedicated to Asklepios, or in the Latin spelling Aesculapius, who was identified with Serapis. Doctors were few and far between, so many sick people went to spend a night in a cubicle there, hoping by this 'incubation' period to be healed by the snake god which is still the symbol of medicine today. Because it became a rich city it had a huge **theatre**, which survives in good condition. When a speech of St Paul's is read from the stage, every syllable is crystal clear from the very back. It was a highly developed, but spiritually hungry, civilization which the apostle confronted. Approximately 66 kilometres (41 miles) south-east of Corinth, the theatre of Epidauros (Palaia Epidavros) is approached on National Road 70.

Mycenae Μυκήνες

The massive stones of Mycenae on their impregnable hilltop were the site of the first mainland European civilization from 1400 to 1100 BC, and the home of Agamemnon in Homer's *Iliad*. They were rediscovered by Heinrich Schliemann (see above under Troy), and bring home graphically the message that the writings of Homer, like the Bible, are more true to history than sceptics used to assume. Drive along the old National Road 7 to Fihti (Φίχτι) and follow the signs to Ancient Mykines.

Opening Times
Epidavros: Tel. 0753 22009, opening daily at 08.00 and closing at 19.00 April to

October; 17.00 November to February, and 18.00 in March. The museum (only) does not open until 12.00 on Mondays. Come out of the museum and turn left to find the toilets
Mycenae: Tel. 0751 76585, opening daily at 08.00 and closing at 19.00 March to October; 17.00 October to March. Toilets on the left near the entrance

Cenchreae

According to Acts 18:18 St Paul sailed from the ancient port of Cenchreae; his vow was probably based on the Nazirites of the Old Testament (Numbers 6:2–21), and he may have been concerned to demonstrate to his Jewish friends that the apostle to the Gentiles had not ceased to observe the law, though he did not impose it on his converts. Phoebe was a Christian woman who ministered in the church at Cenchreae (Romans 16:1–2).

If you drive out of Korinthos by the coast road towards Epidavros, National Road 70, then soon after passing Isthmus, the site of the Isthmian Games, you come to the small town of Kechries (Κεχριες) up on your right. The ancient harbour is on your left; the signboard is only visible when coming from the opposite direction. Extensive remains of quayside buildings have been discovered by excavation and by underwater archaeology. It was the main port for Corinth on the Saronic Gulf.

PAUL'S LETTERS TO THE CORINTHIANS

During his three years in Ephesus, in the course of his third missionary journey, it appears that Paul wrote at least four times to Corinth. Some think that portions of all four letters are included in the two which we have in the New Testament. His human anger shows in his dealings with the Corinthians, but he controls it, and grows and deepens in character as a result.

1 Corinthians 1:12 appears to show that there were up to four versions of Christianity circulating in Corinth:

1. Palestinian Jews had come to Corinth, claiming that they were followers of St Peter, and that it was impossible for a Greek to become a Christian without first becoming a Jew, and obeying the full Jewish law.
2. Some of Paul's followers distorted his teaching, saying that not only was the Old Testament law not binding on Christians, but we are free of any moral restraints whatsoever.
3. Another Christian teacher followed Paul to Corinth, called Apollos. He came from Alexandria, which with its huge library was a centre of Greek learning, and where the Jewish philosopher Philo had taught a mystical version of Judaism. Apollos was brilliant at debating with Greeks and with Greek-speaking Jews, but some people must have thought that Christianity was just another school of philosophy, only properly understood by the highly intelligent.
4. Probably basing themselves on the oriental 'mystery religions' which were so popular, another group claimed that special spiritual powers are given to initiates, especially the gift of speaking in tongues, and those without these gifts are not true Christians. These 'spirit-people' may have thought that only they were 'of Christ', or they may have wrongly thought that they were following the teaching of Apollos.

In his letters Paul diplomatically agrees with each of these groups in turn, and then proceeds to subvert their cherished superiority by showing that each of them is incomplete without the others. Then, out of these appalling rivalries, he produces, in 1 Corinthians 13, the greatest hymn to love in world literature. To read the letters of Paul as one long plea for those who are radically different in their understandings of Christianity to worship together in the unity of mutual love, puts him in direct line with Jesus who sat prostitutes and Pharisees, collaborators and revolutionaries around the same table, and told them the kingdom of God was among them.

A Summary of the Letters to Corinth

The 'previous letter' is referred to in 1 Corinthians 5:9. It is suggested that part of this is contained in 2 Corinthians 6:14—7:1. Reports had reached Paul of immorality among the Christians in Corinth, so he warns the Corinthians not to be 'unequally yoked with unbelievers'. Then Chloe's household reported verbally on immorality in the church and party spirit in Corinth, and this was followed by a list of written questions.

1 **Corinthians** is Paul's reply. Chapters 1–4 deal with party spirit. Paul saw that it was important to unite the different parties, or they would destroy the church.

Chapter 5 deals with immorality. A man was living with his stepmother. Paul's converts were taking his insistence that they were not bound by Jewish law as a liberty to indulge in behaviour which was despised by their neighbours. Because the 'Previous Letter' was misunderstood to mean withdrawal from the world, Paul clarifies what he meant in 1 Corinthians 5:9–11.

Chapter 6 deals with Christians who take each other to court.

Chapter 7 deals with marriage and divorce. Paul believed that Jesus was opposed to divorce, not least because a divorced woman had no means of economic survival except prostitution.

Chapter 8 deals with meat offered to idols; see below under Pergamon.

In Chapter 9 Paul points out that he is entitled to be paid for his ministerial work. But as in the previous chapter, it is sometimes wiser, for the time being, not to take advantage of the freedoms we have as Christians, so as not to offend weak consciences inside and outside the church, until they have had an opportunity to come to a deeper understanding.

Chapter 10 deals with greed at the agape or love feast which preceded Holy Communion.

Chapter 11 is about women covering their heads while they are worshipping: prostitutes were the only women who publicly went bare-headed in the ancient world.

Chapter 12 deals with spiritual gifts. 12:12–30 teaches that we are like limbs in a body, which can only function when united to all the others.

Hence in Chapter 13 the great Hymn to Love arises out of the squabbles of the different parties in Corinth.

Chapter 14 teaches that spiritual gifts must not interrupt orderly worship. (14:34–35 appear in different places in different manuscripts, so may be a later addition; they are contradicted by 11:5.)

Chapter 15 deals with the resurrection. Neither the Jewish belief in physical resuscitation, nor the Greek concept of the immortality of the soul, correspond to the hope brought by the resurrection of Jesus, so a new term, a 'spiritual body', has to be coined to describe an after-life which is not physical, but which is personal, and fuller than this life.

Chapter 16 deals with the collection for the Jerusalem church (see below), Paul's plans, and final greetings.

1 Corinthians was sent by sea, while Timothy went to Corinth by land; he returned with bad news.

The 'severe letter'. Many scholars believe that 2 Corinthians 10–13 is a separate letter which was taken by Titus (2 Corinthians 2:4), calling for moral behaviour, and respect for the apostle.

Paul soon left Ephesus, and travelled to Troas, Philippi and Thessalonica, where he met Titus, who reported that the Corinthians were willing to conform, and by a majority vote had censured the member who had insulted Paul.

The final letter is believed by many to be 2 Corinthians 1–9. It expresses forgiveness, and appeals for a practical demonstration of the unity

between Jewish and gentile Christians by taking up a collection for Paul to take to the Christians of Jerusalem, who were in dire poverty because of a famine (Acts 11:28), and possibly also the early custom of selling up their capital and sharing it with the rest of the church (Acts 4:32).

Spiritual gifts

The Greek word for presents or gifts, is *charismata*. As a result of the generous, loving grace (*charis*) of God, Christians find they are given the ability to do things they had never dreamt of doing. Examples given in 1 Corinthians 12–14 are wisdom, knowledge, faith, healing, miracles, prophecy, discernment of spirits, speaking in tongues, the interpretation of tongues, and love; but all of these come from the same Spirit, emphasizes St Paul. Romans 12 adds ministry, teaching, exhortation, giving, leadership, and compassion. Provided they promote the lordship of Jesus, all of these are given by the Holy Spirit of God. But nobody has all the gifts, so we should respect and not despise those who have different gifts from those we have ourselves. Because we are like limbs of a body, we need each other. Rejoice in those gifts you have, writes Paul, but do not make others feel inferior: love and unity in the church are more important than anything else.

Paul's Third Missionary Journey

After leaving Corinth, Paul sailed to Ephesus where he stayed briefly, then to Caesarea-on-Sea, then went by land to Jerusalem and back to Antioch-on-the-Orontes (Acts 17:18–22). Paul's third journey, the story of which is told in Acts 17:23—21:16, was to strengthen the faith of those he had visited before, so he went from Antioch-on-the-Orontes to 'Galatia and Phrygia': (probably including Derbe, Lystra, Iconium and Antioch-of-Pisidia); then to Ephesus for two years; Troas (2 Corinthians 2:12–13); a circuit of Macedonia organizing the collection for the poor Christians in Jerusalem: probably he visited the churches at Neapolis, Philippi, Thessalonica and Berea. Then he travelled into Achaia – Athens and probably Corinth. It may have been at this time that Paul visited the province of Illyricum (Romans 15:19). He passed through Philippi again, then travelled by sea to Troas. After healing the boy who fell from a window in Troas, Paul asked his friends to go ahead by sea while he walked to Assos (see above in the section on the Troad). From there he sailed to Caesarea-on-Sea, calling at Mitylene, Chios, Samos, Miletus, Cos, Rhodes, Patara, Tyre and Ptolemais (see the section on The Holy Land), then overland to Jerusalem.

EPHESUS (TURKEY)

One of the most visited and most impressive archaeological sites of the Mediterranean world is Ephesus, on a par with Pompeii and Ostia. Many visitors stop in the seaside resort of Kuşadası or in the small town of Selçuk, to go there. The site of the ancient city has been extensively excavated, and gives an impression of the large cities which St Paul visited. Pilgrims travelling in the paths of the apostles will certainly want to spend as long as possible there, and the description which follows will help them to understand what they see. (Armchair travellers may wish to visit http://www.seljuk.gov.tr)

Paul spent two years continuously in Ephesus, longer than at any other church, and wrote to the Christians there one of his most profound letters. His friends there included some of the 'Asiarchs' (Acts 19:31), who held the most prestigious office in the province of Asia, of which Ephesus was the capital.

The history of Ephesus

Ephesus stood at the mouth of the River Cayster (Kücüc

Paul calls at Ephesus on his second missionary journey (Acts 18:18–21)

After staying [in Corinth] for a considerable time, Paul said farewell to the believers and sailed for Syria, accompanied by Priscilla and Aquila. At Cenchreae he had his hair cut, for he was under a vow. When they reached Ephesus, he left them there, but first he himself went into the synagogue and had a discussion with the Jews. When they asked him to stay longer, he declined; but on taking leave of them, he said, 'I will return to you, if God wills.' Then he set sail from Ephesus.

Paul stays at Ephesus on his third missionary journey (Acts 19:1–11, 21–28, 19: 35—20:1)

While Apollos was in Corinth, Paul passed through the interior regions and came to Ephesus, where he found some disciples. He said to them, 'Did you receive the Holy Spirit when you became believers?' They replied, 'No, we have not even heard that there is a Holy Spirit.' Then he said, 'Into what then were you baptized?' They answered, 'Into John's baptism.' Paul said, 'John baptized with the baptism of repentance, telling the people to believe in the one who was to come after him, that is, in Jesus.' On hearing this, they were baptized in the name of the Lord Jesus. When Paul had laid his hands on them, the Holy Spirit came upon them, and they spoke in tongues and prophesied – altogether there were about twelve of them. He entered the synagogue and for three months spoke out boldly, and argued persuasively about the kingdom of God. When some stubbornly refused to believe and spoke evil of the Way before the congregation, he left them, taking the disciples with him, and argued daily in the lecture hall of Tyrannus. This continued for two years, so that all the residents of Asia, both Jews and Greeks, heard the word of the Lord. God did extraordinary miracles through Paul, so that when the handkerchiefs or aprons that had touched his skin were brought to the sick, their diseases left them, and the evil spirits came out of them . . .

Now after these things had been accomplished, Paul resolved in the Spirit to go through Macedonia and Achaia, and then to go on to Jerusalem. He said, 'After I have gone there, I must also see Rome.' So he sent two of his helpers, Timothy and Erastus, to Macedonia, while he himself stayed for some time longer in Asia.

About that time no little disturbance broke out concerning the Way. A man named Demetrius, a silversmith who made silver shrines of Artemis, brought no little business to the artisans. These he gathered together, with the workers of the same trade, and said, 'Men, you know that we get our wealth from this business. You also see and hear that not only in Ephesus but in almost the whole of Asia this Paul has persuaded and drawn away a considerable number of people by saying that gods made with hands are not gods. And there is danger not only that this trade of ours may come into disrepute but also that the temple of the great goddess Artemis will be scorned, and she will be deprived of her majesty that brought all Asia and the world to worship her.' When they heard this, they were enraged and shouted, 'Great is Artemis of the Ephesians!' . . .

But when the town clerk had quieted the crowd, he said, 'Citizens of Ephesus, who is there that does not know that the city of the Ephesians is the temple keeper of the great Artemis and of the statue that fell from heaven? Since these things cannot be denied, you ought to be quiet and do nothing rash. You have brought these men here who are neither temple robbers nor blasphemers of our goddess. If therefore Demetrius and the artisans with him have a complaint against anyone, the courts are open, and there are proconsuls; let them bring charges there against one another. If there is anything further you want to know, it must be settled in the regular assembly. For we are in danger of being charged with rioting today, since there is no cause that we can give to justify this commotion.' When he had said this, he dismissed the assembly.

After the uproar had ceased, Paul sent for the disciples; and after encouraging them and saying farewell, he left for Macedonia.

There are also references to Ephesus in 1 Timothy 1:3–4; 2 Timothy 1:16–18; and 2 Timothy 4:12. When Trophimus was sick, Paul left him to be cared for at Ephesus (2 Timothy 4:20).

Menderes) when it was founded by Greeks in about 980 BC. Rich King Croesus of Sardis in Lydia captured Ephesus and built the Temple of Artemis in about 560 BC. Artemis was not Diana the chaste huntress of later Latin legend, but a fertility goddess: her images show her covered in what were once thought to be breasts, but are now believed to be the testicles of bulls which had been sacrificed to her. Cyrus the Persian ruled Ephesus after he defeated Croesus. The temple was burnt down on the day that Alexander the Great was born in 356 BC,

Artemis of the Ephesians

Ephesus was administered as a vassal state to Pergamon, and from 133 BC by the Romans.

Ephesus was at a meeting of trade routes, and by the time of Caesar Augustus it had grown in importance so much that he made it the capital of the province of Asia. The theatre at Ephesus seats 24,000 people, and theatres in Roman cities had to provide a seat for every free man. Women were not admitted, nor were slaves, and it is reckoned that there were eight slaves for every free couple, so much was the Roman empire built on slave labour. So the population of Ephesus was probably approaching a quarter of a million, the fourth largest city in the empire, after Rome, Alexandria and Antioch-on-the-Orontes.

The government of Ephesus was unlike that of other cities, and Luke's accuracy as an historian is shown by his reference to the 'asiarchs', the town clerk and the proconsuls (in the plural).

Ephesus today

After many ups and downs of fortune, Ephesus was destroyed in the fifteenth century by the Ottoman Turks. By the time Shakespeare set his *Comedy of Errors* in Ephesus it no longer existed. It was excavated by British archaeologists in the nineteenth century, and in the twentieth century by Austrian archaeologists; many of the carvings they discovered are

but although, when he captured Ephesus, he offered to rebuild it at his own expense, the Ephesian people insisted on doing it themselves.

The temple which St Paul knew, the seventh on the site, was 115 metres (377 feet) long, 55 metres (180 feet) wide, and 18 metres (60 feet) high, and visible from far out at sea. It had 127 marble pillars, eight of which have been reused in Agia Sophia in İstanbul. The Temple of Artemis at Ephesus was the largest building yet to be made entirely of marble, and was called one of the Seven Wonders of the World.

On the death of Alexander's successor Lysimachus in 281 BC, Ephesus was ruled by the Seleucid kings from Antioch-on-the-Orontes. From 188 BC

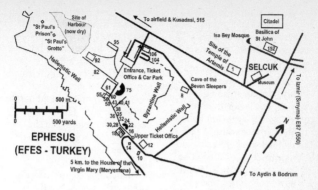

EPHESUS
(EFES - TURKEY)

either in the British Museum or in the Imperial Palace Museum in Vienna. More recent finds are in the **Selçuk Museum** nearby.

The remains of Ephesus are almost all situated on three streets which can be visited in an hour's stroll, though three to four hours is better. An idea of life in an ancient city can easily be grasped here, so they receive four million visitors each year. You are advised to avoid the heat of the day, and take a water bottle.

The buildings remaining in Ephesus today are all drawn and described on the following pages following the sequence as if a visitor is starting at the northern, lower entrance; anyone starting at the upper entrance in the south-east should turn to the last illustration and work back from there. Clear new signs have recently been erected with all the remains numbered, so the numbers in this description

correspond with those on the signs and on the plan in this guide, though only the most important and accessible monuments are listed here.

95. The Church of the Virgin Mary was the first church in Asia to be dedicated to the Mother of Christ. Originally there stood here the 260 metre-long (280 yards) south hall of the Olympeion – an enormous temple, the rest of which was later destroyed, for the worship of Emperor Hadrian as Zeus Olympios. The third ecumenical council was held in Ephesus in 461 to condemn Nestorius. A hairy Egyptian monk named Shenoudi hurled a brass-bound copy of the Gospels at him shouting, 'Thus I refute the heretic with the scriptures'; some Christians today are scarcely more subtle in their use of biblical texts. The council established that the personality of Jesus cannot be divided, so Mary is the 'Mother of God'. They recorded that her body is buried in Ephesus. This council was probably held in the south hall of the Olympeion.

In the fifth century a pillared church half that length was built, having an attached baptistry in the north-west corner, with a large font let into the floor. It was assumed that this council was held here, and so this church was called 'The Church of the Council', but it has now been shown that the church was not built until after AD 474.

In the seventh century a shorter, domed church was built in the western half of the pillared church, and when this collapsed it was used as the forecourt of a church built in the eastern half; it is therefore also called 'The Double Church'. It is reached by a small path turning right after the entrance before reaching the Harbour Street. This is a good place to read and meditate on Paul's letter to the Ephesians.

92. Continuing on the path to the left of the Church of the Virgin Mary you have to pick your way through the undergrowth to reach the remains of the **harbour baths**; the other approach from Harbour Street is not officially open to the public. The baths were built around the end of the first century AD. There was a heated baths complex in the west, a *palestra* (gymnasium or wrestling school) in the east, and a large courtyard surrounded by columned halls with marble panels and floors. Repaired in the reign of Constantine II (AD 337–61) they are also called the Constantine Baths. Until the river silted up they were situated by one of the world's busiest harbours; now they are some five kilometres (3 miles) from the sea.

82. Harbour Street is 500 metres (1650 feet) long and 11 metres (36 feet) wide, and was an early example of a street lit by public lighting. It was built in the first century BC and repaired and widened by Emperor Arcadius (AD 395–408); thereafter it was called the Arcadiana. There

Harbour Street, Ephesus

The Theatre, Ephesus

were shops on either side of this street. At present you can only walk down the section near the theatre.

75. The **theatre** was built, probably around 130 BC on the Greek plan, and enlarged, beginning in the reign of Emperor Augustus (27 BC – AD 14), to make it a Roman theatre with room for over 24,000 spectators; it is the largest Roman theatre in Turkey. The seating is 38 metres (125 feet) high and has a diameter of 158 metres (521 feet). The stage building was three storeys high, of which only the lowest storey survives; animal fights and gladiatorial games were held there in the third and fourth centuries AD. The theatre was where meetings of the *demos*, consisting of all free men in the city, governed its affairs. Pilgrims will want to spend time in the theatre reading the account of the riot over Paul's teaching.

60. **Marble Street** was paved with blocks of marble because it

was the main street from the theatre to the library and part of the processional way. A sign scratched into the pavement on the agora side of the street, with a woman's face, a heart and a left foot, is believed by some to have pointed the way to a brothel. Notice also the different types of fighters in the arena in the reliefs placed along the side of the street: the gladiator with his gladius or sword, the reticulator with his

*Carving of gladiator,
Marble Street, Ephesus*

Commercial Agora, Celsus Library,
Gateway to the Agora and Marble Street, Ephesus

net and trident, etc. These reliefs have been brought here from the gladiators' cemetery near the stadium.

61. The commercial agora was built beginning in the third century BC, with three gateways, and a row of shops, together with store rooms with vaulted roofs, running for 111 metres (364 feet) down each side. It was the marketplace where Demetrius and his friends made their living by selling silver models of the Temple of Artemis and its image. They were losing trade as people became Christians, so they started the riot against Paul. Revelation 18:12–13 could be considered a description of the varied merchandise sold here.

56. The Gate of Mazeus and Mithridates, and south entrance to the commercial agora. The two men whose name it bears were slaves in the household of Emperor Augustus and built this triumphal arch in gratitude when they were given their liberty in about 4 BC. It was reconstructed between 1979 and 1988. An inscription in the south-east conch puts a curse on anyone who urinates against the gate.

55. The Library of Celsus was built between AD 117 and 120 by his son as a tomb for Tiberius Julius Celsus Polemaenus, Consul in Rome and later Proconsul of Asia. It was discovered in 1904 and restored to its original two storeys between 1970 and 1978 using 80% original material; it is the most impressive building in Ephesus today. The statues in the niches of the façade are copies of the originals in the Ephesus Museum in Vienna; they represent Celsus' character: sophia (wisdom); arete (virtue); ennoia (intelligence); and episteme (knowledge). Celsus was buried among his books, under the apse. Niches for the 12,000 scrolls had a gap behind them so that a continuous draught could prevent their becoming damp.

50 and 51. Houses on the slopes. These were the houses of very rich people, plain on the outside but with richly decorated interiors, of two storeys of which the upper storey was used for bedrooms. The oldest dates from the first century BC, and they were used up until the seventh century AD. Now that a large steel and canvas roof has been erected to protect them, even though it does not improve the overall view of Ephesus, they can be visited at the same opening hours as the rest of the site. There is an additional entrance fee but it is worth it as the wall paintings and mosaics are stunning and, unlike those from Pompeii, mostly still in situ. Maybe some of the Asiarchs

who were friends of Paul (Acts 19:31) lived here.

In front of them was a row of *tabernae* or shops, with store rooms above them, fronted by a fine **mosaic pavement (44)** given by a certain Alytarchus, a referee at prize fights. It is nice to think that one of these shops may have been used as tent-making premises by the Roman-Jewish firm of Priscilla and Aquila, in which case Paul will have gossipped the gospel as he sat downstairs by the open doorway. But when he stopped teaching in the synagogue, he found the crowds so great that he had to rent a lecture-hall to teach at siesta time, from 11 am until 4 pm (as one of the manuscripts of Acts tells us); that may possibly have been one of the buildings opening onto the commercial agora.

43. The House of Love. The statue of the phallic god Priapus, the mosaic floors and

Shops and mosaic near the houses on the slopes, Ephesus

Brothel and baths, Ephesus

the frescoes on the walls have led some to believe that this was a second–century brothel, though other archaeologists remain unconvinced.

41. The Baths of Scholasticia, also called the **Varius Bath**, were probably built in the first century AD and were three storeys high, and the hypocaust provided underfloor heating so that visitors could relax in the warm *tepidarium* and discuss the latest news. Scholasticia was a Christian woman who had the baths

repaired in AD 400; her headless statue is in one of the niches.

Latrines, Ephesus

The Latrina. The public toilets from the first century AD had a running water system and

Hypocaust in the Baths of Scholasticia, Ephesus

Temple of Hadrian, Ephesus

as there were no partitions they must also have been a place for discussions. There were probably separate times for men, women and slaves.

40. Inserted into the middle of the Varius Baths, the attractive **Temple of Hadrian** dates from the second century AD. Two columns and two piers at the front, all with Corinthian capitals, supported a semi-circular pediment at the sides. Inscribed bases supported bronze statues of emperors Diocletian, Maximian, Constantius and Galerius. It was reconstructed in the 1950s.

38. The Fountain of Trajan, second century AD, contained a full-sized statue of the emperor and two statues of Dionysos.

Fountain of Trajan, Ephesus

The reconstruction of 1962 is much smaller than the original which was 12 metres (40 foot) high; the statues which were in the niches are in Selçuk Museum.

36. Curetes Street is so named because columns and stones removed from the Pryteneum were placed there in the fourth century AD, inscribed with the lists of the curetes, who were an

the second storey the relief of Nike (Winged Victory) which now stands on Domitian Square.

32. The Memmius Monument, built for Caius Memmius in the late first century BC; the reliefs show Memmius, his father Caicus, and grandfather, the dictator Sulla. Its fragments have been re-erected with no particular

Curetes Street, Ephesus

important class of priests in the Temple of Artemis. The Roman name of the street was either Embolos or Plateia. It was lined on both sides with statues of important people, some of which still stand. The paving was last repaired in the fourth century AD.

35. The Hercules Gate (fourth century AD) marks the southern end of the street of the curetes. It had two reliefs of Hercules in a lion-skin, and on

resemblance to the original monument.

30. The Temple of Domitian, built at the end of the first century AD. Parts of the façade were re-erected in 1975 in the shape of a letter H. The colossal statue, parts of which were found here, was at first thought to be of Emperor Domitian, but is now identified as his brother Titus, who, together with Domitian and their father Vespasian, was

Memmius Monument, Ephesus

worshipped in this temple of the cult of the Emperors. The head and an arm are now in the museum at Selçuk.

28. Pollio monument and Fountain of Domitian. A monument was built in AD 97 to honour C. Sextilius Pollio, who had paid for the erection of the Basilica Stoa and an aqueduct. Adjoining it is a fountain with a large semi-circular room which looked onto the Domitian Square in the agora, and which was built in AD 92. The prominent arch of this has been reconstructed in concrete using original marble fragments.

Temple of Domitian, the Pollio Monument, the Fountain of Domitian, Prytaneion, Basilica Stoa, State Agora, Odeon and Baths, Ephesus

143

24. The Prytaneion or Prytaneum (town hall), built at the end of the first century BC to replace a hellenistic building, was the office of the 'prytaneis' or chief magistrates. The walls of the entrance hall were covered in lists of curetes and others connected with the worship of Artemis. The façade of six thick columns made it look like a temple; a holy fire burnt in the centre of the building, and the three statues of Artemis of Ephesus in the Selçuk Museum were found here.

21. The Basilica Stoa (Royal Colonnade) was constructed along the side of the State Agora in the time of Emperor Augustus, about 11 BC, and contained statues of him and of his wife, Livia, which are in the Selçuk Museum. It was originally a magnificent two-storey building, and many of the columns of the three aisles of the lower storey have been re-erected.

22. A small roofed theatre, holding about 1,500 people, was built in about AD 150. When it was used for concerts it was called the **odeon**, and because the advisory council or 'boule' met there it was also called the **bouleuterion**.

23. The State Agora, used as the centre of administration. It was built in the first century BC, and in its final, Roman form, measured 160 metres long by 58 metres wide (176 by 64 yards).

16. The baths, just inside the upper entrance to the site, and for long incorrectly called the Baths of Varius, were built in the second century AD.

Outside the upper exit, and not normally accessible to the public, are three sites. Behind the upper car park there is a circular structure from the second century AD, converted into a church in Byzantine times. Because a bull, the symbol of St Luke, was carved into the door jamb, it was erroneously called the **tomb of St Luke (14)**. Further down the road towards Selçuk on the left of the road is **the Eastern Gymnasium (12)** from the second century AD, and opposite it on the right hand side of the modern road is the **Magnesia Gate (10)**. This opened onto the Sacred Way leading to the temple of Artemis, which was paved with marble and covered by a roof supported by marble pillars.

Sites close to Ephesus

Returning to the lower northern exit you can see a tower on a small hill to the west above the old harbour. It is part of the second century BC ramparts and since at least the seventeenth century has been known as **'Paul's Prison' (69)**. The only biblical evidence for an imprisonment here is when Paul says he 'fought with wild beasts at Ephesus' (1 Corinthians 15:32), though this can hardly have been meant literally: it is

Reconstruction of the Temple of Artemis at Ephesus. J.T. Wood, 1869

unlikely that a Roman citizen would have been sent into the arena, or have survived if he was. On the hillside below it a cave has been discovered with prayers to St Paul scratched on the walls, and frescos illustrating the story of St Paul and St Thekla. This is called **'St Paul's Grotto' (71)**; neither of these sites is open to the public.

Leaving the lower exit, you pass the **stadium (104)** from the time of Nero (AD 54–68), with a prominent south gate standing above the road, and go straight on past the second century AD **Gymnasium of Vedius (106)** on your right. Going straight on at the crossroads and then turning right onto the main D-515 road from Kusadasi to Selçuk, you pass on your left the single pillar, reconstructed from various fragments in 1970, to mark the site of the great **Temple of Artemis (1)**. In the summer storks nest on top of the pillar.

Turning to the left in Selçuk onto the D-550 (E87) towards İzmir, and then taking the first turning to the left, a steep side street brings you to the remains of the **Church of St John (152)**, which was founded in the fourth century over a chamber believed to be the tomb of the apostle John. The present basilica, 130 metres (427 feet) long and 65 metres (213 feet) wide, was built during the reign of Emperor Justinian (AD 527–65). Walls were built around the church, and a citadel above it (not open to the public), for protection against Arab raids in the seventh century.

If, however, you turn right at the first crossroads after leaving the lower exit, to take the small road eastwards past the Gymnasium of Vedius, you reach the **Cave of the Seven Sleepers of Ephesus (8)** – the legend is that seven Christians were ordered to be walled in

145

Prostitution and Fertility

Worshipping at the Temple of Artemis ensured the fertility of the crops, the herds, and your family. This was a matter of life and death – if the surrounding countryside did not produce meat and grain you would die, and you needed children to support you in old age. So you ensured fertility by sympathetic magic: going with the temple prostitutes was not done mainly for pleasure, it was seen as your civic duty. Prostitutes were usually either women who had been sold as slaves, or who had been widowed or divorced and left with no other means of supporting themselves. It has been suggested that whenever the Bible uses the word we translate as fornication it actually means consorting with prostitutes. Similarly references to homosexuality could refer to using male prostitutes. Today only one reconstructed pillar remains of the Temple of Artemis at Ephesus. The town clerk quelled the riot after two hours by arguing that Paul did not attack the old religions, a lesson which all Christians can learn in their relations with other faiths. The old fertility religions withered of their own accord, when the more reasonable claims of Christianity were set against them.

---

there during a persecution in the reign of Emperor Decius (AD 249–51) and woke up again 200 years later, under Emperor Theodosius II (408–50) to discover that Christianity was now the state religion. When they died, they were buried in the same cave and a church was built on the site, where many other Christians were buried. The cave is closed for repairs, but you can peer through the wire mesh gate.

To visit the **House of Mary** (Meryemana), travelling south from Selçuk on the D-550 (E87) towards Aydın (ancient Tralles), take a turning right after 2 kilometres (1 mile), which brings you to the southern, upper gate of Ephesus

archaeological site. Continue for a further five kilometres (3 miles) towards the summit of Bülbül Dağ. The tradition held here is that John, the beloved disciple, who was commanded by Jesus from the cross to care for Mary, his mother, took her with him to Ephesus. The site of the house, an attractive spot which has foundations dating from the first century, was identified in a vision by a paralysed nun called Katarina Emmerich (1774–1824). The belief that Mary died here assumes that the author of the book of Revelation is the same person as the 'disciple whom Jesus loved' in John 19:27, and is in conflict with the traditions associated with the Dormition Abbey in Jerusalem.

Opening Times

Ephesus site Tel. 0232 892 6010, daily 08.00–18.30. Toilets inside the lower entrance and outside the upper entrance

Artemesion remains daily 08.30–17.30

Church of St John and Hill of Ayasoluk daily 08.00–18.30. For toilets, turn right as you go out and they are on the left

Meryemana Tel. 0232 892 7065, daily 08.00–19.00 May to October; 08.00–17.00 November to April. Mass on Sundays at 10.30 and weekdays at 07.15. Toilets downhill near the shrine

Selçuk Archaeological Museum Tel. 0232 892 6010, daily 08.30–12.00 and 13.00–18.00. Toilets on the right after the ticket desk

Ephesus Museum in the Kunsthistorisches Museum, Burgring, Wien, Austria, Tuesday to Sunday 10.00–18.00

From Ephesus to the whole province of Asia

Paul learnt while he was at Ephesus that instead of fighting the old religions, it was better to present a more attractive alternative. And that he did not have to do everything himself; members of the church at Ephesus probably took the gospel to and founded the churches in the other six cities of Asia mentioned in the Revelation to John, as well as Hierapolis and Colossae (see below), and maybe also at nearby Magnesia-ad-Meander and Tralles (modern Aydın),

mentioned in the letters of Ignatius of Antioch in about AD 110.

Opening Times

Aydın Archaeology Museum Tuesday to Sunday 09.00–12.00, 13.30–17.00

PAUL'S LETTER TO THE EPHESIANS

Paul's letter to the Ephesians, like the other 'captivity epistles', Philippians, Colossias, and Philemon, was written from prison, for he says in 3:1, 4:1 and 6:20 that he is a prisoner in chains. Unlike the others it cannot have been written from Ephesus, and the only imprisonments we know about from Acts were in Philippi (but that was only overnight), Caesarea-on-Sea and Rome. Ephesians is most likely to have been written when Paul was under house arrest in Rome. Unlike the other letters, Ephesians contains no personal greetings, and in the oldest manuscripts 1:1 does not mention Ephesus, so it was probably a circular letter to be taken by Tychicus (6:21) to a number of churches in the province of Asia, perhaps at the same time as Colossians (Colossians 4:7, 16) and Philemon. There are many echoes of Colossians in Ephesians, so that some have suggested that Ephesians is not by Paul; but whereas Colossians was written as an argument in response to a specific crisis, Ephesians seems to be the result of mature reflection on the same themes expounded at leisure in the form of a prayer. In

Ephesians he describes a vision of a world won for love, which could only be achieved if his other vision, that of a church united in love, came first. They both seemed as impossible then as they do now, but Paul believed in them and worked for them.

A Summary of the Letter

(Ephesians 1:1) Paul gives thanks that God has called us to be part of his people, the church, and revealed to us a 'mystery' that he plans to bring the whole of creation together in Christ (1:10). Paul prays that we may know God in Christ, who is the head of the church which is his body (1:15–23). We have been saved from sin and made members of the church, not because we have earned it, but through God's undeserved grace and kindness (2:1–10). God has even included non-Jews, who were previously excluded, in his church which is built into a single structure like a temple (2:11–22). Paul's ministry has been to reveal the mystery that God's plan is for Jews and Gentiles to be united in the church (3:1–13), and he prays that we may know the greatness of God's love (3:14–21). Therefore we must work hard to show love and unity in the church (4:1—5:20). Examples of love and reconciliation which Christians are to show to the world are in the relationships between husbands and wives (5:21–32); children and parents (6:1–4); and between slaves and their

masters (6:5–9). Paul was being guarded by soldiers wearing Roman armour, and he writes that we are under attack from the divisive forces of the universe, so we must defend ourselves with the armour of God (6:10–17). Finally Paul asks for prayer that he may be able to carry this message like an ambassador to the Roman rulers, and prays for his readers (6:18–23).

MILETUS (TURKEY)

The River Meander (today called Büyük Menderes), which gave a word to the language for every river which flows 'meandering with mazy motion', has silted up over the centuries; so that Miletus, which was on the coast in classical times, is now several miles inland. Signposts to 'Milet' from route D-535, about halfway between Bodrum and Selçuk, lead to the isolated site of the ancient city of Miletus, approximately 40 kilometres (25 miles) south of Ephesus. There is an interesting theatre and other fine buildings, but because what was a peninsula at a river's mouth is now only some slightly higher ground several kilometres from the sea, the layout is not easy to recognize. It was on his way back to Jerusalem, at the end of his third missionary journey, that Paul called at Miletus, probably because Ephesus was not safe for him, to say farewell to the elders of the church at Ephesus.

Paul calls at Miletus on his third missionary journey (Acts 20:16–38)

For Paul had decided to sail past Ephesus, so that he might not have to spend time in Asia; he was eager to be in Jerusalem, if possible, on the day of Pentecost. From Miletus he sent a message to Ephesus, asking the elders of the church to meet him. When they came to him, he said to them: 'You yourselves know how I lived among you the entire time from the first day that I set foot in Asia, serving the Lord with all humility and with tears, enduring the trials that came to me through the plots of the Jews. I did not shrink from doing anything helpful, proclaiming the message to you and teaching you publicly and from house to house, as I testified to both Jews and Greeks about repentance toward God and faith toward our Lord Jesus. And now, as a captive to the Spirit, I am on my way to Jerusalem, not knowing what will happen to me there, except that the Holy Spirit testifies to me in every city that imprisonment and persecutions are waiting for me. But I do not count my life of any value to myself, if only I may finish my course and the ministry that I received from the Lord Jesus, to testify to the good news of God's grace.

'And now I know that none of you, among whom I have gone about proclaiming the kingdom, will ever see my face again. Therefore I declare to you this day that I am not responsible for the blood of any of you, for I did not shrink from declaring to you the whole purpose of God. Keep watch over yourselves and over all the flock, of which the Holy Spirit has made you overseers, to shepherd the church of God that he obtained with the blood of his own Son. I know that after I have gone, savage wolves will come in among you, not sparing the flock. Some even from your own group will come distorting the truth in order to entice the disciples to follow them. Therefore be alert, remembering that for three years I did not cease night or day to warn everyone with tears. And now I commend you to God and to the message of his grace, a message that is able to build you up and to give you the inheritance among all who are sanctified. I coveted no one's silver or gold or clothing. You know for yourselves that I worked with my own hands to support myself and my companions. In all this I have given you an example that by such work we must support the weak, remembering the words of the Lord Jesus, for he himself said, "It is more blessed to give than to receive."'

When he had finished speaking, he knelt down with them all and prayed. There was much weeping among them all; they embraced Paul and kissed him, grieving especially because of what he had said, that they would not see him again. Then they brought him to the ship.

The history of Miletus

Miletus was first occupied by the Minoans from Crete, then Mycenaeans from the Peloponnese, then by refugees from Greece during the Dorian invasion. After reaching its zenith in the sixth century BC it was destroyed, together with its sanctuary of Didyma nearby, by the Persians in 499 BC. It was rebuilt, and Emperor Trajan built the sacred way from Miletus to Didyma. The Jewish historian Josephus tells us that the Romans intervened to guarantee freedom of religion to Jews in Miletus. Miletus was the birthplace of the town-planner Hippodamus, the inventor of the grid pattern for laying out city streets at right angles, which was applied first in Piraeus and Rhodes, and later in the northern part of his native city.

Miletus today

On the hill behind the theatre at Miletus is a ruined **Byzantine castle (2** on the map) from which a view of the area may be obtained. This is helpful because the remains, unlike those in Ephesus, are scattered over a wide area, and areas which were formerly in the Meander delta have been drained, so that the original coastline is only visible when seen from above. Then you can see the peninsula on which the city stood, and the two harbours which the captain of the ship in which Paul was travelling had to choose from when he put in there. **The Theatre Harbour** was where the original Cretan inhabitants settled; the theatre was facing it, to the south-west, where the ticket office now stands. The entrance to the other harbour, east of the theatre, called **Lion Harbour**, was guarded by two marble lions; they still stand, rather weathered, near the earth dyke; the Turkish word for lion is Aslan.

The Theatre, Miletus

The theatre (1) is an imposing one, with a façade of 140 metres (460 feet) and to this day still rising to 30 metres (100 feet) above the plain. The first theatre on the site was built in the fourth century BC, but modified in the time of Emperor Trajan, in the second century AD, in the Roman style, and later enlarged to seat 25,000 people. In the theatre, inscribed on the fifth row of seats, are words which could be translated '[Place] of the Jews and of the God-fearers' or '[Reserved] for the Jews who are also God-fearers.' This reflects the report by Josephus about tolerance for Jews at Miletus.

Excavation has revealed traces

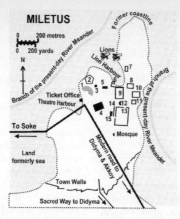

of many buildings, and of the grid pattern of streets, but only the obvious ones are mentioned here. Below the Byzantine castle stands a **heroon (3)**, a monumental tomb to honour an unknown local hero, from the hellenistic period. Paths from the theatre lead to the extensive remains on the right of the path of the **Baths of Faustina (4)**, built on the orders of the wife of Emperor Marcus Aurelius in AD 164, with charming water spouts in the shape of the river god Meander and a small lion.

North of here on the left of the path is the **Byzantine Church of St Michael (5)**, built in the sixth century AD on the site of a temple of Dionysios, easily distinguishable because it is partially roofed over in modern red tiles. The path now leads to the circular plinth which is all that remains of the colossal **Harbour Monument (6)**, probably from 63 BC. The main

building to the north of that is a **Roman baths (7)**, near to the **Lion Harbour**.

There was a colonnade across the head of the bay leading from the harbour monument to the **Delphinion (8)**, a monument dedicated to Apollo in his incarnation as a dolphin; only the base of this remains in the middle of a large square. The harbour gate led from the colonnade into the **northern agora (9)** constructed between the fifth century BC and the third century AD; all three areas are flooded at certain times of year.

The east side of the northern agora is easily distinguished by the reconstructed **Ionic colonnade**, from about AD 50, behind which are remains of a **hellenistic gymnasium (10)** and the **nymphaeum (fountain, 11)** from about AD 79. Facing this across the agora was the **bouleuterion (12)** from between 175 and 164 BC, distinguished by the semi-circular seating for the council members. The massive **Market Gate (13)** from 165 BC, now reconstructed in the Pergamon Museum in Berlin, led from the northern agora to the southern agora which is mostly buried today. However on the west side of the southern agora we can distinguish the foundations of a huge **hellenistic granary (14)**.

The fallen pediment from above the portico of the **Temple of Asklepios or Serapis (15)** is to the south of the granary. Once a year the people of Miletus went in procession from the Delphinion along the **Sacred Way**, leading 20 kilometres (12 miles) south to the Temple of Apollo at Didyma.

Didyma (Didim) was the third largest temple in the ancient world, after Ephesus and Samos. There had been a temple on the site before 1000 BC. Extensive remains, mostly from the hellenistic period, can be visited today; they give an impression of what the temple at Ephesus must have been like. There was a famous oracle there. In around AD 385 a Christian church was built inside the temple and stood until the late Middle Ages. Didyma is now called Yenihisar.

Opening Times
Miletus Tel. 0256 8755562, daily 08.00–18.30 in summer; 08.00–17.30 in winter. Toilets near the ticket office
Didyma Temple of Apollo daily 08.00–18.30. Toilets in the restaurant opposite

Visiting the Aegean coast of Turkey

Bodrum is a centre for the tourist resorts of the Aegean coast of Turkey. Its ancient name was Halikarnassos, its modern name is derived from 'Petrum' because the fort of the Knights Hospitallers there was dedicated to St Peter. It was the site of the 'Mausoleum', the tomb of Mausolus and one of the seven wonders of the ancient world; and the birthplace of the Greek historian Herodotus, whose writings Luke may have used as a model for his Gospel and the Acts of the Apostles.

The coast road north from Bodrum is the D-330 and then the D-525. After crossing the River Meander you pass a sign showing the turning to Milet or **Miletus**, now called Yeniköy or Yeni Balat. Alternatively, continuing north on the D-525 and turning left at Söke you arrive at the seaside resort of **Kuşadasi**. Eighteen kilometres (11 miles) beyond Kuşadasi is the town of **Selçuk**, near the ruins of ancient **Ephesus** or Efes; the main Ephesus Museum is situated in the town. Selçuk is about 177 kilometres (110 miles) north of Bodrum and 80 kilometres (50 miles) by the D-550 or the O-31 (E24) motorway south of İzmir.

15 The Library of Celsus, Ephesus

16 Winged Victory carving, Hercules Gate, Ephesus

17 The Heraion, Samos

18 St Paul's Bay, Rhodes

19 Triumphal gateway, Patara

20 Kali Limones, 'Fair Havens', Crete

21 Statue, St Paul's Island, Malta

22 The tomb of St Peter, the Vatican

23 The Appian Way, near Rome

24 Mosaic, Patmos

25 A shepherd on Patmos

26 Church pillars, Philadelphia

27 The gymnasium, Sardis

Ferries from Bodrum run to Cos (Kos) and from Kusadasi to Samos (Sisam); midway between the two islands is the island of Patmos; although they are so close to Turkey all three islands are part of Greece.

Paul and women

Christian preachers have sometimes given the impression that Paul was opposed to women and sex, largely because they have put their own ideas into his mouth. In Galatians 3:28 he said that 'there is no longer Jew or Greek, there is no longer slave or free, there is no longer male and female; for all of you are one in Christ Jesus'. It must be admitted that passages like 1 Corinthians 14:34–35 (women should keep silence) and 1 Timothy 2:12 (women not to teach) give a negative impression. But the first of these, because it appears at different places in different manuscripts, is probably a later addition and not by Paul; it is contradicted by 1 Corinthians 11:5. Paul gave instructions for specific circumstances; it was not possible to change society overnight, and sudden change in Christian communities would shock their pagan neighbours.

Yet one of the reasons that some scholars think that the first letter which Paul is supposed to have written to Timothy in Ephesus may not be by him is that its teaching on women is so different from that in the letter to the Ephesians. Paul was in fact very progressive for his time, but he used a subtle method of argument. He would quote a commonly held belief, without agreeing or disagreeing, and then show that on the basis of that belief a new approach was needed.

In Ephesians 5:21–32 we see his skill in arguing for mutual submission. The relationship between Adam and Eve was compared with that between Christ and the church. Everyone believed that wives should submit to their husbands because the church must obey Christ. But Jesus sacrificed himself completely for the church, so it follows that husbands must sacrifice themselves, their wishes, their bodies, their time, their possessions, completely to their wives. The old prejudices had been turned on their heads; the change would take centuries to bring about as it gradually dawned on Paul's readers what he was saying.

Mystery religions

The mystery religions by which Paul was surrounded gained their appeal by revealing a secret which, they claimed, explained the purpose of life. A mystery was something which had been a secret but is now revealed. Temples to Mithras, for instance, are found in places as far apart as Caesarea-on-Sea and Britain. Paul, after years of struggling for the acceptance of Gentiles into the people of God, and for unity between Jew and Gentile in the church, realized that God's plan to bring unity to the whole human race through the church, was the 'mystery' which he had to reveal. Therefore unity in the church is not an optional extra, it is the whole purpose of the church's existence as part of God's plan. And this despite all the forces of race, language, politics, sin and refusal to forgive which divide the human race. The Roman empire had tried and failed to unite the world; Paul's task, as he wrote from Rome, was to show the Empire that it could only be done through the love of God in the church; and every Christian's task is to show, by our own life of love, forgiveness, reconciliation, and co-operation with those who are different from us, that God's plan is possible.

Illyricum

During his third missionary journey, probably, and possibly again after his first trial in Rome, Paul visited the province of Illyricum (Romans 15:19). Probably Paul meant by this the cities of **Dyrrhacium** and **Apollonia**, the western termini of the Egnatian Way, where travellers took ship for Brindisi and the Appian Way to Rome. Dyrrhacium had been the capital of the province of Illyricum, but both cities in Paul's day were in the province of Macedonia. Dyrrhacium is modern Durrüs, near Tiranë in

Albania, and Apollonia was about 50 kilometres (32 miles) to the south. At present they are not suitable for visits by tourists.

THE JOURNEY HOME

At the end of his third missionary journey, Paul sailed from Assos, calling at the Greek islands of Mitylene, Chios, Samos, Cos and Rhodes; Miletus (see above in the section under Ephesus) and Patara in present-day Turkey; Tyre (Lebanon); Ptolemais and Caesarea Maritima (Israel), then overland to Jerusalem (Acts 20:14—21:17). The Greek islands are all beautiful, with a wonderful climate, and each has its own unique atmosphere.

Mitylene Μυτιλήνη

Mytilini, as it is now known, is the capital town and port of the island of Lesbos, and the island is often known as Mytilini Island; it is the third largest island in Greece. Many visitors come here for package holidays, trekking or birdwatching, but it is large enough not to seem crowded. Sappho, one of the greatest poets writing in Greek, was born on Lesbos in the fourth century BC. The women of Lesbos enjoyed great independence, and she gathered round her a community of young women who studied music, dance and poetry together. Aristotle and Epicurus also taught philosophy on Lesbos. Paul joined his companions on the ship at Assos

---

The journey home (Acts 20:14–15)

When [Paul] met us in Assos, we took him on board and went to Mitylene. We sailed from there, and on the following day we arrived opposite Chios. The next day we touched at Samos, and the day after that we came to Miletus.

---

and sailed to Mitylene where they appear to have spent at least one night, and possibly changed ships. The town of Mytilini originally stood on an island where the **Byzantine castle** now is, but it is now joined to the mainland. The **ancient harbour** where Paul landed is to the north of this; he will have been able to see the trend-setting **Roman theatre** on the hillside. The **Old Archaeological Museum** contains, among many artefacts from ancient and hellenistic times, some fine terracotta figurines; the **New Archaeological Museum** about 100 metres (110 yards) up the hill behind it has some fine mosaics from Roman times.

There are connections to Mytilini by air and ferry, and buses travel around the island. It is possible to travel by ferry, hydrofoil or catamaran to all but one of the Aegean Islands mentioned in the Bible in a single journey, from Piraeus to Mytilini to Chios to Samos to Cos to Patmos to Rhodes (to Crete) and back again to Piraeus; but in winter the ferries may not run every day on some legs of this route. (For

Samothraki see above under Philippi, and for ferry information websites see under National Tourist Offices: Greece.)

Opening Times
Old Mytilini Archaeological Museum Tel. 0251 22 087, Tuesday to Sunday 08.30–15.00. Toilet on the right in the entrance hall
New Mytilini Archaeological Museum Tel. 0251 40 223, Tuesday to Sunday 08.30–15.00. Toilets on the lower level
Roman theatre and Byzantine castle Tuesday to Sunday 08.30–15.00

Chios Χίος

Chios is a large island between Lesbos and Samos, famed now for shipbuilders, mastic (the original ingredient of chewing gum), and, in the seventh century BC, for its sculptors. It claims to be the birthplace of Homer and had a great shrine to the goddess Cybele. But Paul did not call there, for the Acts of the Apostles tells us that, sailing from Mytilini, the ship carrying the apostolic team arrived on the following day 'opposite Chios'. This probably means somewhere on the coast of Asia Minor, which is as little as 20 kilometres (12 miles) away from Chios.

Opening Times
Chios Archaeological Museum
Tel. 0271 44 239, Tuesday to Sunday 08.30–14.30. Toilets on the left as you enter

Erythrae (Ildır in Turkey)

Erythrae is the most likely place for Paul to have landed 'opposite Chios'. It had a good harbour, protected from storms by some off-shore islands. It was an ancient town where the quiet village of Ildır in Turkey is now situated. From İzmir (see below) it is 88 kilometres (55 miles) along route D-300 or the O-32 motorway to the port of Çeşme; there are ferries to Chios from Çeşme. From here it is about 25 kilometres (15 miles) north through some of the estates of holiday homes which are mushrooming along the Aegean coast, to Ildır. Or you can cut off the corner by going through Kadıavacık; they are all paved roads. Follow the signs to Erythrae up the narrow lanes of Ildır until you reach a small museum. The guardian, who has been there more than twenty-seven years, will direct you to the ancient **theatre**, with an explanatory map and signboard in Turkish, and then on top of the hill to the ruins of a church and a **Temple to Athena**, with a fine view.

Samos Σάμος

Lying to the south-east of Chios, Samos is a much-visited Greek island in the Aegean Sea, often by tourists on their way to or from Turkey, which is only 3 kilometres (two miles) away across the Mykale Straits. It is an attractive island for relaxing or hiking, with sandy beaches, mountain views and unspoilt villages, and it exports orchids and wine. It was the birthplace of Pythagoras and Epicurus among many other distinguished Greek thinkers. The tyrant Polycrates in the sixth century BC gave the Samians a great navy; the **Temple of Hera** (Ηράιον, the Heraion or Ireon, pronounced Ee-**rayon**), 8 kilometres (5 miles) west of Pythagorea, which was included in some old lists of the seven wonders of the world, although as in Ephesus only one pillar remains standing; the 1,200-yard (over a kilometre) long **Eupalinos Tunnel** (Ευπαλινειο Ορυγμα) in Pythagorea, which can still be explored, though it is not recommended for the claustrophobic or those who are large in any direction; and many other building works. The reddish-brown **Samian pottery** found on many Roman archaeological sites was made from Samian earth, a clay found on Samos.

Paul's ship 'touched at' Samos, which probably means they took on supplies but did not go ashore. He and his companions

> ### *Continuing the journey from Miletus (Acts 21:1–7)*
>
> When we had parted from them and set sail, we came by a straight course to Cos, and the next day to Rhodes, and from there to Patara. When we found a ship bound for Phoenicia, we went on board and set sail. We came in sight of Cyprus; and leaving it on our left, we sailed to Syria and landed at Tyre, because the ship was to unload its cargo there. We looked up the disciples and stayed there for seven days. Through the Spirit they told Paul not to go on to Jerusalem. When our days there were ended, we left and proceeded on our journey; and all of them, with wives and children, escorted us outside the city. There we knelt down on the beach and prayed and said farewell to one another. Then we went on board the ship, and they returned home. When we had finished the voyage from Tyre, we arrived at Ptolemais; and we greeted the believers and stayed with them for one day.

probably felt it was too dangerous to go to Ephesus, because there had been a riot there on their last visit, so they sent a message and on the following day met the Ephesian elders at Miletus.

Samos has a busy airport near Pythagorea (Olympic Airways 0273 27 237), and regular ferry services to Piraeus and many of the Greek islands as well as Kuşadasi in Turkey (see Practical Details: Turkey, p. 2). There are three ports: ships from Piraeus and Turkey dock at Samos Town (Βαθύ Vathy), as do those from Chios and islands to the north, sometimes calling first at Karlovasi – don't get off too soon! Ships from Patmos and points south dock at Pythagorio (Πυθαγόρειο) which is probably where Paul called because it was the ancient capital. Some hydrofoils link Vathy to Patmos also.

Opening Times
Samos Archaeological Museum in Vathy Tel. 0273 27 469, Tuesday to Sunday 08.30–15.00. Toilets in the entrance lobby
Eupalinos Tunnel Tuesday to Sunday 08.45–14.45
Hereon Tel. 0273 95 277, Tuesday to Sunday 08.30–15.00. Toilets on the right

Cos Κως

Cos and Rhodes are two of the group of Greek islands which in 1908 were given the title Dodecanese; the word means 'twelve' but there are far more islands than that. Both of them are popular with tourists; both have airports, and share many of the same ferry services. Cos has ferries in summer also to Bodrum in Turkey.
Hippocrates (460–377 BC), the father of medicine and originator of the Hippocratic Oath, was born and lived on

Cos. It was usual in St Paul's day to sail by day and spend the night on land. As he only spent one night in Cos he will not have seen much, but today there are many remains of buildings from his time.

The **west archaeological site**, 400 metres (a quarter of a mile) south of the harbour in Cos town has two fine **Roman streets** at right angles; a large **nymphaeum**; reconstructed pillars from the **hellenistic Xysto**, which was a covered all-weather gymnasium; interesting **mosaics**; a restored **odeon** and a restored third-century AD house called **Casa Romana**, which gives an idea of what a large Roman house must have felt like; much needed repairs are promised 'soon'. Near the medieval castle is the ancient **agora**, with foundations of many buildings, and an ancient **plane tree** where it is said that Hippocrates taught and Paul preached. The large complex called the **asklepion**, 4 kilometres (2½ miles) to the southwest, with a marvellous view from the top, was built in the fourth to the first centuries BC to continue the medical reforms begun by Hippocrates. Between Cos and Rhodes is the island of Patmos (see below under the Seven Churches of the Revelation).

Opening Times
Cos Archaeological Museum
Tel. 0242 28 326, Tuesday to Sunday 08.30–15.00
Asklepion Tel. 0242 28 763,

Tuesday to Sunday 08.30–15.00. Toilets on the right of the entrance
Casa Romana Tel. 0242 23234, Tuesday to Sunday 08.30–15.00

Rhodes Ρόδος

The island of Rhodes is one of the most popular tourist destinations in the Mediterranean, with sandy beaches and year-round sunshine. At the end of the fourth century BC a 32-metre (105-feet) high bronze statue of Helios Apollo was built to commemorate the successful survival of a siege, and known as **The Colossus of Rhodes**. The belief that it stood astride the harbour is now disputed. It only stood for sixty-five years anyway, from 280 to 244 BC, before collapsing in an earthquake, but Paul could have seen it lying in the sea at the entrance to the harbour, where it remained for nearly 900 years. The colourful and complex history of Rhodes has left it, in the **Old Town of Rhodes**, the largest inhabited walled medieval town in Europe, with Byzantine, Turkish and Latin architecture side by side. On the acropolis, in the new town section of Rhodes City, is a **Temple of Apollo**, and at its foot are an impressively restored **theatre** and **stadium**; they are open at all times.

There are three ancient cities on the island of Rhodes. **Ialyssos** has an acropolis with the foundations of an ancient temple next to later Christian remains. **Kamiros** has the foundations of a large area of the hellenistic city rebuilt in 226 BC, which give a good idea of town planning and the layout of houses at the time. The spectacular acropolis of **Lindos**, with sheer cliffs to the sea, is the stage for a hellenistic temple of Athena, with an interesting carving nearby of a trireme battleship from the second century BC. Like many sites in the Dodecanese it was restored in the 1930s using inferior materials and is now undergoing a programme of repairs. It overlooks St Paul's Bay, to the south, with a chapel dedicated to St Paul, which is probably where he landed. Again, Paul only stayed one night. Ialyssos is only 10 kilometres (6 miles) from the town of Rhodes; Lindos is 47 kilometres (29 miles) south of Rhodes city, on the east coast of the island; Kamiros is 34 kilometres (21 miles) down the west coast. Rhodes airport (Olympic Airways Tel. 0241 24 571) has national and international flights, and there are ferries to the other Dodecanese islands, Marmaris, Piraeus, Crete and Cyprus.

Opening Times
Rhodes City archaeological museum Tel. 0241 27 657, Tuesday to Sunday 08.30–15.00. Toilets on the left of the entrance courtyard
Ialyssos Acropolis Tel. 0241 92 202, Tuesday to Sunday 08.30–17.00 in winter;

08.30–18.00 in summer. Enquire at the kiosk outside about toilets
Kamiros archaeological site Tel. 0241 40 037, Tuesday to Sunday 08.30–14.40 in winter; 08.30–18.00 in summer. For toilets turn right at the ticket office
Lindos Acropolis Tuesday to Sunday 08.30–14.40 in winter; 08.00–19.40 in summer. In summer only Monday 12.30–18.30. Toilets down the steps outside the entrance beside the snack bar

Patara (Gelemiş, Turkey)

A magnificent 20-kilometre (12-mile) long stretch of hot white sand on the western Mediterranean coast of Turkey, Patara is mostly visited by young people coming to enjoy a beach holiday. But in biblical times it was the main port for, and the capital of, the independent Lycian Federation, and then the Roman province of Lycia, later amalgamated with Pamphylia, and there are extensive archaeological remains. When he was heading home at the end of his third missionary journey, Paul did not use the ports of Attalia and Perga, as on his first journey, because there was a better chance of getting a boat to the province of Syria from the large harbour at Patara. What was once the **harbour** is now a swamp. Over the centuries the remains at Patara have been covered in sand, and they are only partially excavated.

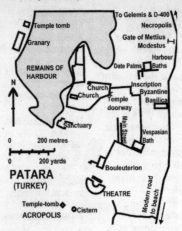

The first thing you see as you enter the site from the north is a group of **tombs** raised above the ground. These are distinctively Lycian, but there are many tombs of different types all over the site: the Lycians liked to keep their dead in the city with them. Then you reach the triple arched **triumphal gateway** dating from about AD 100. It was built to honour Mettius Modestus, the first governor of the combined province of Lycia and Pamphylia. Close to the road on the right are the **harbour baths**, dated some time after AD 50. They stand beside an ancient group of **date palms**, which may be the direct descendants of the date palm in Patara which was linked with the birth of Apollo. Next comes a large **Byzantine basilica** from the sixth century AD, and then there are some **baths** with

an inscription honouring Emperor Vespasian, who ruled from AD 69–79. An earth track leads to the impressive **theatre**. Some of the sand and vegetation has recently been removed, revealing the seating and the stage buildings. A long inscription by the entrance refers to the embellishment of the theatre in 147, but other inscriptions show that it was rebuilt during the reign of Emperor Tiberius (AD 14–37) so it must have been first built on the hellenistic model.

North of the theatre is a large building, identified as a **bouleuterion**, possibly for the parliament of the Lycian Federation in Hellenistic times. The field to the east of this could be the site of the **agora**. North of here there is a 12.6 metre (41 feet) wide section of the **main street**, 98 metres (over a hundred yards) long before it disappears into the marsh. Nearby a unique **inscription** was found giving the distances to all the other cities in Lycia. Buildings to the north from here include a decorated **temple doorway** 6.6 metres (22 feet) high, and various other walls and churches. On the west of the harbour among the sand dunes is a large **granary** with an inscription honouring Emperor Trajan in the second century AD, and an elaborate **temple tomb**. The **acropolis** behind the theatre has an ancient **cistern** for water storage during an attack, and a **Roman temple-tomb**. A visit to the archaeological site can be followed by a relaxing time on Patara beach, where at certain times of the year giant turtles come up from the sea to lay their eggs.

Sixty-three kilometres (40 miles) south of Fethiye, on route D–400 in the direction towards Antalya, is the town of Kınık, and 7 kilometres (4 miles) further south is the village of Ovaköy. Just east of here is a side road turning off to the south, signposted to Patara. The village of Gelemiş, commonly called Patara, is 3½ kilometres (2 miles) along this road, and the archaeological site is a further 1½ kilometres or one mile from there. Then it is another kilometre, less than a mile, to the beach; camping is not allowed. (For Myra,

approximately 50 kilometres to the east, see below under the Journey to Rome.)

Opening Times
Patara archaeological site
daily 07.30–19.00 May to October; 08.00–17.30 November to April. The beach closes at dusk, and the same admission ticket covers both and lasts for several days

Tyre (Sour, Lebanon)

At the time of writing it is quite safe to travel around most of Lebanon; Tyre is in the south of the country on the Mediterranean coast, so one avoids the area near the border with Israel. (See above under Practical Details: Lebanon.) The modern town lies on the north, and the archaeological sites are around the old town to the west. The old port and the Christian quarter are to the south. Now called Sour, it was founded by the Phoenician sea traders as a satellite to Sidon (see below) and soon overshadowed it. Tyrian purple dye, made from the murex shell, became a mark of the clothes worn by royalty and the imperial household; Lydia in Philippi was a dealer in purple-dyed cloth. Hiram king of Tyre helped King David to build a palace (2 Samuel 5:11) and sent wood and gold to help King Solomon build the Temple in Jerusalem (1 Kings 5:1, 10:11). The old town of Tyre is built partly on an island; Alexander the Great captured it in 332 BC by building a causeway from the mainland.

The municipal buildings and magnificent tombs of the city which Paul knew have been excavated. The archaeological remains are on three sites, one on the south of the old peninsula, with **colonnades**, **baths** and **mosaics**; the second a five-minute walk to the north of the first, and the third twenty minutes' walk in a landward direction to the east. The third has a **columned road**; the **Roman necropolis** with decorated tombs; a **monumental arch**; an **aqueduct**; and the largest **hippodrome** for chariot races in the world, which would have seated over 20,000 people.

Paul and his companions landed here after sailing for about 650 kilometres (400 miles) from Patara and passing Cyprus. From Tyre, Paul went to Ptolemais, Caesarea and then on to Jerusalem.

Opening Times
Area 1 (Al-Mina) daily
08.00–19.00 in summer;
08.00–17.00 in winter
Area 2 not at present open to visitors, but visible from the road
Area 3 (Al-Bass) daily
08.00–19.00 in summer;
08.00–17.00 in winter

Sidon (Saida, Lebanon)

Sidon is a port, about 110 kilometres or 70 miles north of Caesarea-on-Sea, which St Paul called at when he sailed, under arrest, on his journey to Rome (see below). But as it is on the Mediterranean coast of Lebanon north of Tyre it is convenient to describe them both together. Often mentioned together with Tyre in the Old Testament, it is now called Saida. It is charmingly situated amid banana and citrus trees, 41 kilometres (25 miles) south of Beirut, and the Old City is a maze of narrow, vaulted shopping streets or souqs. It was founded by the Phoenicians, a race of people who were competent sailors and traded all round the Mediterranean. It remained important under the Persians, Greeks and Romans, and glass was a major export. Its gardens were famous, but there is nothing to see now from biblical times. Stones from the harbour were used by the crusaders to build the **sea castle** and the **Castle of St Louis**. Five kilometres (3 miles) to the north-east is the Phoenician **temple of Echmoun**. The magnificent sarcophagi from the royal tombs are in the İstanbul Archaeological Museum.

Opening Times
Sea castle daily 09.00–18.00 in summer; 09.00–16.00 in winter
Castle of St Louis and the **Temple at Echmoun** always open

The Journey to Rome

The enemies of the Christian movement accused Paul of rejecting the law of Moses, so to show that he still considered it binding on Jewish Christians he paid for some of them to complete the Nazirite vow in the Temple and joined them in the ceremony (Acts 21:17–26; Numbers 6:1–21). But some Jews who had followed him from the province of Asia accused him of bringing non-Jews into the Jewish part of the Temple and provoked a riot. Paul was arrested by the Roman soldiers and taken into the Antonia Fortress, but he got permission to speak to the crowd about his loyalty to Judaism, and gave an account of his conversion. When the Roman tribune discovered Paul was a Roman citizen, he ordered the Jewish council, the Sanhedrin, to appear before him and lay charges against Paul, but Paul provoked a disagreement between the Pharisees and Sadducees in the council over the subject of resurrection. That night some Jews plotted to kill Paul, but Paul's nephew heard of it and warned the tribune, who decided to send Paul for safety to Caesarea-on-Sea for trial before Felix, the governor of the province of Judea (Acts 22–23). This was the beginning of the final journey reported in Acts, the journey to Rome.

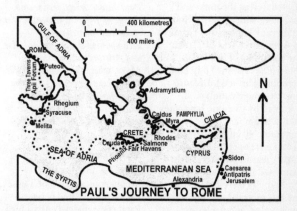

PAUL'S JOURNEY TO ROME

The dividing wall of partition

St Paul, in Ephesians 2:14, may have been referring to the wall in the Jerusalem Temple between the Court of the Gentiles and the Court of Israel, when he wrote of Christ having 'broken down the dividing wall, that is, the hostility between' Jew and Gentile. It was probably the suspicion that Paul had taken Trophimus, a Gentile from Ephesus, past that wall that caused the riot described in Acts 21:27. An example of the stones from that wall bearing an inscription in Greek, Latin and Hebrew has been found, and is in the Topkapi museum in İstanbul. It reads,

> No foreigner may enter within the barricade which surrounds the Temple and its enclosure. Anyone who is caught doing so will only have himself to blame for the consequence, which will be his death.

Overland to Caesarea, and the appeal to the emperor

The Roman military escort started during the night and travelling with a guard of foot soldiers 68 kilometres (42 miles) to Antipatris (Acts 23:31; see the beginning of this book under Places in the Holy Land mentioned in Acts). Because this was rough country, occupied by patriotic Jews, they feared an ambush. The remaining 40 kilometres (25 miles) were open and flat, and mostly gentile country, so they dismissed the foot soldiers, and Paul rapidly travelled the rest of the way escorted only by cavalry. In Caesarea he was tried by Felix, the governor of Syria, because at that time Paul's home town in Cilicia was part of the province of Syria (Acts 24). Felix had married Drusilla, one of the Herodian

royal family. Felix made no decision, and during the frustrating two years detention in Caesarea, some scholars believe Paul may have written some of the 'captivity epistles', and Luke may have taken the opportunity to research accurate details for his Gospel. Felix was recalled to Rome to answer for his mismanagement, and when the new governor Porcius Festus arrived, he too tried Paul, with a second hearing in the presence of King Herod Agrippa II and his sister Princess Bernice (Acts 25–26). Paul exercised his right as a Roman citizen to claim trial in Rome before an imperial court.

BY SEA TO MYRA (TURKEY)

Paul, under arrest, was sent in charge of Julius, a centurion of the Augustan cohort, and accompanied by his friends Luke and Aristarchus, in a ship to Myra, where they could transfer to another ship bound for Rome. (For Adramyttium see above under Troas; for Sidon see above under Paul's Third Missionary Journey.)

Myra (Demre)

Demre is on the west Mediterranean coast of Turkey, and is often visited between Patara (see under Paul's Third Missionary Journey above) and Antalya (see under The Gateway to Galatia above) along route D-400. It is 30 kilometres (20 miles) south-west of Finike, and 182 kilometres (114 miles)

Outline family tree of all the Herods
mentioned in the New Testament

(There were many more wives and offspring than there is space for here)

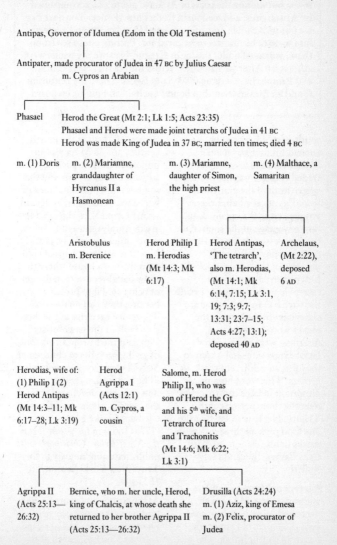

Antipas, Governor of Idumea (Edom in the Old Testament)

Antipater, made procurator of Judea in 47 BC by Julius Caesar
m. Cypros an Arabian

Phasael   Herod the Great (Mt 2:1; Lk 1:5; Acts 23:35)
           Phasael and Herod were made joint tetrarchs of Judea in 41 BC
           Herod was made King of Judea in 37 BC; married ten times; died 4 BC

m. (1) Doris   m. (2) Mariamne,   m. (3) Mariamne,   m. (4) Malthace, a
                granddaughter of   daughter of Simon,   Samaritan
                Hyrcanus II a   the high priest
                Hasmonean

                Aristobulus   Herod Philip I   Herod Antipas,   Archelaus,
                m. Berenice   m. Herodias   'The tetrarch',   (Mt 2:22),
                                    (Mt 14:3; Mk   also m. Herodias,   deposed
                                    6:17)   (Mt 14:1; Mk   6 AD
                                                       6:14, 7:15; Lk 3:1,
                                                       19; 7:3; 9:7;
                                                       13:31; 23:7–15;
                                                       Acts 4:27; 13:1);
                                                       deposed 40 AD

Herodias, wife of: Herod   Salome, m. Herod
(1) Philip I (2)   Agrippa I   Philip II, who was
Herod Antipas   (Acts 12:1)   son of Herod the Gt
(Mt 14:3–11; Mk   m. Cypros, a   and his 5th wife, and
6:17–28; Lk 3:19)   cousin   Tetrarch of Iturea
                                     and Trachonitis
                                     (Mt 14:6; Mk 6:22;
                                     Lk 3:1)

Agrippa II   Bernice, who m. her uncle, Herod,   Drusilla (Acts 24:24)
(Acts 25:13—   king of Chalcis, at whose death she   m. (1) Aziz, king of Emesa
26:32)   returned to her brother Agrippa II   m. (2) Felix, procurator of
                 (Acts 25:13—26:32)   Judea

> ### The first stage of Paul's journey to Rome (Acts 27:1–6)
>
> Embarking on a ship of Adramyttium that was about to set sail to the ports along the coast of Asia, we put to sea, accompanied by Aristarchus, a Macedonian from Thessalonica. The next day we put in at Sidon; and Julius treated Paul kindly, and allowed him to go to his friends to be cared for. Putting out to sea from there, we sailed under the lee of Cyprus, because the winds were against us. After we had sailed across the sea that is off Cilicia and Pamphylia, we came to Myra in Lycia. There the centurion found an Alexandrian ship bound for Italy and put us on board.

south-east of Fethiye. In ancient times it was named Myra, from the myrrh spice traded there; it was the port where most of the grain boats from Egypt called after their voyage across the open sea, to take advantage of the shelter of the Greek islands for the rest of their journey to Rome. It is notable for the Lycian **rock-hewn tombs**, carved to resemble wooden houses, beside the **theatre**. In the theatre are some **carvings** showing the masks worn by the actors; distances were too great for facial expressions to be seen so they put on a different mask, or *persona*. This word became important in later controversies over the three persons of the Trinity: Is it true to say that the one God puts on three different masks in his relationship with us as Father, Son and Holy Spirit?

No visit to Myra is complete without seeing, in a church protected by an ugly iron roof near the centre of Demre, the **tomb of St Nicholas**, who was Bishop of Myra in the fourth century AD. As Myra was an important port he became the patron saint of sailors, and the tomb is empty because most of his bones were stolen by Italian seamen from Bari, though a few are in Antalya museum. Among many other legends, he is said to have thrown three bags of gold secretly into a house where the three daughters were in danger of being sold into prostitution because they had no dowry. This story gave rise to the three gold balls of the pawnbroker's sign, and the European custom of giving presents to children on St Nicholas' day, December 6. (The Santa Claus story, however, was developed from the Saint Nicholas traditions by Clement Clarke Moore (1779–1863) in his poem *'Twas the Night Before Christmas*, published anonymously in the Troy [New York] Sentinel in 1823.)

At the turning off route D-400 leading to the town centre of Demre, a sign reads 'Baba Noel 1, Myra 3'. The Church of St

Myra Rock Tombs, G. Niemann 1881

Nicholas is on a pedestrian street just west of the main square, but the only way to get to the car park is on your way back through the town after visiting Myra.

Opening Times
Rock tombs and theatre daily 07.30–19.00 May to October; 08.00–17.30 November to April. Toilets on the right after the ticket booth
Church of St Nicholas daily 09.00–19.00. Toilets on the left after the ticket booth

Alexandria (Egypt)

St Paul, his companions and the military escort transferred at Myra onto a ship bringing grain from Alexandria to Italy. Alexandria on the Nile delta was the chief port of Egypt. Since at least the time of Joseph the fertile mud of the Nile has produced ample grain for most countries of the Mediterranean, and the Roman Empire was dependent on the regular sailings of the fleet of cargo vessels from Alexandria. It was a great intellectual centre, where Euclid wrote about geometry and Ptolemy drew his maps. Alexandria had a famous library, claiming to have translations of works from every language. It was for this library that seventy-two Hebrew scholars are supposed to have translated the Old Testament into Greek, producing what we know, from the Greek word for 'seventy', as the Septuagint. This is the version from which the New Testament writers often quote, as the Gentiles, and some of the Jews of the dispersion, were unable to read the Hebrew scriptures. Philo (c.15 BC–AD 50) was a Jewish philosopher in Alexandria who interpreted Judaism in terms of Greek philosophy, and Apollos of Alexandria (Acts 17:24; 1 Corinthians 3:4) will have been under similar influences.

The Pharos or lighthouse at Alexandria was one of the seven wonders of the ancient world. The list of these commonly accepted today consists of the Statue of Zeus at Olympia, The Temple of Artemis at Ephesus, the Hanging Gardens of Babylon, the Mausoleum at Halicarnassus, the Colossus of Rhodes, the Great Pyramids in Egypt, and the Pharos at Alexandria. Stones from the Pharos were used in building **Fort Qaitbey** in 1480 on the same site between the western and eastern harbours. The only parts of Roman Alexandria still visible are the **Roman amphitheatre** (Kom al-Dikka) near the railway station, and the **Catacombs of Kom ash-Shuqqafa** in the south-west.

Opening Times
Roman amphitheatre daily 09.00–16.00.
Catacombs of Kom ash-Shuqqafa daily 08.30–16.00
Graeco-Roman museum Tel. 483 6434, daily 09.00–16.00

THE LETTER TO THE HEBREWS

This New Testament book is not, as the older translations suggested, by Paul; it proclaims the gospel in terms which would be understood by Alexandrian Jews, with their emphasis on Moses and angels, and could even have been by Apollos. It assumes a thorough knowledge of the Old Testament in the Greek translation, and uses the sacrifices in the Jerusalem Temple as a metaphor to explain the effects of the death of Christ on the cross.

A Summary of the Letter

1:1—2:9 God has spoken through Jesus, who is more important than the angels. 2:10–18 Jesus became like us, so that his suffering might be a sacrifice of atonement. 3:1—4:13 Jesus is greater than Moses; therefore do not reject God's offer of eternal rest, as the followers of Moses did. 4:14—5:10 Jesus is a high priest, not of the family of Aaron but like Melchizedek (Genesis 14:17). 5:11—6:20 Persistence leads to hope. 7:1–28 A priest for ever like Melchizedek. 7:1–13 Mediator of a new covenant. 9:1–22 Like Plato's 'ideas', there is a perfect sanctuary in heaven, of which the Temple at Jerusalem is an imperfect copy. 9:23—10:39 In the heavenly sanctuary the sacrifice of Jesus on the cross is accepted to remove the sins of all people. 11:1—12:13 Examples of faith. 12:14–29 Do not reject God's grace. 13:1–19 The Christian way of life. 3:20–25 Final greetings.

SAILING INTO DANGER: CNIDUS (TURKEY)

The ship carrying Paul hugged the coast for a while as the seasonal winds were against them, then sailed to Fair Havens in Crete. They tried to move on to the port of Phoenix but were caught by a gale and blown about in the Mediterranean until they were shipwrecked on the coast of Malta.

Cnidus (Turkey)

Ancient Knidos stood at the tip of a promontory of Asia Minor projecting far into the Aegean Sea between the islands of Cos (Kos) and Rhodes (Rodos); in modern Turkish the peninsula is called Reşadiye Yarimadasi. Part of the city was on an island connected to the shore by a narrow strip of land, creating two harbours, one commercial and the other naval. The winds

The story of the shipwreck, told by Luke, a survivor (Acts 27:7–44)

We sailed slowly for a number of days and arrived with difficulty off Cnidus, and as the wind was against us, we sailed under the lee of Crete off Salmone. Sailing past it with difficulty, we came to a place called Fair Havens, near the city of Lasea. Since much time had been lost and sailing was now dangerous, because even the Fast had already gone by, Paul advised them, saying, 'Sirs, I can see that the voyage will be with danger and much heavy loss, not only of the cargo and the ship, but also of our lives.' But the centurion paid more attention to the pilot and to the owner of the ship than to what Paul said. Since the harbour was not suitable for spending the winter, the majority was in favour of putting to sea from there, on the chance that somehow they could reach Phoenix, where they could spend the winter. It was a harbour of Crete, facing southwest and northwest. When a moderate south wind began to blow, they thought they could achieve their purpose; so they weighed anchor and began to sail past Crete, close to the shore. But soon a violent wind, called the northeaster, rushed down from Crete. Since the ship was caught and could not be turned head-on into the wind, we gave way to it and were driven. By running under the lee of a small island called Cauda we were scarcely able to get the ship's boat under control. After hoisting it up they took measures to undergird the ship; then, fearing that they would run on the Syrtis, they lowered the sea anchor and so were driven. We were being pounded by the storm so violently that on the next day they began to throw the cargo overboard, and on the third day with their own hands they threw the ship's tackle overboard. When neither sun nor stars appeared for many days, and no small tempest raged, all hope of our being saved was at last abandoned. Since they had been without food for a long time, Paul then stood up among them and said, 'Men, you should have listened to me and not have set sail from Crete and thereby avoided this damage and loss. I urge you now to keep up your courage, for there will be no loss of life among you, but only of the ship. For last night there stood by me an angel of the God to whom I belong and whom I worship, and he said, "Do not be afraid, Paul; you must stand before the emperor; and indeed, God has granted safety to all those who are sailing with you." So keep up your courage, men, for I have faith in God that it will be exactly as I have been told. But we will have to run aground on some island.'

When the fourteenth night had come, as we were drifting across the sea of Adria, about midnight the sailors suspected that they were nearing land. So they took soundings and found twenty fathoms; a little farther on they took soundings again and found fifteen fathoms. Fearing that we might run on the rocks, they let down four anchors from the stern and prayed for day to come.

But when the sailors tried to escape from the ship and had lowered the boat into the sea, on the pretext of putting out anchors from the bow, Paul said to the centurion and the soldiers, 'Unless these men stay in the ship, you cannot be saved.' Then the soldiers cut away the ropes of the boat and set it adrift. Just before daybreak, Paul urged all of them to take some food, saying, 'Today is the fourteenth day that you have been in suspense and remaining without food, having eaten nothing. Therefore I urge you to take some food, for it will help you survive; for none of you will lose a hair from your heads.' After he had said this, he took bread; and giving thanks to God in the presence of all, he broke it and began to eat. Then all of them were encouraged and took food for themselves. (We were in all two hundred seventy-six persons in the ship.) After they had satisfied their hunger, they lightened the ship by throwing the wheat into the sea.

In the morning they did not recognize the land, but they noticed a bay with a beach, on which they planned to run the ship ashore, if they could. So they cast off the anchors and left them in the sea. At the same time they loosened the ropes that tied the steering-oars; then hoisting the foresail to the wind, they made for the beach. But striking a reef, they ran the ship aground; the bow stuck and remained immovable, but the stern was being broken up by the force of the waves. The soldiers' plan was to kill the prisoners, so that none might swim away and escape; but the centurion, wishing to save Paul, kept them from carrying out their plan. He ordered those who could swim to jump overboard first and make for the land, and the rest to follow, some on planks and others on pieces of the ship. And so it was that all were brought safely to land.

change as ships round the point, so many had to put in there to wait for a change in the wind direction. From Marmaris, a busy resort to which tourists are attracted by the beaches and the mountains, a spectacular mountain road leads 78 kilometres (49 miles) to Datça. Roadworks are underway at the time of writing, but when these are complete a paved road will run almost as far as Knidos, which is 34 kilometres (21 miles) from Datça. However the final section, 5½ kilometres or 3½ miles of earth road, is very narrow and precipitous; unless you have a four-wheel drive vehicle or an intrepid driver, or are prepared to walk it, you had best ask the captain of one of the boats in Datça harbour to take you to Knidos – excursions run daily in summer.

The ruins at Knidos are spread over the peninsula. Near the ticket booth is a **hellenistic theatre** modified in Roman times, and next to that a **Temple of Dionysios**; further up the hill is a **Temple of Aphrodite**, which was famous for the nude statue carved by Praxitiles, and destroyed by the Byzantines, and notorious for the sacred prostitutes associated with the cult. The **Lion of Knidos** is a 7½-ton sculpture from between about 350–200 BC now displayed in the new Great Court of the British Museum in London; portions of the Temple of Artemis from Ephesus and the Mausoleum from Halicarnassus (Bodrum) are also in the British Museum.

Paul's ship would only have travelled as far north as this in order to avoid being blown onto the island of Rhodes if it passed too close. Then it had to tack a long way south.

Opening times
Ruins at Knidos always open. Toilets in the restaurant near the ticket booth
British Museum Monday to Wednesday 10.00–17.30;

Thursday to Friday 10.00–20.30; Saturday to Sunday 10.00–17.30
Great Court Monday to Wednesday 09.00–21.00; Thursday to Saturday 09.00–23.00; Sunday 09.00–18.00, http://www.thebritishmuseum.ac.uk

Loutro (Phoenix), Crete

CRETE (KRITI Κρήτη, GREECE)

The large island of Crete lies in the Mediterranean Sea facing the mouth of the Aegean Sea. It is a popular place for tourists (for practical details of visiting Crete today, see under Greece). In the summer, the resorts on the north coast receive a quarter of all Greece's tourists. As well as the sun, the beaches, the local culture and the wild flowers, the ancient Minoan site at Knossos attracts many visitors to the island.

The history of Crete

Features of Neolithic culture (7000–3000 BC) survived in the early Minoan period in Crete (3000–2100 BC), but in the Middle Minoan period (2100–1500 BC) an advanced

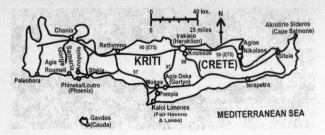

culture developed, revealed by some stunning frescoes seen in the Archaeological Museum in Heraklion (Iraklio, known as Candia during the Venetian occupation AD 1210–1898). Four great palaces were destroyed around 1500 BC, but that at Knossos was rebuilt in the late Minoan period (1500–1100 BC). Its ruins were controversially but vividly reconstructed in the early twentieth century.

According to legend the minotaur, half-man and half-bull, was imprisoned in the labyrinth which Daedalus built at Knossos, and required a yearly sacrifice of seven youths and seven maidens from Athens. Daedalus made wings with which he and his son Icarus could escape from the labyrinth but Icarus flew too close to the sun and fell into the sea. Ariadne, the daughter of King Minos, gave Theseus, prince of Athens, a ball of thread to find his way through the labyrinth and kill the minotaur, but he abandoned her on the island of Naxos.

Inscriptions in Crete are in two scripts known as Linear A and Linear B; the Mycenaean Linear B, an ancestor of the Greek language, has been deciphered, but Linear A is still a mystery.

People from Crete were present in Jerusalem on the Day of Pentecost (Acts 2:11) and Paul's ship called there on his voyage to Rome.

Places mentioned in the shipwreck story

Cape Salmone is the headland at the north-east of Crete, now called Akrotirio Sideros.

Fair Havens is the English translation of Kalolimonias; Kali Limones (Καλι Λιμόνες) is still the name of a small bay about halfway along the south coast of Crete. The harbour was not suitable for spending the winter, and just beyond it the coast turns northward, exposing the ship to the strong north-west wind. The fast referred to in Acts 27:9 is the Day of Atonement, Yom Kippur, which falls after the middle of September which is considered the last safe time for navigation. A small chapel stands on the promontory to the west of the harbour of Kali Limones, dedicated to St Paul because it is believed he preached there. It is still a good natural harbour, but not so beautiful since the largest of the islands which shelter the entrance has been covered by large oil storage tanks, though fortunately not the one known as St Paul's Island.

Lasea or Lasaia was the city for which Fair Havens served as a harbour. At the east end of the beach at Kali Limones there is an ancient breakwater leading to a small island about 100 metres (yards) off shore. The centre of Lasea is considered to have been on top of the cliffs at this point; there has been no official excavation but a survey has shown the site of a temple, a church and the walls of houses.

Gortyna (Γόρτυνα) or Gortys, in Roman times, was the capital of the combined province of Crete and Cyrenaica, and it is believed that Paul preached there and appointed his companion Titus as the first bishop of Crete (Paul's letter to Titus 1:5). The sixth century AD basilica there is dedicated to St Titus. You can take the bus (eight daily) from Bus Station B, by the Hania gate in Iraklio towards the Minoan site of Phaestos, but get off at Agii Deka (Αγιοι Δέκα), where the remains of Gortyna are situated.

There are no buses to Fair Havens; to drive there follow the signs from Iraklio towards Mires (Μόιρες), but after passing Agii Deka look for the excavations of Gortyna on both sides of the road; the basilica is by the ticket office on the north side of the road. About 6 kilometres (4 miles) further on at Mires look out for signs to the left (south) to Kali Limenes. It is a wide road most of the way, though with steep sections and sharp bends.

Phoenix was a city standing on a promontory jutting into the sea about 60 kilometres (40 miles) east of Fair Havens, providing two harbours, one on each side of the promontory. It would have made an ideal port to winter in, but the ship carrying Paul failed to reach it. Today the scant remains of Phoenix are a jumble of stones on top of the ridge, and the tiny modern resort of Loutro has been built in the eastern harbour, but no road leads to it.

To get there today, on highway 90 (E75) about midway between Rethymno and Chania take a turning signposted something like Vrisses (Βρισης) – there are variant spellings. From there follow signs for Sfakia or Chora Sfakion (Χώρα Σφακίων) for a spectacular drive on a winding road over the mountains. From Sfakia there are boats to Loutro. A hiker's path from the Samaria Gorge and Agia Roumeli to Hora Sfakion passes Loutro. Or you can drive up an even more winding road to Anapolis and walk down an extremely steep path to Loutro – allow up to two hours each way for the scramble. There are buses from Chania to Sfakia and Anapolis, enquire at the bus station.

Cauda is a small island approximately 40 kilometres (25 miles) south of Crete, and the southernmost place in Europe; its modern name is Gavdos.

Boats
From Sfakia: Captain 'Giannis' Tel. 0825 91261 or 91028. To Loutro in winter: Mondays, Wednesdays and Fridays, in summer four times a day. To Gavdos Island summer weekends only day trips at 09.30 returning at 16.00
From Paleohora: Interkreta Tourism and Travel Tel. 0823 41 393/888, in summer daily at 09.30 via Sougia, Agia Roumeli, and Loutro to Hora Sfakion returning at 12.30. To Gavdos Island all year Monday and Thursday at 08.30, weather permitting; in summer Monday, Tuesday and Thursday at 08.30

The Syrtis is the old name for the Gulf of Syrte or Sirt, stretching from Leptis Magna to Benghazi on the coast of Libya, which has many dangerous sandbanks and shoals on which a ship could run aground in a storm.

Getting around on Crete
Buses leave the Astoria Hotel on Plateia Eleftherias in Iraklio for the airport, east of the city.

They leave bus station A near the harbour every ten minutes for Knossos, 5 kilometres (3 miles) southeast of Iraklio on National Road 99. Every half hour a bus leaves bus station A in Iraklio for the two and a half hour, 145 kilometres (90 miles) journey west along coastal highway 90 (E75) to the city of Hani or Chania, which also has its own airport 14 kilometres (8 miles) away on the Akrotiri peninsula. It is a Venetian city, and the base for those who wish to trek down the Samaria Gorge.

Opening times
Iraklio Archaeological Museum on Xanthoudidou Street, Tel. 081 226 092, Tuesday to Sunday 08.00–19.00; Monday 12.30–19.00. Toilets beneath the café at the end of the terrace
Knossos Tel. 081 231 940, daily 08.00–17.00. Toilets turn left at the entrance
Gortyna Tel. 081 226 092, daily November to March 08.00–19.00; April to May 08.00–18.00; June to October 08.00–19.00. Toilets through the snack bar

SHIPWRECKED ON MALTA

The popular holiday destination of Malta is an island lying in the Mediterranean south of Sicily, with sunny beaches and rolling hills. First settled in Neolithic times, Malta became part of the empire of Carthage. It was captured by the Romans in 218 BC and named Melita. Since then it

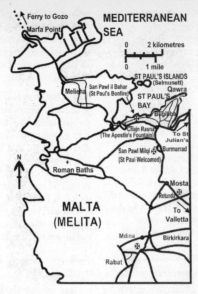

has been ruled by Byzantines, *Arabs, Normans, Moors and Spaniards. The Knights Hospitallers controlled it from 1530, and it was part of the British empire from 1814 until 1964. It was awarded the George Cross for its resistance to German attack from 1940 to 1942. Now it is an independent republic, with a population of mixed Italian, British and Phoenician origin. When St Paul was shipwrecked there on his way to Rome, he was well treated by the islanders and put on another ship which would take them to the Italian port of Puteoli. Luke correctly gives the title of Publius, whose father Paul healed: contemporary inscriptions show his official title was the 'first' or 'leading' man of the island.*

Getting to Malta

Malta is served by international airlines flying into Luqa airport (Tel. 249600, 697800), and there are car ferries into Valletta from Catania and Syracuse in Sicily, Reggio Calabria and Naples in Italy, as well as a passenger service by catamaran from the Sicilian ports of Licata, Catania and Pozzallo. There are ferries from Valletta to the nearby islands of Comoria and Gozo.

Malta today

It has been suggested that 'Melita' in fact refers to an island of the same name off the Dalmatian coast, but it is hard to see in that case why they went to the west coast of Italy to

Church of St Paul Welcomed, Malta

get to Rome. The 'Sea of Adria' (Acts 27:28) included the modern Adriatic, which was then called the Gulf of Adria, but also stretched from Sicily to Crete and from Venice to North Africa. **St Paul's Bay** in Malta is on the north coast of the island about 13 kilometres (8 miles) northwest of Valletta, and can be reached by taxi or bus. The south shore of the bay is occupied by the tourist resort of **Buġibba**, pronounced 'bujibba'.

James Smith, a mariner of Jordanhill, near Glasgow, who published in 1848 a book called *The Voyage and Shipwreck of St Paul*, believed that Paul's ship ran aground trying to negotiate the narrow channel between the mainland and the small island called in English St Paul's Island and known to the Maltese as **Selmunett**, at the north-west end of the bay. On

---

Paul is shipwrecked on Malta (Acts 27:1–11)

After we had reached safety, we then learned that the island was called Malta. The natives showed us unusual kindness. Since it had begun to rain and was cold, they kindled a fire and welcomed all of us around it. Paul had gathered a bundle of brushwood and was putting it on the fire, when a viper, driven out by the heat, fastened itself on his hand. When the natives saw the creature hanging from his hand, they said to one another, 'This man must be a murderer; though he has escaped from the sea, justice has not allowed him to live.' He, however, shook off the creature into the fire and suffered no harm. They were expecting him to swell up or drop dead, but after they had waited a long time and saw that nothing unusual had happened to him, they changed their minds and began to say that he was a god. Now in the neighbourhood of that place were lands belonging to the leading man of the island, named Publius, who received us and entertained us hospitably for three days. It so happened that the father of Publius lay sick in bed with fever and dysentery. Paul visited him and cured him by praying and putting his hands on him. After this happened, the rest of the people on the island who had diseases also came and were cured. They bestowed many honours on us, and when we were about to sail, they put on board all the provisions we needed. Three months later we set sail on a ship that had wintered at the island, an Alexandrian ship with the Twin Brothers as its figurehead.

this island stands a large marble statue of St Paul, erected in 1845. The little church of **St Paul's Bonfire** at the old fishing village of St Paul's Bay, west of Buġibba, is reputed to stand on the site where he was saved from snake bite. Further west at the head of the bay is Għajn Rasul, the **Apostle's Fountain**, with a small roadside statue of the apostle, where he is supposed to have baptized the first converts. Remains of a large Roman villa have been found near the seventeenth-century church of **San Pawl Milqi** (St Paul Welcomed) on the road of the same name off the one way street system in the town of Burmarrad, 2 kilometres (1 mile) south of Buġibba, and it may be on the site of the country house where Publius received the survivors of the shipwreck.

In the ancient walled city of **Mdina**, 'the silent city', in the centre of the island, there are remains of **Roman walls** in the Bacchus Restaurant and behind the telephone exchange, indicating that it was the Roman town of Melita. **Saint Paul's Cathedral** in Mdina is traditionally supposed to be the site of the town house and headquarters of Publius, who is alleged to have become bishop of Malta, and later of Athens. On the south side of Mdina is the town of **Rabat**, with a museum of Roman antiquities, built over the well-preserved **atrium** of a first century BC town house, and the **Grotto of St Paul**, where he is supposed to have sheltered and preached, under the seventeenth-century St Paul's Church. Signposts lead from the church to the third century AD **St Paul's catacombs**, and **St Agatha's catacombs** with frescoes from the twelfth to the fifteenth centuries AD.

Opening Times
St Paul's Cathedral, **Mdina** Tel. 454136 or 456620, Monday to Saturday 09.00–13.00 and 13.30–16.30
Mdina museum of Roman antiquities Tel. 454125, daily 07.45–14.00 from 16 June to 30 September, Monday to Saturday 08.15–17.00 and Sundays 08.15–16.00 for the rest of the year, closed public holidays
St Paul's Church and Grotto, **Rabat** Tel. 454467, and **St Paul's Catacombs**, **Rabat** Tel. 454562, both daily 07.45–14.00 in summer, 08.15–17.00 (or 16.00 on Sundays) in winter, closed public holidays
St Agatha's Catacombs, **Rabat** Tel. 454503, 09.00–17.00 Monday to Friday, 09.00–13.00 on Saturdays, closed Sundays and public holidays, in summer, 13.00–14.00 daily from October to June
Church of San Pawl Milqi, **Burmarrad** Persistence is needed to find the caretaker to give admission to this site

THE JOURNEY THROUGH ITALY

To add to the many good reasons for visiting Italy, including the people, the scenery and the sunshine, the classical remains and the art treasures, the reminders of great figures of the past such as St Francis, the food and the wine, we can now suggest a pilgrimage in the steps of St Paul. From Malta, another grain ship from Alexandria took the centurion, with Paul his prisoner and his companions, to Italy, calling at Syracuse in Sicily and Rhegium on the toe of Italy before disembarking at Puteoli near Naples. From there they travelled by land through the Forum of Appius and Three Taverns to reach Rome, probably in the spring of AD 61.

Syracuse (Sicily)

Syracuse, now called Siracusa, is on the east coast of Sicily, the large island off the 'toe' of Italy, and is a superbly situated port at the head of a beautiful bay, with a regular ferry running to Valletta in Malta. It was colonized by Greeks from Corinth, and was one of the greatest cities of the Greek empire, but was ruled by tyrants. One of these, Denis the Elder (405–367 BC), wished to convince his courtier Damocles that in spite of his great power a ruler could live in mortal fear, and suspended a sword by a single hair above the courtier's head.

Archimedes was born in Syracuse in 287 BC, and it was there he discovered the way to calculate the volume of an object from the water it displaces: he leapt out of his bath crying 'Eureka!' Pindar and Aeschylus also settled in Syracuse. At the time Paul stayed there it had around 300,000 inhabitants.

There is a fifth-century BC **Greek theatre**, one of the largest in the world, and a **Roman theatre**, both cut from the bedrock. They can be seen in the **Zona Archeologica**,

---

Paul travels, under arrest, from Syracuse to Rome (Acts 27:12–16)

We put in at Syracuse and stayed there for three days; then we weighed anchor and came to Rhegium. After one day there a south wind sprang up, and on the second day we came to Puteoli. There we found believers and were invited to stay with them for seven days. And so we came to Rome. The believers from there, when they heard of us, came as far as the Forum of Appius and Three Taverns to meet us. On seeing them, Paul thanked God and took courage. When we came into Rome, Paul was allowed to live by himself, with the soldier who was guarding him.

---

which lies above the city on the Viale Rizzo. The original settlement on the island of **L'Ortigia** is clustered around the site where the nymph **Arethusa** is supposed to have been turned into a spring of fresh water, and has many beautiful buildings, including a seventh century AD **cathedral** which was built into the remains of a Temple of Athena and incorporates Doric columns from the temple in its structure. On their way along the Sicilian coast, Paul and his companions may well have seen the smoking volcano, Mount Etna. The A18 (E45) autostrada from Messina to Catania charges a toll but is faster than the attractive old SS114. The SS114 from Catania to Syracusa however is a good fast road, and free.

Opening Times
Archaeological zone Tel. 0931 66206, daily 09.00 to 16.00. Toilets near the ticket office

Rhegium (Reggio di Calabria)

Rhegium is now Reggio di Calabria, on the toe of Italy facing Sicily across the Straits of Messina. Reggio di Calabria was completely rebuilt after an earthquake in 1908; the only things visible from biblical times are fragments of **Greek walls** and **Roman hot baths** beside the seafront Viale Matteoti, and the interesting **bronze statues** from the fifth century BC found under the sea at Riace in 1972, and now in the

museum. A little way to the north is the rock of Scilla, said to be a mythical sea monster; according to Homer, ships negotiating the straits were often wrecked on this after successfully passing a whirlpool known as Charybdis; hence we say of somebody on the horns of a dangerous dilemma that they are **'between Scylla and Charybdis'**. The A3 (E45) autostrada is toll free from Salerno to Reggio; the old SS18 is beautiful, but hilly and slow. Car Ferries (traghetti) cross from Villa San Giovanni to Messina.

Opening Times
Museo Nazionale della Magna Grecia, Piazza de Nava, Reggio, daily 09.00–19.30, closed on the first and third Mondays of each month, **www.museodellacalabria.com**

Puteoli (Pozzuoli)

The ship bringing Paul to Rome entered the Bay of Naples, where Paul will have seen the active volcano of Vesuvius; but its major eruption which buried Pompeii and Herculaneum was yet to happen in AD 79. Their ship docked at the port of Puteoli, which shared with Ostia the import of the grain supply for Rome. There he was met by a Christian congregation; we do not know who founded it.

Pozzuoli is now a small port close to Naples, with several sites to interest the visitor. It has always been in an area of volcanic activity, known as the **Phlegrian Fields** from a Greek word for 'flaming'. For this reason the area around **Lake Avernus** was considered to have been an entrance to Hades, and Paul may have known the quotation from the Latin poet Virgil (70–19 BC) warning those whose moral path is on a downward spiral that 'Easy is the descent to Avernus: . . . but to retrace one's steps . . . that's the task, that is the labour.' Paul will also have seen the **macellum** or marketplace, and the **Amphitheatre of Augustus**, and on the acropolis the **Temple of Augustus**. Across the bay were the lavish villas of the seaside resort of **Baia**. In 37 BC Agrippa had linked Lake Avernus by canal with Lake Lucrino and the sea to form an extensive dockyard called the **Portus Julius**.

Visiting Pozzuoli today

A walking tour of Pozzuoli taking about half a day can begin at the crater of the **Solfatara Volcano**, just off the Via Solfatara, where jets of steam leave coloured chemical deposits, and in ancient as well as more recent times the sick used to sweat out their diseases in chambers filled with steam. The **Amphitheatre of Augustus** has been cut in half by the railway; fragments of it are visible on the left by the railway bridge as you return along the Via Solfatara, but it is not open to visitors. The later **Amphitheatre of Nero**, completed by Vespasian, is further down on the right. It is one of the largest in Italy, and a visit to the extensive chambers under the arena gives a unique impression of where the Christian martyrs, and the wild beasts to which they were to be thrown, were prepared. Continuing down Corso Terracino takes you past the **Baths of Neptune** on your left, built by Hadrian in the second century AD, and the **Roman necropolis** up Via Celle on the right. Coming down the Via Pergolesi you reach the **macellum** or harbour market, erroneously called the Temple of Serapis because a statue of the god of healing was found there in 1750. This well-preserved marketplace has colonnades and shops round the sides, a temple in the centre, and large public lavatories at one end. Like the baths and the necropolis, the Macellum can be seen from the street but you cannot go inside. The acropolis, now called **Rione Terra**, became unsafe because of volcanic earth movements in 1970, and was closed to visitors; it is now being restored. The Corinthian columns of the Temple of Augustus were found in 1964 to have been incorporated in the **Duomo** or cathedral. Now it can only be glimpsed from the steps which climb up beside a huge archway on the Corsa della Republico. On a clear day you can see the remains of the **Portus Julius** and the resort of

Baia from a glass-bottomed boat, as the volcanic earth movements have caused them to subside below the surface of the sea.

Getting to Pozzuoli

By road from Naples along the coast is congested and confusing, it is better to pay the toll and come off the Tangenziale at the last or last but one exit, or from the north on the Variante SS7 quater; or by train from Naples Metropolitana station at the central railway station, or Cumana station in Piazza Montesanto.

Opening Times
Vulcano Solfatara Tel. 081 526 2341, **www.solfatara.it**, daily 08.30 to one hour before sunset. Toilets behind the building marked 'Bar'
Anfiteatro Neroniano–Flavio Tel. 081 526 6007, daily 09.00 to one hour before sunset
Parco Archeologico di Baia Tel. 081 868 7592, Tuesday to Sunday 09.00 to one hour before sunset
Glass-bottom boats, Associazione Aliseo, Baia, Tel. 081 526 5780, Saturdays and Sundays and at other times by arrangement for groups
Museo Archeologico, **Castello di Baia**, Tel. 081 523 3797, Tuesday to Sunday 09.00 to one hour before sunset
Ercolano (Herculaneum) Tel. 081 90 963, daily 09.00 to one hour before sunset
Pompeii Tel. 081 850 72 55, daily 09.00 to one hour before sunset

The Forum of Appius

It is often pointed out that Christ came at the first moment at which the good news could be taken quickly across most of the known world, with Greek as a common language, the peace enforced by Roman law within the Roman empire, and a magnificent system of Roman roads. 'All roads lead to Rome'; traffic travelling from the east on the Egnatian Way across Greece arrived by ship at Brindisi where it joined the Appian Way (now the SS7) to journey right across Italy. The road from Puteoli, which joined it near Capua, was probably crowded with carts carrying grain.

The modern traveller coming from the south should look at Terracina for the signs 'S7 Rome (Via Appia)'. The side turnings for the next few miles are marked according to the number of miles from Rome. The Appian Way goes straight as a die between two rows of umbrella pines across what used to be, until they were drained, the Pontine Marshes, with a canal following it on the left from Terracina to Faiti.

There was a canal in Paul's time too, and the deputation of Christians who came out from Rome to greet him will not have known whether he was coming by road or in a boat, towed by mules. So they met him where the canal ended, at Appii Forum, a place mentioned by the Latin author Horace, who

Borgo Faiti, the ancient Appii Forum

says it is full of 'rapacious tavern-keepers' – not my experience today. Had the deputation been sent by St Peter, as soon as he heard from the Christians in Puteoli?

The small town of **Borgo Faiti** is near a crossroads with the S156 about 69 kilometres (43 miles) from Rome, and signs on the church, the derelict police post, the restaurant and the memorial to victims of terrorism claim that this was formerly Foro Appii.

Three Taverns

In words which amuse British beer drinkers, Paul 'went to Three Taverns and took courage'. *Taberna* actually means a shop. Maybe the older members of the Christian community in Rome only managed to travel the 48 kilometres (30 miles) or so needed for them to greet Paul there. As well as Priscilla and Aquila who came from Rome, the last chapter of Paul's letter to the Romans shows he knew many Christians there already, at least by name. Paul was encouraged that they came to meet him because he now

realized clearly that he was not alone. The site of Tres Tabernae is probably somewhere in the township of **Cisterna di Latina**; Cicero said it was at the junction with a road to the coastal city of Antium (modern Anzio). Travellers coming from Rome should follow signs marked 'SS7 Veletri, Via Appia'.

ROME

Rome, 'the Eternal City', is still a delight to anyone interested in history, art, and architecture, in spite of the modern traffic and the heat in summer. The legend of the origins of Rome, told by Livy and Virgil, is that Aeneas son of Venus fled from Troy, and founded a settlement at the mouth of the Tiber, which his son moved to Alba Longa. Here a vestal virgin, following her union with Mars, gave birth to the twins Romulus and Remus, who were cared for by a wolf at the foot of the Palatine Hill. Romulus gave his name to the new settlement of Rome on the Capitol, and provided his companions with Sabine wives; a succession of kings were alternately Sabine and Latin.

The Etruscans turned this settlement into a well-organized town, but their last king Tarquin was replaced in 509 BC by the Republic, which was ruled by consuls and the Senate. When the Republic split into rival factions, Julius Caesar took control, but following his assassination in 44 BC he was succeeded by his nephew Octavian, who was granted the title of Augustus Caesar. A succession of Emperors administered the Roman empire, demanding that their subjects should honour them by burning a pinch of incense to the emperor as a god.

In Rome Paul lived under house arrest for two years, and was able to fulfil his ambition to proclaim the gospel at the centre of the Roman empire; and here the narrative of the Acts of the Apostles ends.

Rome was built on seven hills, and by the time the Revelation to John was written it had become so hostile to Christians that it is described as a woman seated on seven mountains (Revelation 17:9).

What happened to Paul afterwards?

We cannot be sure where Paul stayed in Rome – though some suggestions are in the next section – or what happened at the end of the two years there which conclude the Acts of the Apostles. A few scholars have suggested that he lost his appeal and was executed then. More people, however, assume he was released, and went on to minister in Nicopilis (Titus 3:12–15 – see above under Berea), Crete, Troas (2 Timothy 4:13) and even, as he had hoped, in Spain (Romans 15:24 – there was a strong Roman population there producing olive oil and wine for the empire, and the church at Tarragona preserves his memory).

The martyrdom of both Peter and Paul in Rome is supported though not proved by John 13:36, 21:18, and references in the Christian authors Clement, Ignatius and Gaius. The shrines at their reputed burial places are very early, and it was a difficult task to build the basilicas over the cemeteries to enclose them. The memories of persecuted minorities are long, and the early Christians will have proudly shown their grandchildren where their heroes were executed and buried for generations before there were written records.

By about the fourth century the tradition is clear: a fire broke out in Rome on 18 June AD 64. Emperor Nero had wanted to clear some slums to build his new palace, and conveniently that was where the fire began. He had to find a scapegoat, and decided to blame the Christians, with their apocalyptic imagery of the world ending in fire. It is claimed that Peter came to Rome, and wrote his letters from there, then fled under persecution, but met Christ journeying into the city and asked him, 'Domine, quo vadis?' (Lord, where are you going?). Jesus replied that the body of Christ was to be crucified afresh, so Peter returned, and was put in chains. Paul had been arrested and brought to Rome; Peter and Paul were condemned as leaders of the new religion; tradition says that they were both

Paul's arrival in Rome (Acts 27:16–31)

When we came into Rome, Paul was allowed to live by himself, with the soldier who was guarding him. Three days later he called together the local leaders of the Jews. When they had assembled, he said to them, 'Brothers, though I had done nothing against our people or the customs of our ancestors, yet I was arrested in Jerusalem and handed over to the Romans. When they had examined me, the Romans wanted to release me, because there was no reason for the death penalty in my case. But when the Jews objected, I was compelled to appeal to the emperor – even though I had no charge to bring against my nation. For this reason therefore I have asked to see you and speak with you, since it is for the sake of the hope of Israel that I am bound with this chain.' They replied, 'We have received no letters from Judea about you, and none of the brothers coming here has reported or spoken anything evil about you. But we would like to hear from you what you think, for with regard to this sect we know that everywhere it is spoken against.' After they had set a day to meet with him, they came to him at his lodgings in great numbers. From morning until evening he explained the matter to them, testifying to the kingdom of God and trying to convince them about Jesus both from the law of Moses and from the prophets. Some were convinced by what he had said, while others refused to believe. So they disagreed with each other; and as they were leaving, Paul made one further statement: 'The Holy Spirit was right in saying to your ancestors through the prophet Isaiah, "Go to this people and say, You will indeed listen, but never understand, and you will indeed look, but never perceive. For this people's heart has grown dull, and their ears are hard of hearing, and they have shut their eyes; so that they might not look with their eyes, and listen with their ears, and understand with their heart and turn – and I would heal them." Let it be known to you then that this salvation of God has been sent to the Gentiles; they will listen.' He lived there two whole years at his own expense and welcomed all who came to him, proclaiming the kingdom of God and teaching about the Lord Jesus Christ with all boldness and without hindrance.

martyred on 29 June in AD 67. They were detained together in the Mamertine prison; led out of the city gate, on the site of which stands the gate now called the Porta San Paolo. Peter was led to be crucified upside down in Nero's circus, because he said he was not worthy to die in the same way as his Lord, and was buried nearby. Paul, because he was a Roman citizen, could not be crucified, so he was beheaded with a sword at Aquae Silva, and buried where the Church of St Paul's outside the walls now stands.

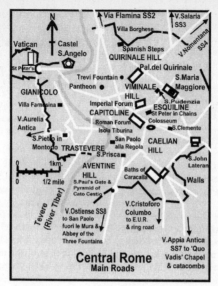

Central Rome
Main Roads

Getting to Rome

Rome is the centre of a road, rail and air network (see the section above on Practical Details – Italy). Motorists will find that travelling round the circular Grande Raccordo Annulare is often faster than shorter, more congested routes, and unlike most Italian autostrada it is free. The Leonardo da Vinci airport is at Fiumicino.

Visiting Rome today

One could spend many weeks in Rome and still not have seen half that is worth seeing. But limiting oneself to sites linked with the apostles Peter and Paul, and buying a day ticket for the Metro and the buses, it would be just possible to cover them on foot in a day, though

less exhausting if longer was allowed. Beware of pickpockets on the Metro.

Starting at the **Vatican**, and omitting the Vatican museums and the Sistine Chapel, which would take a day in themselves, in St Peter's Basilica it is possible to descend a stairway to the left of the high altar to the tombs of Peter and his successors. Now that a glass door has been put in front of Peter's tomb, photography is impossible. The famous square in front of St Peter's is on the site of Nero's Circus, and contains the obelisk which stood at the centre of it.

From there it is about 1¼ kilometres (1 mile) walk along the Viale della Mura Aurelia to

San Pietro in Montorio, which is an ancient site in the Trastevere where most Jews and foreigners lived; Peter may have lived there too. Admiring the fine view over Rome you can walk a further a half of a kilometre (a third of a mile) across the Ponte Sisto to **San Paolo alla Regola,** built in the seventeenth century on a site where Paul may have lived while awaiting trial. It is known to have been used for Christian worship in the early centuries.

From there it is a further 2 kilometres (1¼ miles) to **Santa Pudenziana,** in the Via Urbana just north of Via Cavour. Alternatively, from St Peter's Basilica one could take the Metro at Ottaviano, change at Termini and get off at Cavour which is only a few hundred metres (yards) from Santa Pudenziana. This may be the oldest church in Rome, as the fabric of the walls, up to the blocked off windows, is that of a second-century bath house, known to have been built on the site of the house of a Senator Pudens, and given to the church in 145 by his son. This may have been the Pudens mentioned in 2 Timothy 4:21, and Paul may have rented the house from him; another tradition suggests that Peter lived here. It contains a very ancient mosaic, the oldest in any Christian church, with portraits of Peter and Paul being crowned by women representing the Jewish and

The Forum, Rome

gentile sections of the Christian community.

Returning to the Via Cavour, a flight of steps leads to **San Pietro in Vincoli,** a church much altered since, but originally built in the fifth century to house the chains with which the apostle had been bound in prison, and now containing Michelangelo's masterpiece statue of Moses.

From here you can descend to the **Imperial Forums,** the **Roman Forum** and the **Palatine Hill,** at present undergoing extensive excavation and redisplay. A full day would be needed to explore these. Facing the Arch of Septimus Severus (but not in the area covered by the Forum admission charge) and underneath the **Church of San Giuseppe dei Falegnami,** is the **Mamertine Prison,** where Peter and Paul, and many other state prisoners, are believed to have been imprisoned.

Passing south of the **Colosseum,** begun in AD 72, into the narrow street of San Giovanni in Laterano – which leads to the magnificent basilica of that name, originally built in the fourth century – the pilgrim finds the church, or rather churches one above the other, of **San Clemente**. St Clement was the fourth bishop of Rome, from 88–97, and at the lowest level there are fascinating remains of first-century houses, as well as a marketplace, and it is quite conceivable that St Peter walked along one of these narrow alleys to visit his friend's home. It is certain that this was the site of one of the original twenty–five house churches in Rome in about 200, listed as 'titular churches'. Clement wrote an epistle to the Corinthians, rebuking them for deposing their presbyters. He may be the Clement mentioned in Philippians 4:3. The remains of a temple of Mithras also survive at the lowest level, which seems to have coexisted next door to the church for many years.

The Metropolitana underground railway can be taken from Colosseo to Circo Massimo. The **Circus Maximus** was laid out around the sixth century BC for chariot races. From here it is a short walk up the Via d. Fonte di Fauno to the **church of S. Prisca**, which may be on the site where Paul's companions Aquila and Priscilla lived when they worked in Rome.

From there a pilgrim can walk to Porta San Paolo, **St Paul's Gate**, with, nearby, the **Pyramid of Caio Cestia** from 12 BC, which the apostle will

certainly have seen, and the much later **Protestant cemetery** where Keats and Shelley are buried. From the Pyramide station one can take the Metro to **San Paolo fuori le Mura**, which was built originally by Emperor Constantine over the cemetery where St Paul was buried. Beneath the altar is a marble slab with the name of the apostle, and during repairs many years ago some reported seeing beneath it the metal casket in which Constantine enclosed the saint's remains. The enormous basilica was last rebuilt, following a fire, in 1854.

From Basilica San Paolo you could take the Metro to Laurentina to visit **Aquae Silva**, also known as **Abbazia della Tre Fontane**. In this peaceful spot surrounded by eucalyptus trees and cared for by Trappist monks and the Little Sisters of Jesus, is a church over the spot where Paul is supposed to have been beheaded, and where three springs are alleged to have immediately welled up.

Returning to San Paolo fuori le Mura you can also take a couple of buses to the **catacombs**. The Catacombs of **Domitilla** on Via Ardeatina, **Marcellina and Pietro** on Via Casilina, **Priscilla** on Via Salaria, and **Callisto** on Via Appia Antica were all used for the burial of Christian martyrs, and that under the **Church of St Sebastian**, also on Via Appia

Antica, is reported to have held the bodies of Peter and Paul for a while, perhaps to protect them from grave robbers until they were returned to their original burial places.

Tunnels were made when digging out the volcanic tufa rock (see above under Cappadocia), soft when wet and hard when it dries, from which many of the buildings of ancient Rome were constructed. With admirable economy these tunnels were then used by all faiths for burials, to save space on the surface, and often decorated with inscriptions and paintings. Christians and pagans would hold memorial feasts around the tombs of their family members, but for the Christians these took the form of the Eucharist. Contrary to popular legend, though Christians may have hidden from their persecutors here briefly, they never lived in them for any length of time. The Church of St Sebastian was known as 'Kata Cymbas', meaning 'near the hollows', and the name of 'catacombs' was later applied to all Christian underground burial places. Visiting them is fascinating, but not recommended for the claustrophobic.

Nearer to the city centre on the Via Appia Antica is the charming little chapel of 'Domine, quo vadis?', with appropriate mosaics. The whole of the Via Appia Antica, from the **Circus of Maxentius** to the **Tomb of Cecilia Metella** from the beginning of the first century AD, has just been turned into Europe's largest pedestrian precinct.

On other days one could visit the **Baths of Caracalla**, the **Colosseum**, the **Pantheon**, **San Giovanni in Laterano**, **Santa Maria Maggiore**, the **Sistine Chapel**, the **Trevi Fountains** and the **Spanish Steps**, as well as any number of fascinating museums and galleries. The **Museo del Civilta Romano** at the EUR has fascinating models of Roman sites and Roman life.

Opening Times
Museu d'Història de Tarragona, Catalunya, Spain
(four Roman sites): June to September Tuesday to Saturday 09.00–20.00; Sunday 10.00–14.00; October to May Tuesday to Sunday 10.00–13.30 approximately

Rome (many sites give free admission to visitors under 18 years old and over 60):

Baths of Caracalla Tel. (06) 57 58 626, daily 09.00 to one hour before sunset, or till 14.00 on Sundays, Mondays and public holidays

Catacombe de San Sebastiano Tel. (06) 78 50 350, Thursday to Tuesday 08.30–12.30, 14.30–17.30 or till 17.00 in winter. Closed on Sundays mid-November to mid-December. Guided tours only

Catacombe di San Callisto Tel. (06) 51 36 01 51, and

Catacombe di Domitilla Tel. (06) 51 10 342

www.catacombe.domitilla.it, have the same opening hours as San Sebastiano. Toilets near the entrance
Colosseum Tel. (06) 70 04 261 and 70 05 469, daily 09.00 to 16.30
Foro Romano and Palatino Tel.(06) 69 90 110, daily 09.00 to 16.00
Foro Imperiale Tel.(06) 67 90 048, closed for restoration
Pantheon Tel. (06) 68 30 02 30, Monday to Saturday 09.30–19.30; Sunday 09.00–18.00
Basilica di San Giovanni in Laterano Tel. (06) 77 207 991, daily 07.00–19.30
Basilica di Santa Maria Maggiore Tel. (06) 48 31 95, daily 07.00–19.00 except during church services
Basilica di San Paolo Fuori le Mura Tel. (06) 54 0910 374, daily 07.00–18.30 in summer; 07.00–18.00 winter, toilets through door to right of altar
Basilica di San Pietro, Vaticano Tel. (06) 69 88 1662, daily 07.00–18.00 except during church services. Toilets in the square in front of the church
Mamertine prison, **Chiesa di San Pietro in Carcere** daily 09.00–12.00, 14.00–17.00
Museo Capitolino in the Palazzo Nuovo, Capitol Hill Tel. (06) 67 10 2071 Tuesday to Sunday 09.00–19.00 – pieces are sometimes temporarily displayed in the ACCA Arts Centre in the Via Ostiense, open 10.00–18.00 Tuesday to Friday; 10.00–19.00 Saturday and Sunday
San Pudenziana Tel. (06) 48 14 622, Monday to Saturday

08.00–18.00. If closed ring the bell to the left of the entrance
St Prisca daily 08.00–12.00 and 16.00–18.30. Enquire at the Parish Office next to the church, or contact the Centro Servizi per l'Archeologia Tel. (06) 48 15 576
San Pietro in Vincoli Tel. (06) 48 82 865, daily 09.30–12.30 and 15.30–19.00 or until 18.30 in winter
San Clemente Tel. (06) 70 45 10 18, Monday to Saturday 09.00–12.30 and 15.00–18.00, Sundays and holidays 10.00–12.30 and 15.00–18.00
Museo della Civilta Romana, EUR, Tel. (06) 59 26 135, Tuesday to Saturday 09.00–19.00; Sundays 09.00–13.30

THE LETTERS OF PETER

The first letter of Peter is a circular letter to be carried by Sylvanus (probably the same as Silas who travelled with Paul) to Christians throughout the area we know as the Jewish Dispersion (1:1); it was written from 'Babylon' (5:13) which is usually considered a symbolic name for Rome (Revelation 17:5, 9). Some people have seen it as the summary of a sermon delivered by Peter at an Easter baptism service. The second letter of Peter speaks of the letters of Paul (3:15) which were probably not collected and circulated until after his death, so that many people think this letter, although intended to honour Peter, was written by someone else much later.

A Summary of the Letters

1 Peter 1 begins with a great thanksgiving for the resurrection of Jesus, and a call to live a life of reverence. (Chapter 2) We are living stones in God's temple, so we must live as slaves of God. (2:18—3:7) This is to be shown in the relationship of slaves to their masters, and of husbands and wives to each other. (3:8—4:19) We must be willing to suffer for being a Christian. (Chapter 5) Leaders in the church are to be shepherds of the flock.

2 Peter 1:1–15 says that we are called to share in the nature of God. (1:16–21) We were eye-witnesses of Christ's glory. (2:1–22) warns against false prophets. (3:1–13) In spite of the promises of Jesus delivered through the apostles, the day of the Lord has been a long time coming, but it will come. (3:14–18) In the meantime you are to grow in grace.

PAUL'S LETTER TO THE ROMANS

Unlike all his other letters, this is written to a church which Paul had not yet visited. It is to prepare the way for a hoped for visit to the centre of the Roman empire, on his way to Spain. It justifies his position as apostle to the Gentiles, and summarizes his preaching. There is no space here to enter the debate on the meaning of 'justification by grace through faith, not by works of the law'. It is a good rule to ask first what a passage of scripture meant to the one who wrote it, and to the community to whom it was first read aloud. Only then can we know what it means to us as individuals today. Romans has rightly been called 'the gospel according to Paul'.

Paul may have written this letter from Corinth or Ephesus at the end of his third missionary journey (Acts 20). He knew many people from Rome, and greets them by name in the last chapter. His colleagues in building the church at Ephesus and Corinth, the tent-makers Priscilla and Aquila, were among the Jews who had been expelled from Rome by Emperor Claudius (Acts 17:2); according to the Roman historian Suetonius this was as a result of their rioting about someone called 'Chrestus'. They must have told Paul there was a deep division there between the Jewish Christians and the gentile Christians, and his purpose in writing was to make a passionate plea for unity.

The Jews are God's chosen people, the descendants of Abraham, with whom God had made a covenant based on their keeping God's laws. So even some Christian Jews despised the rest of the world, whom they called the Nations (*goiim* in Hebrew, Gentiles in Greek), as lawless and immoral. The Jews, they claimed, unlike the Gentiles, were regarded as good people by God because they keep the law given to Moses.

God would only love the Gentiles if they became part of the chosen people, by circumcision and obedience to all the Jewish laws. Paul insisted that God's covenant was for the world, and it could only become a world faith if the Gentiles were admitted without being required to keep the divisive food, sabbath and circumcision laws. Nevertheless they must aim at perfection in their moral behaviour.

A Summary of the Letter

(Romans 1:1) Paul works to build a united and multi-ethnic people of God by subtly arguing that all alike, Jews and Gentiles, need God's forgiveness, and this is only found through faith in Jesus Christ. This is the gospel or good news that Paul preached.

(1:18) Jews despise Gentiles for the widespread worship of idols, and 'unnatural' sex. But greed, jealousy, competition, lying, pride, disobedience, and breaking promises – vices found among Jews as well as Gentiles – are contrary to the will of God and therefore equally unnatural. (2:1) And the most unnatural vice of all is judging others.

(2:17) God hates it when we hurt each other. Jews and Gentiles alike deserve a guilty verdict, either by the law of Moses or by their own consciences. The law was an essential part of God's plan, to show us that he cares about the way we treat each other. (3:9)

The scriptures (Psalms 14:1–3 and 53:1–3) say that nobody is righteous, regarded as good by God. (3:21) But God will regard us as good, even though we have not been good, and admit us to his chosen people, if we have faith in Jesus. (4:1) Even Abraham was not justified by the Law, which had not yet been given to Moses, but by faith (Genesis 15:6). So he became, according to the Jewish scripture, not just the ancestor of the Jews but the father of many 'Nations' – Gentiles.

(5:12) We are all guilty, the Jews believed, because we are descended from disobedient Adam; but we are all regarded as good, says Paul, because of our faith in obedient Jesus. (6:1) Our guilt was removed when Jesus was nailed to the cross. It was as if we had been contracted as slaves to our sinful habits, and by an act like that when someone else pays for a slave's freedom ('redemption'), Jesus has set us free. Our only obligation now is to live a good life in gratitude for what he has done. (7:1) After the person who makes a contract dies, nobody is bound by it. We are part of the body of Christ, and Jesus has died, so we are no longer bound by our contract as slaves to sin.

(7:7) To live a good life we have to struggle against our selfish desires, but this is possible if we are controlled by the Holy Spirit. The Old Testament law was powerless to restrain our

191

natural selfishness, but the Spirit empowers us to live in a loving way. Freed from the negative restrictions of the law we can live in a positive and loving manner.

The Jewish Christians were not the only ones to be obsessed with Law; the Gentiles were very proud of the Roman law. So Paul uses a lawcourt metaphor: 'justification' is what happens when the judge declares the accused to be 'not guilty'. (7:31) Paul says that Jesus is our advocate, pleading for us with God the judge, who therefore declares us to be not guilty even though in fact we are guilty.

(9:1) The Jews were God's chosen people, and they still are, even though many of them have rejected Jesus. (10:5) God's plan is to bring the Gentiles to faith through the teaching of the Jews, and then to bring the Jews to faith through the example of the Gentiles.

As in many of his letters, Paul in Romans teaches, first, what God has done for us, and therefore second, what we must do for each other. Beginning with 'therefore' in (12:1), Paul's moral teaching concerns love for (12:3) our fellow-Christians, limbs in the body of Christ; (12:14) our enemies; (13:1) the state authorities, even when hostile; (13:8) our neighbours; (14:1) Jewish and Gentile Christians, who may have different dietary customs; (15:1) and those whose faith is weak. As always, his aim is to build a world community founded on unity in love between those who are different.

(15:7) Paul is writing to the Romans to explain why he is the apostle to the Gentiles, and to prepare them for a visit he hopes to make, after he has carried some money collected by the Christians in Greece to the poor Christians of Jerusalem. (16:1) Because he has never yet visited Rome he finishes with a longer than usual list of personal greetings to leading Christians he knows there.

PAUL'S PERSONAL LETTERS

Paul's very personal first and second letters to Timothy and his letter to Titus are quite unlike the letters which he wrote to congregations; they are often referred to as the Pastoral Epistles. A decision on when they were written depends on what we think happened to Paul after he went to Rome for the first time. If he died at the end of his time there, the Pastorals must have been written during that imprisonment or earlier. If he was released and went back to work in Asia Minor, then 1 Timothy and Titus could have been written from there and 2 Timothy after he was rearrested (see 2 Timothy 4:16–18). Or if he went to Spain as he hoped (Romans 15:28) they could all have been written after his second arrest.

The style and language of 1 and 2 Timothy and Titus are very different from that of the other letters, the teaching of Paul and his opponents appears more rigid, and it is not clear whether he is giving basic training to young missionaries or reminding senior bishops of what he had told them years before. He appears to be quoting from earlier Christian authorities, and is more legalistic, particularly on the position of women. For these and other reasons, some who accept the authenticity of most of the other letters have doubted whether the Pastoral Epistles, or some of them, are really by Paul. If they are, then he must have adopted a very different style in writing to individuals. If not, they could have been written during or after his lifetime by someone else acting on his instructions, or seeking to honour him.

A Summary of the Letters

1 Timothy is addressed to the young assistant who had joined Paul at Lystra, and now appears to be in charge of the church at Ephesus; it could be that Paul was in Macedonia when he wrote it (1 Timothy 1:1–3). He warns against false teachers and those who reject the law (1:3–11). He is grateful for God's mercy (1:12–20) and gives instruction in prayer (2:1–15). He describes the qualifications of bishops and deacons (3:1–13), and since he emphasizes they must be the husband of one wife, one wonders whether many Christians had more than one. Paul quotes a formula in 3:14–16 which he describes as the mystery of our religion. 4:1–5 warns against false asceticism; the rest of the chapter gives instruction to a young minister. Chapter 5 and 6:1–2 give advice on dealing with different groups within the congregation, and the rest of the epistle is about false teaching, true riches and fighting the good fight of faith.

2 Timothy is written when Paul is a prisoner (2 Timothy 1:8), possibly in Rome (1:17), and he believes he is near the end of his life (4:6). He gives encouragement to Timothy, urging him to be a good soldier (2:1–13) and a worker approved by God (2:14–26). Paul warns him of godlessness and false teaching in the last days (3:1— 4:8). His final instructions contain revealing personal details; Paul wants Timothy to come to him (4:9–22).

The letter of Paul to Titus is addressed to a Greek disciple (Galatians 2:3) who is in charge of the church in Crete (1:5–16). Paul is writing from Nicopolis nearby (Titus 3:12–15). The letter contains exhortations to sound doctrine and good deeds, and advice for dealing with old and young in his congregation, slaves and those who cause divisions (2:1—3:11).

A LIFETIME'S ACHIEVEMENT

Less than forty years had passed since Jesus the Nazarene died alone on Calvary, yet in that time the Christian church had spread and was growing right across the then known world, largely due to the labours and suffering of the apostles whose paths we have traced in this book. St Paul's life story is amazing. Why should anyone travel those distances, endure those beatings and imprisonments, and argue with the finest minds of the day, just to propagate a philosophy which he himself had invented? All ideas have to be expressed in words drawn from the culture of the people among whom they arise. But in order to convey a world view to people of another culture, not just the words but the whole set of thought patterns have to be translated. St Paul was a pioneer in the translation of Christianity from a Jewish sect into a World Faith. More exciting than any single cultural expression of the faith, is to see the sparks which fly when two cultures clash in a single mind, and the new ideas which are generated in the process.

So I now see Paul as going beyond the not-so-simple religion of Jesus in translating it into non-Jewish terms. But that is not to say he invented a new religion. Rather he was captivated and driven half way across the known world by the figure who appeared to him on the road to Damascus, prepared to face any hardship to challenge the Roman empire with the claims of the crucified Jesus.

Jews of widely differing views shared the belief that God made a covenant with the Jewish nation in order to redeem the whole world, and was shortly about to intervene decisively in history to bring that about. What made Jesus distinctive was his teaching that this would be achieved by his own death and resurrection. Paul's preaching was that this had already happened, and that Paul's own task was to spread the blessings it brought to all the people of the world. For this it was essential that non-Jews could be accepted on terms of equality into the covenant community, without being required to keep the Jewish law. His experiences in places he visited showed him that to preserve the unity of Jew and Gentile in the young and troubled Christian church was essential to its task of uniting the whole world through Christ to God. His message is needed as much today as it was then: if people are to stop hurting and harming each other, they need to take responsibility for their actions, confess them to God, and accept the forgiveness and eternal life offered through Jesus. And if the human race is to survive, people from different races and cultures must learn to live together in love, without demanding that others should adopt our cultural norms as though they were the unchanging will of God.

The Letters to the Seven Churches of the Revelation

Pilgrims who visit Turkey in the steps of St Paul often visit those towns, all in the former Roman province of Asia, mentioned in the Revelation to John. The Revelation is also called The Apocalypse, which means the revealing of something which had been hidden. So although not all of them are mentioned in the Acts of the Apostles, these towns deserve a place in this book. To understand the symbolism of Revelation a thorough knowledge of the Old Testament, and other apocalyptic writings, is needed. But to understand the letters of the risen Christ to the seven churches, in chapters 2 and 3, a visit to the sites of the actual towns is invaluable.

Who wrote Revelation?

In Acts and the letters of Paul the Roman empire is seen as a defence for the Christians against persecution by non-Christian Jews, and Paul's aim is to convert the empire to Christ. But in Revelation it is the empire which is persecuting the Christians, and they are consoled by the promise that

the empire will not last for ever. The author himself in the first chapter tells us his name was John and he was writing from the island of Patmos. For many centuries Christians accepted that a life of John, claiming to be written by his secretary Prochorus, one of the Seven mentioned in Acts 6:1–6, was a genuine account; the Greek

---

The introduction to the letters to the seven churches (Revelation 1:9–20)

I, John, your brother who share with you in Jesus the persecution and the kingdom and the patient endurance, was on the island called Patmos because of the word of God and the testimony of Jesus. I was in the spirit on the Lord's day, and I heard behind me a loud voice like a trumpet saying, 'Write in a book what you see and send it to the seven churches, to Ephesus, to Smyrna, to Pergamum, to Thyatira, to Sardis, to Philadelphia, and to Laodicea.' Then I turned to see whose voice it was that spoke to me, and on turning I saw seven golden lampstands, and in the midst of the lampstands I saw one like the Son of Man, clothed with a long robe and with a golden sash across his chest. His head and his hair were white as white wool, white as snow; his eyes were like a flame of fire, his feet were like burnished bronze, refined as in a furnace, and his voice was like the sound of many waters. In his right hand he held seven stars, and from his mouth came a sharp, two-edged sword, and his face was like the sun shining with full force. When I saw him, I fell at his feet as though dead. But he placed his right hand on me, saying, 'Do not be afraid; I am the first and the last, and the living one. I was dead, and see, I am alive forever and ever; and I have the keys of Death and of Hades. Now write what you have seen, what is, and what is to take place after this. As for the mystery of the seven stars that you saw in my right hand, and the seven golden lampstands: the seven stars are the angels of the seven churches, and the seven lampstands are the seven churches.'

Orthodox still do. This states that John, son of Zebedee, one of The Twelve, was the Beloved Disciple who was asked by Jesus to look after his mother (John 19:26–27). After she had been taken up to heaven and St Paul had been martyred, John went to Ephesus and wrote the Gospel of John and the three Letters of John. He is called St John the Divine, which is the old English word for a theologian. Then, under the persecuting Emperor Domitian in AD 95 he was sent in exile to Patmos, where he received a vision in a cave and dictated it to Prochorus as the book of Revelation. It begins with letters from the risen Christ to seven churches in the province of Asia, each of them a strategic postal town from which copies could be distributed to other churches in the same district. John returned to Ephesus after the death of Domitian and died there aged over a hundred.

Against this account, there is some evidence that Revelation could have been written during the persecution organized in the reign of Emperor Nero in AD 68: when the words 'Nero Caesar' are written in Hebrew letters the corresponding numbers add up to '666', the 'mark of the beast' in Revelation 13:18. Moreover modern western scholars are sceptical whether the Gospel and the Revelation could have been written by the same person, because the style and approach are so different, and that either could have been written by a Galilean fisherman. John was a very common name. Yet it is possible that someone would adopt a very different style for writing what we call apocalyptic visions.

An Apocalyptic Vision?

Much effort has been expended trying to work out exactly what events are predicted by the book of Revelation, and when they will occur, based on the assumption that it is a literal prediction of what will happen 2,000 years later. There is little agreement between those who take this literal approach.

At first, people believed that the gods lived above the clouds in 'the heavens'. While never quite denying this, most of the Jewish people by the time of Christ had moved to a belief that God is everywhere. They believed that those who have died are sleeping in a place called Sheol, and the Pharisees thought that

they would be resurrected to life again on earth. In the Greek and Roman world the gods were thought to live on Mount Olympus, and the dead to have a ghost-like existence in the world of the shades (Hades). The Greek philosopher Plato had given another interpretation to the idea of heaven: it was an ideal world where the perfect ideas of everything in the material world existed. Many Jewish books have been discovered in recent centuries which show how common it was to write of a vision in which 'the heavens were opened'. What is seen in the vision is usually a series of symbols which give a true understanding of what is happening on earth. They are called 'apocalyptic' which means revealing, unveiling or uncovering what was hidden. These visions are a form of prophecy, which can be thought of either literally, as a 'foretelling' of what will happen in the future; or metaphorically, as a literary genre for 'forth-telling' God's view of what is happening in the present; or as a combination of the two. Examples in the Bible are parts of Ezekiel, Daniel and Zechariah; Mark 13 and parallels, 2 Thessalonians 2 and the book of Revelation.

Paul's letters to the Thessalonians are among the earliest he wrote, and in them he assumed that the Day of the Lord, and the physical resurrection of believers on earth, was coming very soon. But he had already discovered that some Christians concluded that in this case their manner of life did not matter, and others gave up work altogether as they thought the end was near. As relations between Jews and Romans deteriorated, Christians came to see that in predictions like those in Mark 13 Jesus may have been warning about the inevitable destruction of Jerusalem, which eventually happened in AD 70, rather than about the end of the world. By the time he wrote 1 Corinthians 15, Paul had moved to a more metaphorical view: 'flesh and blood cannot inherit the kingdom of God', he wrote.

Possibly neither Paul nor the writer of the book of Revelation thought it important to distinguish between literal prediction and metaphorical interpretation of history, even if they would have understood the question. Maybe nor should we, so long as it doesn't become an excuse for being idle, making elaborate speculations, ignoring the needs of the contemporary world, or postponing a decision to follow Christ.

If you choose to interpret Revelation in a more metaphorical way, you will see it as a superb sequence of poetic symbols, tailor-made to give hope to the Christians in the seven churches of Asia in the first century. Images with which they were familiar from the Old Testament are recycled to suggest that the Roman empire, under which they were suffering persecution, was under the judgement of God, and would not last for ever. If they would remain faithful to their Christian faith, they would receive their reward, if not in this life, then after their death, because they were playing their small but important part in a huge cosmic drama.

PATMOS (GREECE)

The author of Revelation says he was on Patmos. This Greek island is one of the Dodecanese Group, yet it is only about 50 kilometres (30 miles) from the coast of modern Turkey, where the seven churches are situated to which John wrote. It is only 13 kilometres (8 miles) long, and to the pilgrims who have visited it for centuries to honour the author of the Apocalypse, are now added holiday-makers in search of sun and sea.

Getting to Patmos

There are ferries and hydrofoils on various days to Patmos from Pythagoria or Vathy in Samos, and from Cos, Rhodes and Piraeus. To travel between Patmos and Kuşadası in Turkey it is necessary to change ferries in Samos.

Getting around on Patmos

The port is in the small town of Skala, and almost opposite the quay a road is signposted to Hora, 4½ kilometres (3 miles).

After climbing this road, by bus, taxi, hire car or on foot for 2.2 kilometres (1.3 miles) you reach the **Cave of the Apocalypse**. The roof of the cave is split by three great fissures, through which St John is supposed to have heard the voice of God, the Holy Trinity. The saint's bed, kneeling place and table are pointed out. Continuing up to Hora, you reach the colossal fortress **Monastery of St John the Theologian**, which dominates the island. It was built in 1088 on the site of earlier churches and a Temple of Artemis, and fortified for protection against pirates. The treasury contains a priceless collection of manuscripts, icons, embroideries and other ecclesiastical ornaments. An old rock-surfaced path shortcuts the loops of the modern road but it is not well signposted; from the bottom it starts with some steps up to the right some 100 metres (yards) past the football pitch on the road to Hora; from the top where a signpost off the road points to the Cave of the Apocalypse; but to visit the cave you have to turn off the rock path down a flight of steps past the theology school.

Opening Times
Patmos Monastery of St John the Theologian Monday to Saturday 08.00–13.00; Sunday 08.00–12.00; and on Tuesday, Wednesday and Sunday 16.00–18.00, but times vary so telephone 0247 31398 to check. Toilets off the central courtyard
Patmos Cave of the Apocalypse same times, Tel. 0247 31234

Travelling round the seven churches

A coach tour from Ephesus round the sites of the seven churches takes about three days. The approximate distances by road are as follows:

Ephesus (Selçuk) to Smyrna (İzmir) 68 kilometres or 42 miles on route D-550 or motorway O-31

Smyrna to Pergamon (Bergama) 88 kilometres or 55 miles on route D-550 (E87)

Pergamon to Thyatira (Akhisar) 72 kilometres or 45 miles on route D-240

Thyatira to Sardis (Sart) 48 kilometres or 30 miles on route D-555, then D-300 (E96)

Sardis to Philadelphia (Alaşehir) 48 kilometres or 30 miles on route D-300 (E96) then D-585

Philadelphia to Laodicea (near Pamukkale) 65 kilometres or 40 miles on D-585, then D-320 (E87), then D-320 and local roads

Pamukkale to Selçuk 173 kilometres or 108 miles on route D-320 (E87).

> ### *When the Lamp of Love Grows Dim (Revelation 2:1–7)*
>
> To the angel of the church in Ephesus write: These are the words of him who holds the seven stars in his right hand, who walks among the seven golden lampstands: 'I know your works, your toil and your patient endurance. I know that you cannot tolerate evildoers; you have tested those who claim to be apostles but are not, and have found them to be false. I also know that you are enduring patiently and bearing up for the sake of my name, and that you have not grown weary. But I have this against you, that you have abandoned the love you had at first. Remember then from what you have fallen; repent, and do the works you did at first. If not, I will come to you and remove your lampstand from its place, unless you repent. Yet this is to your credit: you hate the works of the Nicolaitans, which I also hate. Let anyone who has an ear listen to what the Spirit is saying to the churches. To everyone who conquers, I will give permission to eat from the tree of life that is in the paradise of God.'

EPHESUS

(See pages 131–47 for notes on the history of Ephesus and visiting Ephesus today.)

Praise

Each of the letters to the seven churches is addressed to 'the angel' of that church, who may be the pastor or bishop of the church, or the messenger who would carry the letter to them, or its heavenly representative. All but two of the letters begin with praise for the Christians of that town. For those in Ephesus it is long: 'I know your works . . .'. They have built on the firm foundations laid by Saint Paul when he founded the church in Ephesus; they have spread the gospel to the towns around, enduring criticism and maybe rioting and persecution like that which broke out when he was

there (Acts 19). They will not tolerate those who claim to be Christians but continue to harm their neighbours, and they are praised for rejecting false apostles and the works of the Nicolaitans. See below under Pergamon for a suggestion about the Nicolaitans; they obviously taught false beliefs, and Bishop Ignatius of Antioch wrote to the Christians of Ephesus at the beginning of the second century, 'You all live according to truth, and no heresy has a home among you; indeed you do not so much as listen to anyone if they speak of anything except concerning Jesus Christ in truth.'

Rebuke

Usually, however, the praise is followed by rebuke. Jesus is the one 'who holds the seven stars in his right hand, who walks among the seven golden lampstands'. The meaning of the 'lampstands' has been explained earlier in Revelation 1:20: they are the seven churches. The image is based on Exodus 25:37 and Zechariah 4:2, verses which also gave rise to the seven-branched Jewish menorah. Although wax candles were known in the first century, the word used here refers to oil-lamps. Jesus said, 'Nobody lights a lamp to put it under a basket, but on a lamp-stand to give light to the whole house' (Matthew 5:15). Like the foolish virgins in Jesus' parable (Matthew 25:1–13), the Ephesians had no 'oil in my lamp' to keep them 'burning till the break of day', for (2:4) they had 'lost their first love'. So love is the oil, and it is running low. The reason may have lain in their virtues, as hinted at in 2:2: 'I know how hard you have worked'. Workaholics are too busy to love. Also in 2:2 we read: 'You will not tolerate wicked people'. Maybe they were too judgemental and fault-finding – which destroys love. The loss of their first love shows that the Christian honeymoon was over. This is a risk for individual Christians, congregations and denominations, especially in big cities like Ephesus. So in 2:7 we are told to 'Hear what the Spirit says to the churches' – us included.

Remedy

With the rebuke is given the remedy: the solution to the problem of loss of initial enthusiasm is given in verse 5: 'Remember how far you have fallen': think back to how you used to love Jesus. 'Repent': learn to depend on God, not on your own efforts. 'Live as at first': simply behave as one who is obedient to God; very often if you behave as though you love someone the feelings will follow later. Remember, repent and obey.

Warning

If you do not remember, repent and obey, your love for God dries up, the lamp goes out, and is removed from God's presence.

Promise

But if you overcome, you can eat from the tree of life, which stood in the Garden of Eden (Genesis 2:9, 3:22) which gives back to us the promise of eternal life which the human race forfeited by our disobedience.

SMYRNA

Smyrna was the name in biblical times of the city now called İzmir, today Turkey's third largest city and a NATO naval base. The hill now called Old Smyrna was settled around 3000 BC by people whose culture resembled that of Troy, because of its unique situation as a port on the Gulf of İzmir. Greek settlers came in the eleventh century BC, and it is

---

Suffering Amid Riches (Revelation 2:8–11)

And to the angel of the church in Smyrna write: These are the words of the first and the last, who was dead and came to life: 'I know your affliction and your poverty, even though you are rich. I know the slander on the part of those who say that they are Jews and are not, but are a synagogue of Satan. Do not fear what you are about to suffer. Beware, the devil is about to throw some of you into prison so that you may be tested, and for ten days you will have affliction. Be faithful until death, and I will give you the crown of life. Let anyone who has an ear listen to what the Spirit is saying to the churches. Whoever conquers will not be harmed by the second death.'

---

claimed that Homer wrote the Iliad here. In the sixth century it was taken by the Lydians, the Medes and the Persians in succession. In the fourth century BC Alexander the Great ordered the building of a stronghold on Mount Pagos, which was then 5 kilometres (3 miles) south of the town, and a new hellenistic city grew up on the north-western side of the hill. In the first century AD, under Roman rule, Smyrna was 'the Glory of Asia', with its straight streets, fine temples, a marketplace lined with pillars, and the biggest stadium in the region, on the northern slopes of Mount Pagos, where a crown was given to the winning runner – often the one who kept on going when others gave up. In 195 BC they built a temple to Dea Romana, and in AD 25 they were allowed to build a temple to Emperor Tiberius as a god.

Getting to İzmir

Pilgrims beginning a tour of the seven churches or of the sites associated with St Paul can fly to İzmir from İstanbul or Ankara. Adnan Menderes airport is 18 kilometres (11 miles) south of İzmir. There are two railway stations in İzmir, the Alsançak station near the Ferry Port at the north of the city, on Ziya Gökalp Bulvari, and the Basmane station in the town centre on the Anafartalar Caddesi. İzmir is at a road junction on route D-550 (E87) which runs north towards Bergama (Pergamon) (104 kilometres or 65 miles) and İstanbul (565 kilometres or 353 miles), and south towards Selçuk (Ephesus, 85 kilometres or 53 miles). The O-31 motorway travels south to Aydın (ancient Tralles). The D-300 (E96) leads east to Salihli (Sardis) (113 kilometres or 71 miles) and Ankara (579 kilometres or 362 miles). Route D-565 runs north–east to Manisa with the ancient site of **Magnesia-ad-Sipylus**, where Tantalus was king, (42 kilometres or 26 miles). Route D-300 and the O-32 motorway go west to **Çeşme**, a seaside town and port lying opposite

The Agora, Smyrna

the island of Chios (88 kilometres or 55 miles; for the nearby remains of **Erythrae** see above under Paul's Third Missionary Journey). **Ferries** run from Çeşme to Chios, and car ferries to Piraeus near Athens, Patras in the Peloponnese, and Brindisi in Italy. Car ferries sail from İzmir to Venice on Wednesdays and from Venice to İzmir on Saturdays, consult **www.idi.com.tr**

İzmir today

On the south-east side of the city, up a road signposted Kadifekale, where there is a small parking area for buses and other vehicles, is the medieval **hilltop citadel** on top of Mount Pagos. Stones from the Macedonian acropolis and Roman, Byzantine, Genoese and Ottoman periods are incorporated in the walls, and there is a superb view of the city and Gulf of İzmir from the top. The bowl of the **stadium** can just be traced on the northern slope, although the area is built over with houses. St Polycarp (see below) is supposed to be buried above the stadium. North-west of the citadel, on Sokak 816, is the ancient **agora** or marketplace. It originally dated from the Greek period but was destroyed in an earthquake in AD 178; remains can be seen of the structures built mostly in the reign of Emperor Marcus Aurelius in the second century AD. A 165-metre (180 yards) long colonnade on the north side supported on a vaulted basement was originally a two-storey city administration hall called the **basilica**; a fine row of pillars survives. On the east side a row of **shops** opened onto the main street of the city.

Halfway down the steep winding road called M. Rifat Paşa Caddesi is the **archaeological museum**, with remains from the agora at Smyrna as well as other nearby sites. There is practically no parking space in central İzmir, so these sites are best visited on foot or by taxi. There is a **Franciscan church** dedicated to St Polycarp in İzmir today, and the **Anglican church** there has a long and distinguished history. Also there is a small Turkish **evangelical congregation** which keeps a low profile.

Opening Times

İzmir agora daily 08.30–12.00 and 13.00–17.00
İzmir archaeological museum Tel. 0232 489 0796, daily 09.00–18.30. Toilets at the rear of the entrance hall

Praise

The risen Christ writes to the church in Smyrna: 'I know your affliction and your poverty, even though you are rich.' Some of those who were economically rich were spiritually poor. Yet in the midst of this rich city, the Christian faith was also found among those who were economically poor. Those who have nothing are most attracted by a God who 'for your sakes became poor, so that by his poverty you might become rich' (2 Corinthians 7:9). Jesus said, 'Blessed are the poor in spirit' (Matthew 5:3) – those who do not depend on their possessions because spiritual riches make material gain unimportant. In this letter alone there is no rebuke or remedy.

Warning

Smyrna was famous as a centre of **emperor worship** (see below under Pergamon). People who lived in the Roman empire would burn a pinch of incense before a statue of the emperor as if he were a god. But it became a test of loyalty: burn incense or die. Jews said they had only one God. They were therefore granted a unique exemption as a 'registered religion'; anyone of the Jewish race was excused from sacrificing to Caesar. The Christians, however, were of many races, so they could not become a *religio licita* (legal religion). 'Those who say they are Jews and are not' were probably Jews who betrayed the Christians to the authorities:

Christians appeared to be teaching Jews not to obey the law, and teaching non-Jews that they could become part of God's chosen people simply by being baptized, so they put the Jews' status (as a *religio licita*) at risk. The risen Christ warns the Christians of Smyrna that some of them would be imprisoned because of these accusations; they must 'be faithful until death': refuse to sacrifice even if they are executed for disloyalty.

Promise

If they will keep the faith, even if it means dying for it, Jesus will give them a crown as a prize, like that of the winners in the Smyrna games. They will be unharmed by the second death, the death of the soul, which follows the death of the body for those who do not have the life of God within them. To those who keep going when the rest have dropped out – the faithful, regular worshippers who attend church Sunday by Sunday even when it is inconvenient, and who show their faith by patient service to their neighbours – Jesus promises a crown, like that of the winning athlete; only in your case the crown will consist of eternal life. Maybe others who are less committed will enjoy eternal life also, but for those who are faithful, we can be certain because Jesus has promised it.

Polycarp of Smyrna

Christians in Smyrna did die; one of them, who may have been a young man when the letter from Christ in Revelation was first read out there, became the Bishop of Smyrna. His name was Polycarp; he was martyred when aged 86 in about 155 AD:

When the armed men came to arrest him . . . Polycarp gave instructions that a table should be spread for them with as much to eat and drink as they wished, and persuaded them to allow him an hour to pray undisturbed. When they agreed, he stood up and prayed, being so full of the grace of God that for two hours he could not keep quiet. The armed men who heard this were amazed, and some of them felt very sorry that they had come to arrest such a wonderful old man. But when at last he had finished praying, after remembering all whom he had ever met, small and great, high and low, and the whole Church throughout the world, they took him away . . .

In the stadium the magistrate tried to persuade him: 'Swear by Caesar as a God and I will release you; curse this Christ.' Polycarp replied, 'I have been his servant for eighty-six years and he has never mistreated me. Then how can I blaspheme the King who saved me?' . . .

When he was tied to the stake, before they lit the fire, Polycarp looked up to heaven and said, 'O Lord God almighty, the Father of your beloved and blessed Son Jesus Christ, through whom we have our knowledge of you, the God of the angels and all the heavenly powers and of all creation and of all those righteous people who live in your presence; I bless you for giving me this day and this hour, so that I might inherit a place among the martyrs who have shared Christ's cup of suffering to bring them resurrection to imperishable and eternal life of soul and body in the Holy Spirit. Receive me into your presence today, as a valuable and acceptable sacrifice, as you have already told me I would be, dependable and true God. For this and everything I praise you, I thank you, I glorify you, through the eternal heavenly high-priest Jesus Christ, your beloved Son. Through him and with him and the Holy Spirit be glory both now and ever and for the ages to come. Amen.'

– From *The Letter from the Church in Smyrna on the Martyrdom of St Polycarp* 7, 8 and 14

PERGAMON / PERGAMUM

The small Turkish town of Bergama, north of İzmir, is dominated today by the steep 275 metres (900 feet) high hill which formed the acropolis of ancient Pergamon, in most Bible translations given its Latin spelling, Pergamum. There was a small settlement on the top of this hill from the fifth century BC. Lysimachos, the general who controlled this area after the death of Alexander the Great, kept a huge treasure of 9,000 talents here, and left a treasurer, called Philetairus, in charge of it. When Lysimachos died Philetairus held on to the treasure and declared himself the first king of the independent territory of Pergamon (283–263 BC). King Eumenes II (179–159 BC) formed an alliance with Rome, and created a library of 200,000 volumes.

The rival library of Alexandria in Egypt became jealous, and cut off the supply of papyrus from the Nile, so the people of Pergamon scraped down goat skins and invented 'Pergamenta charta' or parchment (2 Timothy 4:13). Unlike papyrus, which had to be rolled into a scroll, parchment or vellum can be folded without cracking, so it made possible the development of the codex or book. When Mark Antony offered the library of Pergamon to Cleopatra, however, the contents were absorbed into the library of Alexandria.

The city was attacked by the wandering Celtic tribes who gave their name to Gaul and Galatia.

A famous marble statue of 'The Dying Gaul', copied from a bronze set up in Pergamon, is in the Museo Capitolino in Rome (see above under Rome for opening times). To commemorate the defeat of the Galatians, King Eumenes II built, between 180 and 160 BC, the huge Altar of Zeus – in fact a temple with an 18-foot high podium, with a great frieze, showing a battle between gods and giants, running for 136 metres (446 feet) around the base. It has been reconstructed to form the centrepiece of the Pergamon Museum in Berlin, Germany; there is a model of it in the archaeology museum at Bergama.

Pergamon is not on the coast, and is of no commercial significance, except as a centre for the wool from the hills. So King Attalos III voluntarily gave up their independence and bequeathed the Pergamene kingdom to Rome, who turned it into the Province of Asia.

In 29 BC Pergamon was allowed to build a temple to Augustus – this was the first temple outside Rome dedicated to a living emperor. Although other centres for emperor worship were later built at Smyrna and Ephesus, Pergamon remained the principal centre for the whole province of Asia.

The Temple of Healing at the foot of the hill represents a very early worship of the snake god Serapis, whose image remains the symbol of the medical profession in the intertwined snakes of the cadduceus.

> ### *Where Satan Dwells (Revelation 2:12–17)*
>
> And to the angel of the church in Pergamum write: These are the words of him who has the sharp two-edged sword: 'I know where you are living, where Satan's throne is. Yet you are holding fast to my name, and you did not deny your faith in me even in the days of Antipas my witness, my faithful one, who was killed among you, where Satan lives. But I have a few things against you: you have some there who hold to the teaching of Balaam, who taught Balak to put a stumbling block before the people of Israel, so that they would eat food sacrificed to idols and practice fornication. So you also have some who hold to the teaching of the Nicolaitans. Repent then. If not, I will come to you soon and make war against them with the sword of my mouth. Let anyone who has an ear listen to what the Spirit is saying to the churches. To everyone who conquers I will give some of the hidden manna, and I will give a white stone, and on the white stone is written a new name that no one knows except the one who receives it.'

Getting to Pergamon

Bergama lies on route D-240 near the junction with the D-550 (E87), 88 kilometres (55 miles) north of İzmir, 30 kilometres (20 miles) from the coast and 3 kilometres (2 miles) north of the Caicus River in southern Mysia. The top of the acropolis is 6 kilometres (4 miles) north of the **archaeology museum** in the centre of the town, and the asklepion is 3½ kilometres (2 miles) south of the museum. A turning near the Red Basilica signposted to Kozak leads to a beautiful forest road heading north which joins the D-550 (E87) south of Edremit.

Pergamon today

The remains of the Roman city lie mostly underneath the modern town. At the foot of the steep road leading up the acropolis is the large **Red Basilica**, built of bricks but originally covered in coloured marble. Because some of the pillars are in an Egyptian fashion with male and female figures back to back, it is generally thought to have been built by Emperor Trajan (AD 117–38) as a temple to the Egyptian gods. It was later used as a church dedicated to the apostle John. It had a huge courtyard, now buried under houses, with the river flowing through a tunnel underneath. From there, those who are prepared to walk up the hill will pass the **gate of the acropolis**; the **lower agora** (second century BC) which had an **odeon** and a covered **stadium** beside it; the **gymnasium** on three terraces for different age-groups; the **Roman baths**; the **Temple of Hera** (second

PERGAMON
Bergama - Turkey

Acropolis
Arsenal
Royal Palaces
Temple of Trajan
Library
Temple of Athena
Temple of Dionysos
Heroon
Theatre
Altar of Zeus (site)
Upper Agora

N

Gymnasium

0   500 m.
0   500 yards

Lower Agora

Theatre
Sacred Way
Library
Porch
Asklepios
Temple
Telesphoros
Temple
Tunnel

Red Basilica
Site of courtyard

Museum

D-240 to Akhisar

River Selinus

D-240 to Izmir

century BC), the **Temple of Demeter** (third century BC) where the Eleusinian mystery religion was celebrated; and the **upper agora**.

Those who drive up the steep motor road (4 kilometres or 2½ miles), however, will walk down from the car park to the upper agora, then pass the foundations of the **Altar of Zeus** (now in Berlin). Climbing up again they will see on their right the remains of the **palaces of the kings of Pergamon**, and on their left the steep auditorium of the **theatre**, which would hold an audience of 15,000 with a magnificent view and a little Ionic **Temple of Dionysos** next to the stage; the **Temple of Athena** (fourth century BC); the **library** (170 BC); the **Temple of Trajan** (built

between AD 117 and 138) – in this huge temple there was an enormous statue of the emperor, of which only a hand and a foot remain – and the **arsenal**, where 900 rounds of spherical shot were stored for use in catapults. From the arsenal you can see parts of the **aqueduct** which brought water 45 kilometres (28 miles) and then in a siphon of lead pipes, which would withstand a pressure of twenty atmospheres, to the summit of the acropolis.

South-west of the town of Bergama, the healing temple or **asklepion** – Asklepios was another name for Serapis – was founded in the fourth century BC; the physician Galen (AD 129–199) practised here. It is approached by an 800 metres (875 yards) long **sacred way**, and on a pillar near the entrance is a carving of a snake. The **northern colonnade** leads from the **library** to the **theatre**, which could seat 30,000. There will probably be time in the theatre there for groups to worship and take a

The Theatre, Pergamon

group photograph. In the square at the centre of the temple was a **sacred well** with a pool for therapeutic washing; and a **tunnel**: it is said that as the patients passed through this tunnel the priests would whisper oracles of healing through the openings above their heads. The tunnel leads to a two-storey round **Temple of Telesphorus**, another god of healing, who had two daughters Hygeia and Panacea. Here bathing and incubation, where sick people spent the night and were treated on the basis of their dreams, were practised. It is said that tame snakes, which were considered an incarnation of the god, would crawl over them as they slept. North of this is the round **Temple of Asklepios** where departing patients gave thanks for their healing.

Opening Times
The Red Basilica (Kızıl Avlu) Tel. 0232 631 2885, daily 08.30–18.30. Toilets round the back of the ticket office
The acropolis daily 08.30–17.30. Note that the road closes half an hour after the site is closed. Toilets opposite the ticket office
The archaeological museum Tel. 0232 631 2884, daily 08.30–18.30. Toilets on the right in the forecourt
The asklepion Tel. 0232 631 2885, daily 08.30–18.30. Toilets in the car park
The Pergamon Museum on the Museum Island in Berlin, Germany (entrance from Am Kupfergraben) Tuesdays to Sundays 10.00–18.00. Toilets on the lower level, down the stairs from the entrance hall

Praise

The Christians of Pergamon continued to answer 'yes' when asked 'Do you believe in the name of Jesus?', even though one of them had been killed 'where Satan lives'. Some have suggested that this is a reference to the snake image in the temple of Serapis, for Satan is called 'that ancient serpent' in Revelation 12:9 and 20:2. But it is unlikely that Antipas would be killed in a healing temple; more likely he refused to sacrifice in the centre of emperor worship, for 'the Satan' means the tempter, and the temptation to compromise must have been strong. The altar of Zeus, where the cult was centred, shows the giants with serpents' tails instead of legs.

Rebuke

Some of them held the teaching of Balaam. In the Old Testament, Numbers 22—24 paints a favourable picture of Balaam, but Numbers 31:16 was taken to mean that Balaam advised the Jews to eat meat sacrificed to the god Baal-Peor at orgies with their non-Jewish wives. Maybe the Nicolaitans, who are also mentioned in Ephesus (see above), were similar to the Balaamites. 'Balaam' in Hebrew and 'Nicolaos' in Greek both mean 'conqueror of the people'. Could they have been followers of the Nicolaos mentioned in Acts 6:5? They obviously perverted Paul's gospel of freedom into lax moral standards.

Remedy

Christians in Pergamon who have compromised with false teaching and loose morality are called to repent. The Greek word for repentance *metanoia* does not mean remorse, though remorse may lead to repentance. Rather it is a change of mind or attitude, a different way of looking at things. The Jewish historian Josephus around this time was negotiating with the Roman army, and appealed to some rebel Jewish generals to 'repent and believe'; this shows that the real meaning of the words is 'stop relying on your own efforts and trust me'.

Warning

The risen Christ is the one 'who has the sharp two-edged sword', and if people do not repent he 'will make war against them with the sword of my mouth'. Jesus does not use violence to overcome evil, but only words of love. Tolerance is better than fanaticism, but the church at Pergamon was stretching tolerance to the point of syncretism (mixing up several religions). Jesus has a two-edged sword which will put an end to that. Most swords were hacking tools, but a two-edged one will cut the flesh off the bone on the back-stroke. The sword is the word of Jesus: compare Revelation 1:15 and 19:15: 'out of his mouth comes a sharp sword'; Hebrews 4:12: 'The word of God is sharper than any two-edged sword, piercing to the division of soul and spirit, like cutting the marrow out of a bone, and discerning the thoughts and intentions of the heart'; Ephesians 6:17: 'the sword of the Spirit which is the word of God'. This is an image drawn from the Old Testament. In Isaiah 49:2 God's servant says, 'He made my mouth like a sharp sword'; Wisdom 17:15 'the word [of God] leaped down from heaven . . . carrying the sharp sword of your authentic command'. So the Bible judges us: it distinguishes our motives.

Promise

God's word judges the motives behind our actions, but also

Emperor worship

What was the attraction of emperor worship? People wanted to give thanks for the pax Romana. They thanked their many gods for other blessings by burning a pinch of expensive incense in the temple; why not do the same for the Emperor? The Christians refused, but they were not a legal religion (see above under Smyrna). So the governors of provinces wrote to the emperor asking what to do:

> One day an unsigned paper was given to me, which listed the names of many people whom it accused of being Christians. This is the procedure I have followed with those who were brought before me on this charge. First I asked them whether or not they were Christians, warning them of the punishment if they were. If they confessed that they were, I gave them a second and third chance to deny it. If they still said they were Christians, I sent them away to be executed. Some said they were not Christians and never had been. I ordered a statue of your Royal Highness to be brought into the court, together with the images of the gods. I dictated a prayer to the gods and made the accused repeat it after me; then I had them make supplication with incense and wine to your statue. Moreover I made them curse Christ. These are all things which, so it is said, those who are really Christians cannot be made to do. Then I thought it right to let them go.'

From *Pliny to Trajan, Letter X.96*, in Bythinia c. AD 112

gives us grace to resist temptation. 'Manna', which means 'what is it?', was the name given to the bread provided by Moses in the wilderness (Exodus 16), which was placed in the temple (Exodus 16:33); some Jews believed it was hidden by Jeremiah at the time of the exile, and expected that it would be brought back by the Messiah. Christians will have seen in this a reference to Holy Communion, through which we are strengthened with God's grace. God also gives us a white stone to declare us innocent if we overcome. The Jewish high priests wore in their breastplate two stones called Urim and Thummim with the name of God engraved on them, used to find out the will of God (Exodus 27:30). Some people wore an amulet with the name of their god in strange writing; the secret name of Jesus is 'Love'. Or this could be the stone ticket to a feast; or the stone with which the jury gave a verdict of innocent, the opposite of being 'black-balled'.

Meat offered to idols

The church at Pergamon is rebuked for compromising about meat offered to idols. Because there were no abattoirs or slaughter houses, most beasts were slaughtered in the temples and offered to the god of that temple before the meat was sold. The old gods were being abandoned by the young because they were thought to have no relevance to the new age; yet private parties and trade guild feasts were still held in temples; and the meat eaten there had previously been offered to idols. Many said that to eat such meat meant that you believed in the power of that god, whereas for Christians, Jesus is the only power.

Paul, in 1 Corinthians 8, points out that other gods 'don't exist', and you have no need to ask about the source of your food. Nevertheless, for those who are uncertain, to see Christians knowingly eating such meat might lead to the assumption that Christians worship other gods also. So he says, in effect, don't ask, but if you are challenged, don't eat; it is better to be a vegetarian than to cause someone, who is not quite sure whether the other gods exist, to turn aside from faith in Jesus because they see you eating in a temple. Many temptations come from peer pressure: 'everybody's doing it'. Christians must be prepared to be non-conformists, to stand up and be counted.

THYATIRA

Akhisar is a modern city on the site of the ancient town of Thyatira. The Roman author Pliny the Younger tells us that Thyatira was founded by the Lydians and called Pelopia, then renamed by Seleucus Nicator in the third century BC and garrisoned with Macedonian troops. It was on the border between the kingdom of Pergamon and the Seleucid empire, and changed hands several times. The Jewish author Josephus writes that Seleucus also settled a colony of Jews there to provide craftsmen and an economic life for the town. Lydia, the merchant of purple cloth at Philippi, was from Thyatira. Thyatira was a small place. Its only claim to fame was the number of trade guilds referred to in its inscriptions.

Getting to Thyatira

Akhisar, called by its Greek name 'Axari' by the local Turkish population, stands at a crossroads between the roads from Bergama (Pergamon / Pergamum, route D-240, about 72 kilometres or 45 miles); Salihli (Sardis, route D-555, about 48 kilometres or 30 miles); İzmir (Smyrna, route D-565, 95 kilometres or 60 miles) and Balikesir (route D-565, 88 kilometres or 55 miles). There are two small brown signs

Tempted by Jezebel (Revelation 2:18–29)

And to the angel of the church in Thyatira write: These are the words of the Son of God, who has eyes like a flame of fire, and whose feet are like burnished bronze: 'I know your works – your love, faith, service, and patient endurance. I know that your last works are greater than the first. But I have this against you: you tolerate that woman Jezebel, who calls herself a prophet and is teaching and beguiling my servants to practice fornication and to eat food sacrificed to idols. I gave her time to repent, but she refuses to repent of her fornication. Beware, I am throwing her on a bed, and those who commit adultery with her I am throwing into great distress, unless they repent of her doings; and I will strike her children dead. And all the churches will know that I am the one who searches minds and hearts, and I will give to each of you as your works deserve. But to the rest of you in Thyatira, who do not hold this teaching, who have not learned what some call 'the deep things of Satan,' to you I say, I do not lay on you any other burden; only hold fast to what you have until I come. To everyone who conquers and continues to do my works to the end, I will give authority over the nations; to rule them with an iron rod, as when clay pots are shattered – even as I also received authority from my Father. To the one who conquers I will also give the morning star. Let anyone who has an ear listen to what the Spirit is saying to the churches.'

pointing to 'Thyateira' high up on the central reservation of the D-565, pointing down a side turning to the south-east. Coaches should pass these travelling north-east then follow another similar sign on the roadside which leads to an area reserved for parking tourist coaches. The site lies on Cemal Ilgaz Caddesi on the corner with Mustafa Abut Caddesi.

Thyatira today

Akhisar has practically nothing to show of the old town of Thyatira today, except a jumble of ancient stones surrounding the walls of a **Byzantine church**, which may have been converted from a first-century BC Roman secular basilica, with an agora and a colonnaded street in front of it. Pilgrims can read the letter of the risen Christ to Thyatira in the ruins of the church.

Opening Times

Thyatira site daily 08.30–midnight. Toilets by the ticket booth

Praise

Coins from Thyatira show that they worshipped the emperor as an incarnation of Apollo the sun god, and we know that the guild of workers in bronze was an important one. The description of the risen Christ in Revelation 2:18 shows how words are always chosen which will have a special meaning for each town. The Christians of Thyatira are praised not only for their deeds of love, faith, service and patient endurance, but because these deeds are increasing.

Rebuke

The Christians of Thyatira are rebuked for tolerating 'Jezebel'. In 1 Kings 16:31, etc., Jezebel was a king's wife who taught the Israelites to worship idols. If you identify your god with a statue, your god is too small. You may think god can only hear you if you pray in the temple, and god will not care what you do when he or she cannot see you. Second, if you have more than one god you can play them off against each other, choosing to obey the god of sex on some days and the god of war on others. Polytheism has no moral imperative, you can do what is right in your own eyes.

The Jezebel in Thyatira could have been a travelling prophetess who claimed to know better than the church leaders. She was teaching the congregation to eat meat sacrificed to idols, contradicting the decision of the church in Jerusalem recorded in Acts 15:6–29. But to earn your living in Thyatira you had to practise a trade: carpenter, shopkeeper

and so on. It was illegal to practise a trade unless you were a member of a trade guild. Members of guilds had to attend the annual dinner. The dinner was always held in a temple. The meat served had always been sacrificed first to the god of that temple. What was a Christian Thyatiran to do? If you refused you might become unemployed and unemployable, which meant starvation for your family.

Warning

'Jezebel' seems to have recommended a complete compromise with the pagan feasts, and lax sexual morals, though 'fornication' might be symbolic language for idolatry (Hosea 9:1). If the other Christians followed her example, this could have been the end of Christianity in Thyatira. So she is warned by the risen Christ that if she goes on like this, she will indeed be thrown into bed with her followers, but in her case a bed of pain. And the Christians are warned not to tolerate her.

Remedy

The Thyatirans are told to hold on and refuse to compromise. Tolerance is not indifference to truth and morality. Tolerance means 'I disapprove of what you say, but I will defend to the death your right to say it' (Voltaire). An American humorist wrote that you should always respect a man's religious beliefs, in the same way you respect his belief that his wife is beautiful and his children are clever; you admire him for holding them, but you don't need to agree with them. Christians should rejoice in a multi-cultural society and oppose any form of discrimination, but we must not let the vulnerable be misled. It is misleading to teach that it doesn't matter what you believe, because beliefs affect the way you behave. It is misleading to teach that it doesn't matter how you live, because, for example, promiscuity is damaging to the emotional maturity of individuals and to the stable family atmosphere that children need. Christians are taught to hate the sin and love the sinner. Holiness includes tolerating other faiths and many individual beliefs, but it forbids distorting the truth which we believe, and compromising in our personal morality. It is wrong to dilute the truth of God's love, which is what idolatry does, and to treat the opposite sex as being there for our gratification, which is what is sinful about fornication.

Promise

Yet 'to the one who overcomes temptation I will give the morning star,' which is the guarantee that a new day will follow the night; in Revelation 22:16 Jesus himself is described as the morning star.

SARDIS

The hamlet of Sart, ancient Sardis, lies on the busy highway from İzmir to Ankara. The remains of a large Temple of Artemis stand at the foot of a steep acropolis, and on the other side of the main road the gymnasium has been extensively restored. The legend of the origins of Sardis are found in Aesop's Fables. King Midas had asked the god Bacchus to cause everything he touched to turn to gold. When he found that he could not eat or drink, he asked for the gift to be taken away, and was told to wash in the River Pactolos. From then on, it was said, the sand of the river was full of gold, and the town built on the bank became enormously rich. It was named Sardis. The gold was extracted from the stream by allowing it to settle on sheepskins, which may have given rise to the legend of the Golden Fleece.

Moving from legend to history, the King of Lydia, with his capital in Sardis, was Croesus (reigned 560–546 BC), which is why we say 'rich as Croesus'. Gold coinage is supposed to have been invented during his reign in Sardis. It was also at a road junction, and grew rich with the wool trade. Croesus built the first temple of Artemis in Sardis, which was destroyed by the Greeks in 498 BC. Aesop is said to have written his Fables while living at Sardis at the court of King Croesus. In 546 BC Croesus asked the oracle at Delphi whether he should attack Cyrus, the emperor of Persia, and received the

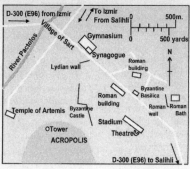

SARDIS (SART - TURKEY)

'Delphic' reply: 'If you attack, a great army will be defeated.' He did so, only to discover that it was his own army which was destroyed.

Cyrus, who is praised in Isaiah 44:28—45:7 because he allowed the Israelites to return to Jerusalem from their exile in Babylon, was attacking the acropolis of Sardis. It is so steep that the attackers could find no way up, and the defenders relaxed their guard. Then a defender dropped his helmet, and picked his way down a secret path to retrieve it. The attackers now knew the way in, and the next night they found the people of Sardis sleeping and the walls undefended, believing they could never be attacked.

In 334 BC Alexander captured Sardis and rebuilt the temple of Artemis. But by their failure to watch, the people of Sardis allowed the acropolis to be scaled again by Cretans in 218 BC.

Getting to Sardis

Sart lies on the river Ecelkapiz or Sart Çayi, ancient Pactolos, and on the D-300 (E96) highway from İzmir (Smyrna) to Ankara, 94 kilometres (59 miles) from İzmir, between the towns of Turgutlu and Salihli.

The Temple of Artemis and the Acropolis, Sardis

Salihli is also on the railway between Konya (Iconium) and İzmir. Sardis is about 60 kilometres (37 miles) from Thyatira and about 45

The Gymnasium, Sardis

fine **Temple to Artemis**. The temple is 100 metres (330 feet) long by 48 metres (155 feet) across, with the largest Ionic columns in the Hellenistic world. A small **Christian church** was built into the ruins in around AD 400. Across the road is a large **gymnasium** complex, completed in the second century AD, which controversially has been partly reconstructed. A second to seventh century AD **synagogue** was built on the site. Along the side nearest the modern road are the remains of some Byzantine shops and the Roman marble road, 18.5 metres (20 yards) wide. There are remains of a few **houses**, a **theatre** and a **stadium** from the Roman period.

kilometres (28 miles) from Philadelphia. A new by-pass means that traffic from Salihli is diverted away from the archeological sites, and you must be careful to turn off the bypass at the sign pointing into the village centre.

Sardis today

The **acropolis** is the steep rocky summit, with a superb view, north of the ruins of the

Opening Times
The Artemision is open most of the hours of daylight, pay for

---

Wake Up! (Revelation 3:1–6)

And to the angel of the church in Sardis write: These are the words of him who has the seven spirits of God and the seven stars: 'I know your works; you have a name of being alive, but you are dead. Wake up, and strengthen what remains and is on the point of death, for I have not found your works perfect in the sight of my God. Remember then what you received and heard; obey it, and repent. If you do not wake up, I will come like a thief, and you will not know at what hour I will come to you. Yet you have still a few persons in Sardis who have not soiled their clothes; they will walk with me, dressed in white, for they are worthy. If you conquer, you will be clothed like them in white robes, and I will not blot your name out of the book of life; I will confess your name before my Father and before his angels. Let anyone who has an ear listen to what the Spirit is saying to the churches.'

admission near the gateway to the site. Toilets by the gate **The gymnasium, baths and synagogue** daily 08.00–19.00. Toilets on the right of the ticket office

Rebuke

The letter to Sardis begins with rebuke, and saves the praise, for a faithful minority, until later. They were a wealthy church, and had a reputation for being a lively one, but spiritually they were dead.

Remedy

The remedy, couched in words which would remind them of the shameful history of their town, was a call to wake up! You think you're rich and safe, says the risen Christ, but death could attack at any time, like the Persians attacking Sardis. Wake up, as in Cyrus' day, strengthen what remains, remember, obey, repent. Becoming a Christian makes a change in our way of looking at things. There has to be a clear decision to look at my life in the way that Jesus does, not in the way that the world does. This may or may not involve remorse, and it may or it may not be public; but at some stage a decision is needed: are you on the side of Jesus, 'Do you turn to Christ?'

Warning

Jesus warns: 'I will come like a thief'. Perhaps because of the prevalence of burglary, this is an image for the suddenness of judgement used frequently in

the New Testament: Matthew 24:43; Luke 12:39; 1 Thessalonians 5:2–4; 2 Peter 3:10; Revelation 16:15.

Praise

Praise is limited to a few who have clean clothes, the image used in Revelation for good deeds (Revelation 19:8). There may be a comparison here with those who walk, dressed in white, beside a king at his triumphal procession.

Promise

If you walk with Christ your name will be written in the book of life: the list of those who are going to have eternal life with God in heaven. This is a metaphor found in Exodus 32:32, Psalm 69:28; Daniel 12:1; Philippians 4:3; Revelation 20:15. It is very powerful, because the opposite is the death list. Deletion from the register of synagogue members (John 9:22, 12:42, 16:2) removed the protection of the legal religion and carried probable condemnation to death.

PHILADELPHIA

In the Turkish town of Alaşehir today, all that remains of the Christian buildings after a succession of frequent earthquakes are three massive pillars of an ancient basilica. Once it was the town of Philadelphia, which means brotherly love. King Attalus II of Pergamon had sent Macedonian troops to occupy the Lydian hill settlement of

---

The Key, the Open Door and the Pillar (Revelation 3:7–14)

And to the angel of the church in Philadelphia write: These are the words of the holy one, the true one, who has the key of David, who opens and no one will shut, who shuts and no one opens: 'I know your works. Look, I have set before you an open door, which no one is able to shut. I know that you have but little power, and yet you have kept my word and have not denied my name. I will make those of the synagogue of Satan who say that they are Jews and are not, but are lying – I will make them come and bow down before your feet, and they will learn that I have loved you. Because you have kept my word of patient endurance, I will keep you from the hour of trial that is coming on the whole world to test the inhabitants of the earth. I am coming soon; hold fast to what you have, so that no one may seize your crown. If you conquer, I will make you a pillar in the temple of my God; you will never go out of it. I will write on you the name of my God, and the name of the city of my God, the new Jerusalem that comes down from my God out of heaven, and my own new name. Let anyone who has an ear listen to what the Spirit is saying to the churches.'

Callebetus. Attalus was known as Philadelphus because of his loyal affection for his brother Eumenes, who was the previous king. Philadelphia was on the border of three regions, Mysia, Lydia and Phrygia, like a doorway opening onto the trade routes to the East. The town had been founded only 200 years earlier to spread Greek culture into the wilds of Phrygia and Lydia.

Getting to Philadelphia

Alaşehir is just off route D-585, which joins Salihli (Sardis, on the D-300 [E96]), with Denizli (on the D-320 [E87]), the junction for Hierapolis. It is about 45 kilometres (28 miles) east of Sardis and about 90 kilometres (52 miles) north-west of Laodicea. It is also on the railway between Konya (Iconium) and İzmir (Smyrna). There are two small yellow signs to 'Saint Jean Iskelesi' pointing left at the second traffic island after you leave the main road, then right just after the next one.

Church pillars, Philadelphia

Pillars of the church

The three pillars of the basilica are the remains of a Byzantine church dedicated to St John.

The caretaker of the site will allow you the use of his courtyard for worship, and offer to sell you Christian books.

Praise

The Christians in the city of brotherly love are praised for their deeds, and because they have 'kept my word, and not denied my name' – their lives were based on the scriptures, and they were not afraid to admit that they were Christians.

Opportunity

There is no rebuke in this letter. The risen Christ writes to the Christians in Philadelphia about the open door before them; this is a phrase Paul had used of opportunities for evangelism (1 Corinthians 16:9; Colossians 4:3). Their strategic situation gave them an opportunity to spread, not Greek culture but Christian love, to those who do not know about it. He also quotes from Isaiah 22:22: 'I will place on his shoulder the key of the house of David; he shall open, and no one shall shut; he shall shut, and no one shall open.' Jesus is the key who opens all doors to us, to spread the good news of God's love, to people around the world, and to the homes and hearts of people in our own area. Once a census enumerator asked me, 'What is your employer's business and how long has he been doing it?' I replied, 'He's been in the love business ever since he created the world, and my job is to help him spread it around a bit.'

Christians have an open door to spread brotherly love.

Obstacles

What was hindering them from taking this opportunity was that they were weak, and suffering from Jewish opposition – as elsewhere the Jews felt their position as a tolerated ethnic community was threatened by the multi-racial Christian group claiming the same exemption from sacrifice to Caesar.

Warning

The church in Philadelphia are warned about imminent persecution; they must keep the faith, 'Hold on to what you have!'

Promise

If they are faithful Christ will keep them from the hour of trial – this is what we mean when we pray that he will 'lead us, not into temptation'. 'I am coming,' he promises; if they understood this to mean that the end of the world would happen within their lifetime they were cruelly deceived; but if they understood it as a promise of Christ's invisible presence with them in their times of testing, they will have found it to be gloriously true. They are also promised that they will be made pillars in Christ's temple, with a new name ('love') written on them. In Galatians 2:9 Paul calls James and Cephas and John 'pillars'; today we talk about people as being 'pillars of the church'; not only do they support the

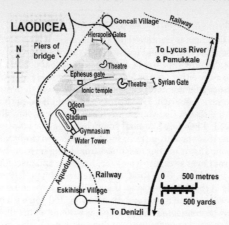

LAODICEA

N

Goncali Village — Railway

Hierapolis Gates

Piers of bridge

To Lycus River & Pamukkale

Theatre

Ephesus gate

Theatre

Ionic temple

Syrian Gate

Odeon

Stadium

Gymnasium

Water Tower

Aqueduct

Railway

Eskihisar Village

To Denizli

0   500 metres

0   500 yards

community spiritually, sadly they are sometimes the only ones left when all else are gone.

LAODICEA

Pamukkale is a popular resort for Turkish and foreign holiday-makers, where the gleaming white terraces of calcium deposits, known as travertine, from the hot springs, form one of the most photographed images of Turkey. The name of the resort means 'cotton castle'. It is surrounded by the remains of the hellenistic city of Hierapolis. Hierapolis, Laodicea and Colossae were three neighbouring towns, mentioned in the Bible, in the valley of the River Lycus, a tributary of the River Meander; they all became rich because they were on the main trade route between Ephesus and Syria. Polycrates, who was Bishop of Ephesus at the end of the second century, mentions that Philip was killed in Hierapolis in AD 80; but the tradition is not clear whether this is one of The Twelve (Acts 1:13) or one of the Seven (Acts 6:5). Papias from the next generation, who told us how the Gospels were written, is also buried in Hierapolis.

Laodicea was founded in the third century BC by King Antiochus II of Syria, who named it after his wife. It drew its water from more hot springs to the south. There was a rebellion in Laodicea in 220 BC against Antiochus III the Great; to prevent a recurrence he settled 2000 Jewish families from Babylon in the region. In the first century BC the Latin orator Cicero defended the governor of Laodicea who was charged with seizing twenty pounds of gold which the Jewish community of Laodicea were sending to the Temple in Jerusalem, which represents a rich Jewish community of around 7,500 men.

The people of Laodicea reckoned they had no need to draw on the

221

The Lukewarm Church (Revelation 3:14–22)

And to the angel of the church in Laodicea write: The words of the Amen, the faithful and true witness, the origin of God's creation: 'I know your works; you are neither cold nor hot. I wish that you were either cold or hot. So, because you are lukewarm, and neither cold nor hot, I am about to spit you out of my mouth. For you say, "I am rich, I have prospered, and I need nothing." You do not realize that you are wretched, pitiable, poor, blind, and naked. Therefore I counsel you to buy from me gold refined by fire so that you may be rich; and white robes to clothe you and to keep the shame of your nakedness from being seen; and salve to anoint your eyes so that you may see. I reprove and discipline those whom I love. Be earnest, therefore, and repent. Listen! I am standing at the door, knocking; if you hear my voice and open the door, I will come in to you and eat with you, and you with me. To the one who conquers I will give a place with me on my throne, just as I myself conquered and sat down with my Father on his throne. Let anyone who has an ear listen to what the Spirit is saying to the churches.'

Christians in Colossae, Hierapolis and Laodicea (Colossians 4:12–16)

Epaphras . . . greets you. . . . he has worked hard for you and for those in Laodicea and in Hierapolis. . . . Give my greetings to the brothers and sisters in Laodicea, and to Nympha and the church in her house. And when this letter has been read among you, have it read also in the church of the Laodiceans; and see that you read also the letter from Laodicea.

earthquake relief fund which the Roman Senate had set up in AD 60, they thought they were rich enough to pay for the repairs to their city themselves. They had a medical school which produced a famous eye ointment made from collyrium; possibly Luke 'the beloved physician' studied medicine there. The Laodiceans were proud of their wealth derived from banking, clothing made from the naturally black wool of the local sheep, eye ointment, and from visitors who came to drink or bathe in the healing waters. But the water cooled down on its way, and furred up the pipes; they advertised it as hot, but it was lukewarm.

Getting around in the Lycus Valley

Highway D-320 (E87) comes into Denizli from the north-west, and just before the railway station, where you can also catch a Dolmuş minibus, there is a sharp left turn onto the D-320 heading north-east, and

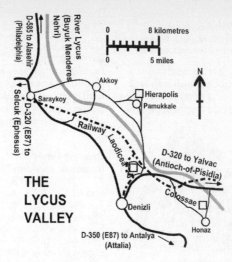

THE LYCUS VALLEY

then another left turn soon after onto an unnumbered road, both signposted towards Pamukkale. On this road there are two signposts left to **'Laodikeia'**; the first leads over a railway crossing to the stadium and baths, the second arrives quite quickly at the theatres. The main road through Pamukkale village bypasses **Hierapolis**, but two special approach roads have been made leading to the two **visitor centre** entrances. Then, returning towards Denizli, you turn left (east) at the junction onto the D-320 towards Afyon. Avoid the first road off this marked to Honaz, but take the second turning 12 kilometres (7½ miles) from the junction, to the right, signposted 'Honaz 6 km, Collesae 1 km'. In spite of this it is 3 kilometres (2 miles) to the mound of Colossae, which is easily identifiable on the right. There is also a view of the village of Honaz on the site of Khonai, where the last Byzantine inhabitants of Colossae moved in the ninth century because it was more easily defended.

The Lycus Valley towns today

In **Hierapolis**, you can visit the **Roman street** leading to the extensive **necropolis** or cemetery, some of the graves and buildings being marked with Christian symbols. Or you can swim in the **hot spring water** in the Thermal Centre. Or you can view the **travertine terraces**, though you are not allowed to walk on them. The **museum** is built into the **Roman baths**. The **theatre** and the octagonal **martyrium of St Philip** are up the hill. At times Hierapolis is full of tourists.

Laodicea is a partially excavated hill which is about 2 kilometres (1 mile) square. The **aqueduct**, a system of pipes at

Water Tower, Laodicea

ground level bringing the water from the hot springs to the south, can be easily seen coming down the hill to the approach road. Shortly after this an earth road turns off to the right over another railway crossing – beware of trains, this crossing has no signals or gates. The earth road takes you up onto the tel, to an extensive **gymnasium complex**, and on to the two **theatres** (one Greek and one Roman in design). At the end of the gymnasium is a **water tower**; readers of Revelation will notice that the pipes can be seen to have 'furred up' with the deposit of the salts as the water cooled down on its long journey from the hot springs. There were several **gateways** to the city; perhaps the risen Christ

described himself as knocking for admission at one of these.

Colossae is a totally unexcavated mound. The founding of Laodicea led to the gradual decline of Colossae until it was abandoned. Of what was once named as a 'colossal' city, practically nothing is to be seen.

Opening Times
Hierapolis Museum Tel. 0258 272 2034, daily 08.30–12.30 and 13.30–18.00. Toilets in the Thermal Centre. The archaeological site and the terraces are always open but there is a substantial admission charge payable at the east or west visitor centres
Laodicea and Colossae are always open

Rebuke

For this prosperous and successful church there is no praise. The risen Christ declares that the Laodiceans are wretched, pitiful, poor, blind, naked, and their faith is lukewarm, like their water. They need eye salve, they need white clothes. Christ hits them below the belt by attacking the things they are most proud of. They were lukewarm Christians, with a conventional, one-day-a-week religion, and scared of enthusiasm. Jesus loves atheists, because there is a chance they will become converts. But he can't stand lukewarm Christians, because they are not hot enough to be any use.

Remedy

So he invites them to buy from him what they thought they already had in abundance: gold, white clothes and eye ointment. But he means treasure in heaven, good deeds and spiritual insight.

Warning

To us as to the Laodiceans Christ says, 'Behold, I stand at the door and knock . . . if you hear my voice, I will come in and share a meal with you.' He invites us to eat at his table at Holy Communion. But he also wants to eat at our table, in our homes and our daily life, and he can't get in. Holman Hunt's famous picture 'The Light of the World' shows why: there is no handle on the outside, the door can only be opened from the inside.

Promise

To those who overcome the tendency to be merely lukewarm, Christ promises that we shall share his throne. Emperors like the Seleucids of Antioch, when they conquered a vassal state, would appoint a king to rule over that part of their kingdom by inviting him to sit next to them on a bench-like throne. Christ invites us to look after a part of his kingdom, so that we may reign with him in eternity.

THE REST OF REVELATION

We have discovered the life of the churches to which the first three chapters of Revelation were addressed, the persecutions and temptations to which they were subject, and the difficulty of maintaining a distinctive witness amid many competing religions. Now we shall be more able to interpret the use of Old Testament imagery in the rest of Revelation to see how its picture of the heavens opened, the world of ideals, and the world of their day as God saw it, will have been an encouragement to the readers for whom it was intended. Then we can go on to deduce that the risen Christ is telling us, too, that although we shall have to suffer in this life, God is ultimately in charge of this world and the life to come.

PAUL'S LETTERS TO THE COLOSSIANS AND TO PHILEMON

The church at Colossae, like those at Laodicea and Hierapolis, seems to have been founded by Epaphras under Paul's guidance (Colossians 1:7, 4:13). Colossians is one of the 'captivity epistles' (Colossians 4:18), and it may be that Epaphras and Onesimus had brought news to Paul in his prison of the 'heresy' which was disturbing the church in Colossae. This was a set of beliefs which seems to have combined pagan mythology, speculative philosophy, and elements of mystical Judaism. Its teachers will have claimed that theirs was a philosophy going beyond Christianity; that the material world was evil and opposed to the spiritual world of the angels. Therefore it apparently demanded the observance of festivals, kosher diet, asceticism and self-denial, and the worship of angels. They thought that the human Jesus could only represent a part of the nature of God. Paul refuted these beliefs by teaching the pre-eminence of Jesus Christ, calling him the image of God and the creator of everything, including the angels. The fullness of the church leads us to the fullness of Christ who is the fullness of God. The way for the Gentiles to reach God is therefore not by circumcision but by baptism, in which we are raised with Christ; so we must 'seek the things which are above', meaning not the angelic powers but a holy life.

A Summary of the Letter

Colossians 1:1–2 Greetings. 1:3–8 Paul thanks God for the love and the hope of the Christians in Colossae. 1:9–14 He prays for their growth in good works, endurance, and in knowledge of God who has rescued us from the powers of darkness. 1:15–20 Christ is the head of all things: this is a typically Jewish exploration of the first words of the Bible, 'in the beginning God', which in Hebrew could mean 'in, through or by the head is God'. 1:21–23 Paul is a minister of the gospel of reconciliation. 1:24—2:4 He reveals to the Gentile nations the mystery that Christ is in us. 2:6–23 The fullness of God is found in Christ 'bodily', not in the Colossian heresy. 3:1–17 Because of your baptism you have died to earthly things, so clothe yourselves in love, when there are no distinctions between people but all are one in Christ. 3:18—4:1 Mutual submission of wives and husbands, parents and children, slaves and slave-owners. 4:2–18 Further instructions and greetings.

Paul's letter to Philemon

In this short personal letter, Paul writes about a runaway slave named Onesimus, which means 'Useful'. A slave who asked a friend of his owner to seek a reconciliation could not be punished as a fugitive. Because a slave had no legal rights and was the property of his owner, Paul sends Onesimus back to his slave-owner, Philemon. But he requests him to welcome his slave, who has been converted, as a Christian brother, and therefore his equal, thereby undermining the whole institution of slavery. If Onesimus stole anything, Paul writes to Philemon, charge it to my account: after all, you owe me your whole life because I told you about Jesus! Because Onesimus is described as 'one of you' in Colossians 4:9, it seems probable that Philemon lived in Colossae.

The Legends of the Twelve

Jesus appointed twelve of his disciples 'to sit on twelve thrones judging the twelve tribes of Israel' (Matthew 19:28; Luke 22:30). Judging in this context means ruling, as in the book of Judges. Apparently these men were intended to symbolize the twelve sons of Jacob, and to be leaders of the people of God after Jesus had risen, just as the patriarchs had led the twelve tribes of the original chosen people. It is sometimes pointed out that Jesus did not choose any of the many women among his disciples to be among the Twelve, but if he had done so the symbolism of the sons of Jacob would have been lost. All who followed Jesus are called disciples; these twelve disciples are usually referred to as the Twelve, and it is almost entirely in Luke and Acts that they are called the apostles.

In Luke's writings several people other than the Twelve are called apostles: James the brother of the Lord, Barnabas, Andronicus and Junia (or Julia), and above all Saul of Tarsus. The word apostle simply means one who has been sent; in modern times we would be more likely to use the Latin word which means the same thing, 'missionary'. And there were many missionaries in the early church; when Paul writes about the tasks and the suffering of the apostles, he is describing the missionary vocation down the ages. After the Twelve were driven out of Jerusalem by persecution they seem to have left the leadership of the church there to James the brother of the Lord, and concentrated on the apostolic task of being travelling missionaries.

The legends of the early church, which may or may not have some truth in them, tell us where the various disciples went. The lists of the Twelve in Matthew 10:2-4; Mark 3:16-19; Luke 6:14-16; and Acts have some differences but we can harmonize them as follows:

1. **Simon Peter** who became the apostle to the Jews of the Dispersion, was crucified upside down in Rome in AD 67.
2. **Andrew**, Peter's brother; early traditions claim he worked in Scythia north of the Black Sea, or Patras in Greece. In 337 his body was supposed to have been taken from Patras to Byzantium (İstanbul); his bones are alleged to have been stolen from there and brought by crusaders to St Andrews in Scotland. Alternative stories claim that his remains were taken in 1206 to Amalfi, or that they are in Rome.

3. **James**, son of Zebedee, killed with a sword by King Herod Agrippa (Acts 12:2). He is believed to have preached in Spain, and his bones are supposed to have been rediscovered at Santiago de Compostella (James is the English version of Jacob, Iago is the Spanish spelling.)

4. **John**, son of Zebedee and brother of James (to both of whom Jesus gave the nickname Boanerges or Sons of Thunder). It is assumed that he was 'the disciple whom Jesus loved' and that he cared for the Virgin Mary on Mount Zion in Jerusalem, or that he took her to Ephesus where his remains are buried.

5. **Philip** may have preached in Hierapolis and have been buried there.

6. **Bartholomew** may be the surname of the disciple called **Nathanael** in John's Gospel. He is said to have worked in Hierapolis, or to have been flayed alive in India; the hospital of St Bartholomew on the Isola Tiberina in Rome also claims he had a healing ministry there at what was previously a pagan healing centre.

7. **Thomas** whose name means 'the twin', is called Doubting Thomas but was the first to come to faith in the risen Jesus as Lord and God. There is very good evidence to show he went to India, built up a church there (the Syrian Orthodox) and is buried in Madras.

8. **Matthew** the tax collector. Since the same stories are told of him as of **Levi** the tax collector, son of Alphaeus, we may presume they are the same person and Matthew was Levi's nickname (it means 'Gift of God'; may we guess that this was the joke Levi used to make when asked where his wealth came from?). He is supposed to have worked among Jewish Christians for whom he wrote his Gospel; there are many different accounts of his death.

9. **James**, son of Alphaeus, and therefore apparently brother of Matthew. Known as James the Less or Little James, there is no reason to identify him with James the Just, the brother of the Lord who presided over the church in Jerusalem and wrote the Letter of James. One of the women at the empty tomb was called 'Mary the mother of James', and one of the women at the cross was called 'Mary, wife of Alphaeus', some have thought that Cleopas is an alternative spelling of Alphaeus, so that the two disciples on the road to Emmaus could have been the parents of James and Matthew.

10. **Thaddaeus** is presumed to correspond to the disciple called in other lists **Judas, son of James**. He is said to have worked in Edessa (Şanlıurfa in Eastern Turkey), died and been buried there.

11. **Simon** the Cananaean, who was called the Zealot, was one of the freedom fighters who wanted to drive out the Roman army by force. He worked in Persia and was beaten and stoned to death there.

12. **Judas**, son of Simon Iscariot. Iscariot could mean 'the man from Kiriath Jearim', which would make him the only Judean among the Galilean disciples; or it could be from the word *sicarius*, the short dagger carried by the Zealot assassins, which would imply that he betrayed Jesus to start the revolution against Rome. He hanged himself (Matthew 27:5) or died from a fall (Acts 1:18). Because it was important to keep the symbolic number of twelve, he was replaced by Matthias (Acts 1:26).

Getting by in Turkish and Greek

TURKISH PRONUNCIATION

a	'a' as in part		hear; occasionally 'ch'
â	'ia' as in tiara		as in loch
ay	'i' as in fight	I, ı	(without a dot) a
c	'j' as in jam		neutral vowel like the
ç	'ch' as in chatter		'a' in around
e	as in 'met'	İ, i	(with a dot) 'i' as in fit
e	at the end of a		or 'ee' as in feel
	Turkish word is	j	's' as in pleasure
	always pronounced,	o	as in cot
	e.g. bile is	oğ	'o' as in owner
	pronounced 'beeleh'	ö	'ur' as in burn
ey	'ay' as in say	öy	'uh-i' run together as
g	always hard as in		a single sound
	gather	s	'ss' as in press
ğ	generally silent, but	ş	'sh' as in shop
	lengthens the	u	'u' as in pull
	preceding vowel	ü	like the German ü,
h	always pronounced,		between ooh and ee
	sometimes 'h' as in		

MODERN GREEK PRONUNCIATION

Words of two or more syllables have an acute accent to show where the stress is.

A	α	a as in	hand; e.g.	άνθρωπος	anthropos	human being
Αι	αι	e	met	αίμα	ema	blood
Αυ	αυ	av	lavatory	μαύρος	mavros	black
B	β	v	vine	βούτυρο	vooteero	butter
Γ	γ	gh	ghoul	γάλα	ghala	milk
Γγ, Γκ	γγ, γκ	g	good (initial)	γκάζι	gazee	gas
	γγ, γκ,	ngg	angle	Αγγλία	anggleea	England
Γη	γη	yee	year	γη	yee	earth
Γι	γι	y	yes	για	ya	because of/for
Γυ	γυ	yee	year	γυναίκα	yeenekha	woman
Δ	δ	TH	THis	δάκτυλος	THakhteelos	finger
E	ε	e	met	έτοιμος	eteemos	ready

Ει	ει	ee as in	meet e.g.	είδος	eeTHos	character
Ευ	ευ	ef	effervesce	ευχαριστώ	efharisto	thankyou
Ζ	ζ	z	zone	ζώνη	zonee	zone
Η	η	ee	meet	ήλιος	eeleeos	sun
Θ	θ	th	thin	θέατρο	theatro	theatre
Ι	ι	ee	meet	ίππος	eepos	horse
Κ	κ	kh	khan	και	khe	and
Λ	λ	l	log	λάδι	laTHee	olive oil
Μ	μ	m	mat	μάτι	matee	eye
Μπ	μπ	b	beer (initial)	μπύρα	beera	beer
	μπ	mb	amber	κάμπος	khambos	countryside
	μπ	mp	ample	σύμπαν	seempan	universe
Ν	ν	n	not	νύχτα	neehta	night
Ντ	ντ	d	door (initial)	ντομάτα	domata	tomato
	ντ	nt	bent	συναντώ	seenanto	attach
	ντ	nd	bend	πέντε	pende	five
Ξ	ξ	x	rocks	ξένος	ksenos	foreign
Ο	ο	o	cot	όχι	ohee	no
Οι	οι	ee	meet	οίκοι	eekhee	houses
Ου	ου	oo	food	που;	poo	where?
Π	π	p	pat	πόλη	polee	city
Ρ	ρ	rr	trrill	ρόδα	rroda	wheel
Σ	σ, final ς	s	sat	σήμα	seema	sign
Τ	τ	t	top	τράπεζα	trapeza	table
Τζ	τζ	dz	friends	τζάμι	dzamee	mosque
Υ	υ	ee	meet	ύπνος	eepnos	sleep
Φ	φ	f	fat	φούστα	foosta	shirt
Χ	χ	h	lough	χάνω	hano	lose
Ψ	ψ	ps	lapse	ψάρι	psari	fish
ω	ω	o	ordinary	ώρα	ora	hour

Some pairs of vowels are pronounced separately if the first has an acute accent or the second has a diaeresis, e.g. Κάιρο kha-ee-ro Cairo, and γαϊδουράκι gha-ee-THurakhee little donkey.
The Greek question mark is a semi-colon e.g. που; (poo) where?

Learn a Phrase a Day in Turkish and Greek

There are many fluent English-speaking people among the populations of Greece and Turkey. It is a sign of friendliness, however, to make some attempt to learn the local language. It can make the visitor feel at home, without overtaxing the memory, to learn a few simple phrases each day during a fourteen-day holiday. Here are some suggestions; ask a native speaker to demonstrate the pronunciation:

1. Good morning. Good evening. Hello.

    Günaydın. İyi akşamlar. Merhaba.

    Καλημέρα **khaleemera**. Καλησπέρα **khaleespera**. Γειά σου **yasu**.

2. Where is the toilet? Men. Ladies.

    Tuvalet nerede? Bay (Baylar). Bayan (Bayanlar).

    Πού είναι οι τουαλέτες; **pu eene ee tualetes**. Αντρών. **Andron**. Γυναικών. **Yeenekhon**.

3. Good bye.

    Hoşça kalın (by one leaving). **Güle güle** (by one staying).

    Αντίο **andeeo**.

4. How much does that cost? One, two, three, four, five, six, seven, eight, nine hundred thousand Turkish lire / nine hundred euros.

    Kaç lira? Bir, iki, üç, dört, beş, altı, yedi, sekiz, dokuz yüz bin liradır.

    Πόσο κοστίζει; **Poso khosteezee?** ένα, **ena**, δύο, **THeeo**, τρία, **treea**, τέσσερα, **tesera**, πέντε, **pende**, έξη, **eksee**, επτά, **epta**, οχτώ, **ohto**, εννέα, **enea**, εκατό χίλια εύρω, **ekhato heeleea efro**.

5. Yes. It costs ten, eleven, twelve, thirteen, twenty, twenty-one, thirty, a hundred and one million lire / a hundred and one euros. No, it is too dear.

    Evet. On, on bir, on iki, on üç, yirmi, yirmi bir, otuz, yüz bir milyon lira. Hayır, çok pahalı.

    Ναι **ne**. Κάνει **khanee** δέκα **dekha**, ένδεκα **enTHekha**, δώδεκα **THoTHekha**, δεκατρία **THekhatreea**, είκοσι **eekhosee**, είκοσι ένα **eekhosee ena**, τριάντα **treeanda**, εκατό ένα εύρω **ekhato ena efro**. Όχι, είναι πολύ ακριβό, **ohee, eene polee akhrivo**.

6. We would like two beers / three coffees with milk, please. No, no sugar, thank you.

İki bardak bira / üç fincan sütlü kahve istiyoriz, lütfen. Hayır, sade teşekkür ederim.

Θα ήθελα δύο μπύρες / τρείς καφέδες με γάλα, σας παρακαλώ. Tha eethela THeeo beeres / trees khafeTHes me gala, sas parakhalo. Όχι ohee, Θα ήθελα ζαχαρή tha eethela zaharee, σας ευχαριστώ sas efhareesto.

7. What time is it? One o'clock, a quarter past ten.

Saat kaç? Saat bir, onu çeyrek geçiyor.

Τι ώρα είναι; Tee ora eene? Είναι ένα η ώρα μετά μεσημύρίας, eene ena ee ora meta meseemvreeas, δέκα και τ έταρτο, THekha khe tetarto.

8. Half past four, a quarter to six, tomorrow morning.

Dört buçuk, altıya çeyrek var, yarın sabah.

τέσσερεις και μισή teserees khe meesee, έξη παρά τέταρτο eksee para tetarto, πρωινός άυριο preenos avreeo.

9. Where is there some hot water? Cold water? Mineral water? Thank you very much. It's a pleasure!

Sıcak su / Soğuk su / Maden suyu nerede? Çok teşekkür ederim. Bir şey değil.

Πού υπάρξει ζεστό νερό; κρυό νερό; μεταλλικό νερό; Pu eeparhei zesto nero? Khreeo nero? Metalikho nero? Σας ευχαριστώ πολύ. Sas efhareesto polee. Ευξαριστήση μου. Efhareesteesee moo.

10. Sorry (I apologize). Excuse me (I didn't understand).

Özür dilerim. Efendim?

Συγγνώμη seeghnomee. Δεν καταλαβαίνω THen katalaveno.

11. We need a double room with bathroom or shower.

Çift kişilik banyolu / duşlu bir oda.

Θά θέλαμε ένα δωμάτιο για δύο άτομα με μπάνιο ή ντους. Tha thelamee ena THomateeo ya THeeo atoma me baneeo ee dus.

12. Breakfast. Lunch. Dinner. A drink.

Kahvaltı. Öğle yemeği. Akşam yemeği. İçki (alcoholic) / Içecek (non-alcoholic)

Πρωϊνό pro-eeno. Μεσημεριανό meseemereeano. Βραδυνό VraTHeeno. Ποτό poto.

13. Help! Danger. Police. Fire! Doctor. Dentist.

İmdat! Tehlike. Polis. Yangın var! Doktor. Dişçi.

Βοήθεια! voeetheea! Προσοχή prosohee. Αστυνομία asteenomeea. Φωτια fotia! Γιατρός yatros. Οδοντιάτρος oTHondeeatros.

14. I am ill. Stomach ache. Heart trouble. Headache.

Rahatsızım. Mide ağrısı. Kalp ağrısı. Baş ağrısı.

Ασθενώ. Astheno. Στομαχόπανος. Stomahopanos. Καρδιακή προσβολή. KharTHiakhee prosbolee. Πονοκέφαλος. Ponokhefalos.

Words ending in -ion or -eum
Many words which we use today ending in -ion when they come from Greek, or -eum if they come from Latin, mean a building celebrating a thing or the statue of a god contained within it. Can you work out what these contain? See if you can think of any not on this list:
atheneum, colosseum, delphinium, gymnasium, herodeum, mausoleum, museum, mithraeum, nymphaeum, odeon, palladium, pandemonium, pantheon, planetarium, serapion, stadium.

Further Reading

John C. Allen, *The Journeys of St Paul*, Hulton Educational Publications Ltd, Amersham 1973

Roland Allen, *Missionary Methods: St Paul's or Ours?* Robert Scott, London 1912

M.H. Ballance, 'The site of Derbe: A new inscription' in *Anatolian Studies* 7, Ankara 1957, pp. 147–51,

M.H. Ballance, 'Derbe and Faustinopolis' in *Anatolian Studies* 14, Ankara 1964, pp. 139–40.

William Barclay, *Letters to the Seven Churches*, SCM Press, London 1957.

William Barclay, *The Daily Study Bible*, Saint Andrew Press, Edinburgh, and Westminster Press, Philadelphia 1959.

William Barclay, *The Mind of St Paul*, Wm Collins Sons & Co. Ltd, London 1958.

Charles Kingsley Barrett, *New Testament Background: Selected Documents*, SPCK, London 1956.

Charles Kingsley Barrett, *The Acts of the Apostles*, International Critical Commentary, T & T Clark, Edinburgh, in two volumes 1994 and 1998.

Susan Baykan, translated by Anita Gillett, *Priene Miletus Didyma*, Kaskin Color Kartpostalcilik Ltd, İstanbul 2000.

Edward Musgrave Blaiklock, *The Seven Churches*, Marshall Morgan & Scott, London 1956.

Edward Musgrave Blaiklock, *Cities of the New Testament*, Pickering & Inglis, London 1965.

Edward Musgrave Blaiklock, *The Archaeology of the New Testament*, Pickering & Inglis, London 1970.

Edward Musgrave Blaiklock, *Acts, the Birth of the Church*, Fleming H. Revell Co., New Jersey 1980.

Everett Blake and Anna G. Edmonds, *Biblical Sites in Turkey*, Sevyay, İstanbul 1977.

Leonard Boyle OP, *A Short Guide to St Clement's*, Collegio San Clementi, Rome 1989.

Ronald Allen Brownrigg, *Pauline Places*, Hodder & Stoughton, London 1989.

Ronald Allen Brownrigg, *The Twelve Apostles*, Wiedenfeld & Nicolson, London 1974.

Frederick Fyvie Bruce, *The Acts of the Apostles*, Tyndale Press, London 1951.

Ivor Bulmer-Thomas (ed.), *St Paul, Teacher and Traveller*, Faith Press, Leighton Buzzard 1975.

Fatih Cimok, *Antioch on the Orontes*, A Turizm Yayınları, İstanbul 1980, 1994.

Fatih Cimok, *St Paul in Anatolia and Cyprus*, A Turizm Yayınları, İstanbul 1999.

For Further Reading

Walter Conrad, *Christliche Stätten in der Türkei von İstanbul bis Antakya*, Verlag Katholisches Bibelwerk GmbH, Stuttgart 1999.

Hans Conzelmann, translated by James Limburg et al., *Acts of the Apostles*, Fortress Press, Philadelphia 1987.

W.D. Davies, *Paul and Rabbinic Judaism*, SPCK, London 1970.

Lindsey Davis, *The Silver Pigs* (and others in the 'Didius Falco' series of historical detective novels, for an amusing but well-researched idea of how common people lived in the Roman Empire), Sidgwick & Jackson, London 1989; Pan London 1990; Macmillan 1996. Other books in the Falco series are now published by Century, Random House UK Ltd, London.

Martin Dibelius, edited by Heinrich Grieven, *Studies in the Acts of the Apostles*, SCM Press Ltd, London 1956.

Charles Harold Dodd, *The Meaning of Paul for Today*, Fount Paperbacks, London 1958.

John W. Drane, *Paul*, Lion Publishing, Berkhamstead 1976.

G.S. Eliades, translated by B.E. Newton, *The House of Dionysus: The Villa of the Mosaics in Paphos*, Paphos Archaeological Museum, Cyprus 1980 (2nd edition 1984).

Jack Finnegan, *The Archeology of the New Testament: The Mediterranean World of the Early Christian Apostles*, Westminster Press, Colorado, and Croom Helm, London 1981.

Stanley Fiorini et al., *Mdina, the Old City of Malta*, Midsea Publications Ltd, Malta 1991.

Luca Giannini (ed.), *Holy Rome*, Fodor's Travel Publications Inc., Touring Editions srl, Milan 1999.

James Harpur and Marcus Braybrooke, *The Journeys of St Paul*, Marshall Publishing, London 1997

Colin J. Hemer, 'The letters to the seven churches of Asia in their local setting' in *Journal for the Study of the New Testament*, Supplement Series 11, JSOT Press, University of Sheffield 1986.

Colin J. Hemer, *The Book of Acts in the Setting of Hellenistic History*, JCB Mohr (Paul Siebeck), Tübingen 1989.

Fahri Işik, translated by Merik Çobanoğlu, *Patara: The History and Ruins of the Capital City of the Lycian League*, Universal Holding, Antalya 2000.

Vassos Karageorghis, *Salamis in Cyprus*, Thames & Hudson, London 1969.

Kim Ju-Chan and Kim Han-Ki, *Biblical Routes of Turkey*, Chung Dam, Seoul, Korea 1998.

Joochan Kim, *Seven Churches in Asia Minor*, Okhap Publishing Co., Korea 1999.

Lonely Planet Publications, Melbourne, Oakland, London and Paris. *Cyprus* (1st edition), *Greece* (4th edition), *Israel and the Palestinian Territories* (4th edition), *Jerusalem* (1st edition), *Lebanon* (1st edition), *Malta* (1st edition), *Middle East* (3rd edition), *Rome* (1st edition), *Syria* (1st edition), *Turkey* (6th edition), *Turkey Travel Atlas* (1st edition), *Western Europe* (4th edition). [I have used many other guide books but this series has useful details of opening times etc., and is regularly updated on the Internet at **www.lonelyplanet.com**]

Hyam Maccoby, *Paul and Hellenism*, SCM Press London and Trinity Press International, Philadelphia 1991.

F.G. Maier and V. Karageorghis, *Paphos History and Archeology*, A.G. Leventis Foundation, Nicosia 1984.

Malta Tourism Authority, *Malta in the Footsteps of St Paul*, Valetta 2000.

Otto Friedrich August Meinardus, *St Paul in Greece*, Lycabettus Press, Athens 1972, (2nd edition 1995).

Otto Friedrich August Meinardus, *St Paul in Ephesus and the Cities of Galatia and Cyprus*, Lycabettus Press, Athens 1973.

Otto Friedrich August Meinardus, *The Greeks of Thyatira*, Lycabettus Press, Athens 1974.

Hieromonk Sofronios G. Michaelides, *St Lazarus, the Friend of Christ and First Bishop of Kition: The History of His Church at Larnaca*, Larnaca, Cyprus 1990.

Stephen Mitchell, *Anatolia, Land Men and Gods in Asia Minor*, Vol. I, *The Celts in Anatolia and the Impact of Roman Rule*, Clarendon Press, Oxford 1993.

Stephen Mitchell and Marc Waelkens, *Pisidian Antioch*, Duckworth and the Classical Press of Wales, London 1998.

Hugh Montefiore, *Paul the Apostle*, Collins Fount Paperbacks, London 1981.

H.V. Morton, *In the Steps of St Paul*, Rich & Cowan Ltd, London 1936.

Jerome Murphy-O'Connor OP, *Paul: A Critical Life*, Oxford University Press, Oxford and New York 1996.

William Neil, *The Acts of the Apostles*, Oliphants, London 1973.

Timothy Pain, *Dear Theo*, Scripture Union, London 1993.

Nicos Papahatzis, translated by Kay Cicellis, *Ancient Corinth*, Ekdotike Athenon s.a., Athens 1977.

Wolfgang E. Pax, *In the Footsteps of St Paul*, Nateev Printing and Publishing Enterprises Ltd, Tel Aviv 1977.

John Pollock, *The Apostle*, Lion Publishing plc, Tring 1969.

Sir William Mitchell Ramsey, *St Paul the Traveller and Roman Citizen*, Hodder & Stoughton, London, New York, Toronto 1895.

John Arthur Thomas Robinson, *Redating the New Testament*, SCM Press, London 1976.

Felix Sammut OFM Conv., *St Paul in Malta*, Conventual Franciscans, Rabat, Malta 1967 (5th edition 2000).

E.P. Sanders, *Paul* (Past Masters), Oxford University Press, Oxford and New York 1991.

Peter Scherrer, translated by Lionel Boier and George M. Luxon, *Ephesus: The New Guide*, Ege Yayınları (Zero Prod. Ltd.), İstanbul 2000.

Prof. Dr Umit Serderoğlu, *Behramkale Assos*, Arkeologi ve Sanat Yayınları, İstanbul 1995.

James M. Scott, *Paul and the Nations*, JCB Mohr (Paul Siebeck), Tübingen 1995.

For Further Reading

James Smith of Jordanhill, *The Voyage and Shipwreck of St Paul*, Glasgow 1848.

John Stott, *What Christ Thinks of the Church*, Angus Hudson Ltd, London, new edition 1990.

Dr Mehmet Taşlialan, *Pisidian Antioch: The Journeys of St Paul to Antioch*, Ankara 1997.

Cengiz Topal, *Derbe, Bimbir Kilesi, Manazan Mağaralari, Alahan Monastiri*, T.C. Karaman Valiliği il Kültür Müdürlügü, Karaman 2000.

Joannis Touratsoglou, translated by David Hardy, *Macedonia, History, Monuments and Museums*, Ekdotike Athenon s.a., Athens 1998.

Hüseyin Uluarslan, *Assos (Behremkale)*, Okullar Pazarı, Çanakkale no date.

M. Vehbi Uysal, *Karaman Derbe Kerlihöyük*, Ok Ofset Matbaacılıc, Kayseri 1990.

Norman Wareham and Jill Gill, *Every Pilgrim's Guide to the Holy Land*, Canterbury Press, Norwich 1992, 1996.

Bruce W. Winter, Series Editor, *The Book of Acts in its First Century Setting*, William Eerdmans, Michigan, and The Paternoster Press, Carlisle:

1. *The Book of Acts in its Ancient Literary Setting*, Bruce W. Winter and Andrew Clark 1993.
2. *The Book of Acts in its Graeco Roman Setting*, David W.J. Gill and Conrad Gempf 1994.
3. *The Book of Acts and Paul in Roman Custody*, Brian Rapske 1994.
4. *The Book of Acts in its Palestinian Setting*, Richard Banckham 1995.
5. *The Book of Acts in its Diaspora Setting*, Irina Levinskaya 1996.

Gilbert Wiplinger and Gudrun Wlach, *Ephesus: 100 Years of Austrian Research*, Österreichisches Archäologisches Institut, Vienna 1996.

Tom Wright, *What St Paul Really Said*, Lion Publishing plc, Oxford 1997.

Herbert Brook Workman, *Persecution in the Early Church*, Charles H. Kelly, London 1906; Epworth Press, London 1960.

Edwin Masao Yamauchi, *The Archaeology of the New Testament: Cities of Western Asia Minor*, Pickering & Inglis, London 1980; Baker Book House, USA 1980.

Levent Zoroğlu, translated by G. Kuzan, *A Guide to Tarsus*, Donmez Offset, Ankara, no date.

W. Zschietzschmann, *Hellas and Rome: The Classical World in Pictures*, A. Zwemmer Ltd, London 1959.

Maps and Plans

Note: In the plans of modern towns only the more significant streets are shown.

Index

Index

Index